The Buddhist Religion

A Historical Introduction

Second Edition

RICHARD H. ROBINSON
formerly of
University of Wisconsin

WILLARD L. JOHNSON
University of California,
San Diego Extension

DICKENSON PUBLISHING COMPANY, INC.
Encino, California, and Belmont, California

To Sītā and Neil,
my daughter and my son,
kuladuhitre ca kulaputrāya

Here, never are acts of hate
calmed by hatred,
But by love.
This is the primordial Dharma (sanātana-dhamma).
Dhammapada

ISBN-0-8221-0193-9
Library of Congress Catalog Card Number: 76-49233

Printed in the United States of America
Printing (last digit): 9 8 7 6 5 4 3 2 1

Illustrations by Merilyn Britt

Contents

Foreword

THE RELIGIOUS LIFE OF MAN series is intended as an introduction to a large, complex field of inquiry—man's religious experience. It seeks to present the depth and richness of religious concepts, forms of worship, spiritual practices, and social institutions found in the major religious traditions throughout the world.

As a specialist in the language and culture in which a religion is found, each author is able to illuminate the meanings of a religious perspective and practice as other human beings have experienced it. To communicate this meaning to readers who have had no special training in these cultures and religions, the authors have attempted to provide clear, nontechnical descriptions and interpretations of religious life.

Different interpretive approaches have been used, depending upon the nature of the religious data; some religious expressions, for instance, lend themselves more to developmental, others more to topical studies. But this lack of a single interpretation may itself be instructive, for the experiences and practices regarded as religious in one culture may not be the most important in another.

THE RELIGIOUS LIFE OF MAN is concerned with, on the one hand, the variety of religious expressions found in different traditions and, on the other, the similarities in the structures of religious life. The various forms are interpreted in terms of their cultural context and historical continuity, demonstrating both the diverse expressions and commonalities of religious traditions. Besides the single volumes on different religions, the series offers a core book on the study of religious meaning, which describes different study approaches and examines several modes and structures of religious awareness. In addition, each book presents a list of materials for further reading, including translations of religious texts and detailed examinations of specific topics.

We hope the reader will find these volumes "introductory" in the most significant sense: an introduction to a new perspective for understanding himself and others.

Frederick J. Streng
Series Editor

Preface to the Second Edition

This second edition is a revision of the book left authorless by the untimely and tragic accidental death, in 1970, of Richard H. Robinson. Reviewers fairly well agreed on its merits but thought it difficult for introductory students; they also felt that it had unfortunate omissions. I have left much of Robinson's text substantially the same, but have also tried, by adding new sections and editing old ones, to make it more complete and easier to use.

New in this edition is a glossary of key Sanskrit terms. Here one may find definitions of all Sanskrit doctrinal terms which occur anywhere in the book not in parentheses. Students should remember as they read this book to refer often to definitions of terms in the glossary, especially while they are first becoming acquainted with the Sanskrit vocabulary of Buddhist thought. The bibliography has been revised and expanded to be more useful to student and teacher alike. Maps, charts, and diagrams, some provided by Kathryn Cissell, have been added. The written word has been supplemented with line drawings done by Merilyn Britt and taken from the rich treasure store of Buddhist art, allowing a closer witness to the actual Buddhist experience. Corresponding to the original author's prologue is an epilogue describing some of my own experiences of Buddhism. Finally, this textbook was originally designed to be used with a supplementary reader which would make available to students some of the key texts upon which this historical account of the Buddhist religion is based. The companion volume is now available in Stephan V. Beyer's *The Buddhist Experience: Sources and Interpretations,* in this same Dickenson series. Footnotes, gathered at the end of the text, indicate subjects referred to in this work which Beyer anthologizes in his companion volume.

I would like to thank all reviewers for helping me to avoid error, omission, and confusion; and beg all readers to excuse remaining errors, misleading statements, or ill-founded ideas that herein masquerade as truth. Their appearance in print doesn't mean that they cannot be challenged and improved.* My special thanks go to Bernice L. Lifton who so skillfully edited the entire manuscript before it went to the printer, to Pat Rounds who prepared the index, and to Fred Streng, who, as Senior Editor of *The Religious Life of Man* Series, advised and helped me on this project.

Willard Johnson
Pacific Beach, California

*I thank in advance any students, teachers, or other readers who would send me, via the publisher, comments, suggestions, and criticisms for the improvement of this book.

Note on Linguistics

The reader will notice that terms transliterated from foreign languages in this book often appear with diacritical marks. Occasionally, when a transliterated word may not be recognized and has an accepted English spelling, proper transliteration form is dropped (as Krishna for the more proper Kṛṣṇa).

The reason for diacritical marks is that only by using them can our orthography (writing system) closely approximate the original spelling of these foreign terms. For instance, the term *nirvana,* when spelled without diacritics indicating that the first *ā* is long and that the *ṇ* is retroflex (represented by the dot under the n), is not a close approximation of the original spelling of the term, since Sanskrit distinguishes long *ā* from short *a* and a retroflex *ṇ* from a dental *n*.

The diacritical marks also aid pronunciation of terms. For their correct use consult the pronunciation guide below.

Buddhists have used many and quite diverse languages for canonical purposes, ranging from the north Indian languages of Sanskrit and one of its literary vernaculars, Pali (in which the oldest Buddhist Canon is preserved), to Chinese, Korean, and Japanese. To simplify matters this text uses Sanskrit so as to present the basic vocabulary of Buddhism in its original language, although terms transliterated from other non-Indic languages also occur.

Though Pali was the first canonical language of Buddhism, all Indic words and names are given in their Sanskrit rather than their Pali form so that the beginning student will not have to learn two forms for each term. The few exceptions to this rule occur when a word has been left in Pali because it is misleading to use its less-usual Sanskrit form. In such cases the word is either clearly marked as being Pali or is required by the context to be in its Pali form. Many words are identical in the two languages, for example, *Bodhi, Buddha, Māra, Piṭaka, Rāhula, samādhi, Saṅgha, Tathāgata, Vinaya.* Common Sanskrit-Pali correspondences: *Abhidharma—Abhidhamma, arhant—arahant, bhikṣu—bhikkhu, bodhisattva—bodhisatta, dharma—dhamma, dhyāna—jhāna, Gautama—Gotama, Kauṇḍinya—Koṇḍañña, Kuśinagara—Kusināra, maitrī—mettā, Maitreya—Metteya, nirvāṇa—nibbāna, prajñā—paññā, Śakra—Sakka, Siddhārtha—Siddhattha, skandha—khandha, śramaṇa—samaṇa, sthavira—thera, Sūtra—Sutta Udraka Rāmaputra—Uddaka Rāmaputta, vijñāna—viññāna, yakṣa—yakkha.* Sanskrit /ś/ and /ṣ/ become Pali /s/, e.g., *Aśoka—Asoka, Tuṣita—Tusita.*

The following guide to pronunciation of Sanskrit is intended to help the student to pronounce this new Buddhist vocabulary without too great divergence from its proper form. Completely proper pronunciation is nearly impossible since it would require distinctions between sounds not current in our ordinary English speech. Thus, the differences between retroflex, *ṇ* and dental *n*, and among the palatal *ś*, the retroflex *ṣ* and the dental *s*, are slight but quite distinct to a speaker of the language, as is the distinction between unaspirated and aspirated consonants, such as between *dāna* and *dharma*.

The Sanskrit alphabet was designed by ancient Indian phoneticians to accurately represent all the sounds of the language.

THE SANSKRIT ALPHABET

Vowels

a ā i ī u ū ṛ ṝ ḷ e ai o au

Consonants

k	kh	g	gh	ṅ	(gutteral)
c	ch	j	jh	ñ	(palatal)
ṭ	ṭh	ḍ	ḍh	ṇ	(retroflex)
t	th	d	dh	n	(dental)
p	ph	b	bh	m	(labial)

Semivowels

y r l v

Sibilants

ś ṣ s

PRONUNCIATION

Sanskrit vowels may be short or long, a long vowel being marked by a horizontal line (macron) over it. The diphthongs *e, ai, o, au* are not marked but are long also. Of the short vowels, *a* is pronounced as the *u* in *cut* and not like the *a* in *sat, i* like *see* or *bit, u* as in *bull* or *full*. For the long vowels, *ā* is pronounced as in *father* or *calm, ī* as in *machine, ū* as in *rule* or *pull, ṛ* is vocalized as in *litter*, and *ḷ* follows the second *l* in *little*. The diphthongs follow *train* or *prey* for *e, aisle* or *time* for *ai, go* or *know* for *o*, and *cow* or *house* for *au*.

Among the consonants, Indian speakers distinguish unaspirate from aspirate stops, the aspirate being pronounced with a strong emission of breath and written as a separate letter. Of the gutterals (or velars), *k* is pronounced as in *kill*, or the *ck* in *luck* (not aspirated), while *kh* is the same but aspirated, as in English *come* or the *ck-h* of *blockhead; g* follows *gun* or *go, gh* is aspirated as in *loghead*, and *ṅ* is the nasal of this series, following *sing* or *king.* Among the palatals, *c* is pronounced as the second *ch* in *church,* while the aspirated *ch* is pronounced like the first sound of *church* but with stronger emission of breath to produce aspiration, or like the *ch h* in *witch hook; j* as in *jay* or *jug, jh* the same but aspirated, and *ñ* as *singe* or *canyon.* Of the retroflex (or cerebral) series, *ṭ* is pronounced as in *tear, ṭh* the same but aspirated; *ḍ* is as *dumb, ḍh* the same but aspirated, and *ṇ* follows *morning.*

Pronunciation of the dental series *t* is as in French *entrée, th* being the same only aspirated, not as in English *thing* or *this,* but rather like *pothook; d* follows *adhere, dh* the same only aspirated, and *n* is as in *nudge.* Of the labials, *p* is pronounced as in *pear, ph* the same only aspirated, not as in English *phial* or *f,* but rather like *shepherd* or *uphill; b* is as in *bear, bh* the same but aspirated, and *m* follows *map.* Among the semivowels, *y* follows *yellow* or *you, r* is like *rear, l* like *lead* or *long,* and *v* is not like English *v,* but is like *w* in world.

Of the three sibilants in Sanskrit, it is difficult to distinguish palatal *ś* from retroflex *ṣ;* both are pronounced like *sh* as in *shut,* contrasting with *s* which follows *stand.*

In pronouncing Sanskrit words, stress the last long syllable other than the last syllable which is never accented. Length is determined either by a long vowel, or a vowel followed by more than one consonant. If the next to last syllable is short, stress the previous. Examples: *Himálaya,* stressed on penultimate long vowel; *Śakúntalā,* stressed on penultimate short vowel followed by two consonants.

The Buddha, seated in samādhi, his hands in the meditation gesture. (After a sculpture found at Anurādhapura, Ceylon, of the third century A.D.)

Prologue:
The Scene Today

INDIA

Bodh-gayā lies seven miles from the Hindu holy city of Gayā, a railway point in the backward central area of Bihar State. The tourist-pilgrim who goes by cycle rickshaw emerges from the crumbling old city, past lotus ponds and tall palms, away from the little mountains that crop out of the plain, and along the sandy flats of the Phalgu River. The road passes shrines to obscure folk deities, mud-and-thatch huts, then a dusty little one-street bazaar. The rickshaw stops at the top of a slight rise. The visitor walks a few yards to the Mahā Bodhi Temple, the 170-foot spire of which has held his gaze for the last mile. The four-sided tapering stone tower is substantially the same as when the Chinese pilgrim Hsüan-tsang saw it in 635 A.D. It was renovated in the eleventh century in the last period of splendor that Buddhism enjoyed in eastern India before the cataclysmic onslaught of the Muslims about 1200 A.D. In its heyday this holy place was visited by pilgrims from Ceylon, Indonesia, Tibet, and China. For over fifteen hundred years, kings of India offered worship and donations here and left their traces in sculptured stone.

This is the site where, about 530 B.C., Gautama Siddhārtha Śākya attained supreme, perfect enlightenment and became a Buddha. The event is as central and as momentous for Buddhism as the Resurrection is for Christianity, and equally fraught with mystery. Devout Buddhists aspire to attain that liberation from transmigration which Gautama declared he achieved while sitting on the "Diamond Seat" under the Bodhi Tree. Every event in the legend of the Enlightenment *(Bodhi)* is associated with some spot on this site, and ancient donors erected a monument on each, as if seeking to render perceptible the presence that had once graced the spot.

Hindu boys at the gateway to the main shrine sell rosaries made of Bodhi Tree nuts. The pīpal, of which the revered tree is a specimen, is widespread in South Asia, but Buddhists offer special reverence to progeny of *the* tree. The one now growing at Bodhgayā is a descendant of the tree under which Gautama sat.

CEYLON

Anurādhapura, capital of Ceylon from the fifth century B.C. till the ninth A.D., is today a city of resplendent ruins. It lies among vast artificial irrigation lakes in the now sparsely populated plain of northern Ceylon. When seen from the peak of Mahintale, eight miles to the east, white domes of *stūpas* (reliquary mounds) glimmer along the jungle skyline against the sunset. But Anurādhapura, though in ruins, is far from deserted. It is only 125 miles by rail from Colombo, and in February 1966, the prime minister and the entire cabinet went by special train to celebrate the installation of a golden railing around the venerable Bodhi Tree said to be a slip brought in the third century B.C. from the one at Bodh-gayā.

The Sinhalese philosophy professor takes his two young daughters and the Western visitor in through the outer wall and up to the inner complex surrounding the Bodhi Tree. (Buddhist shrines, unlike Hindu ones, are open to people of all nations and creeds.) There all four take lotus buds, fold the petals back, and place the flower offerings on a marble niche. The tree's branches are visible above the golden railing, which surmounts a high protective wall. The small chapel just to the left is quite ordinary. The interest of the shrine is not art but the hedged-in, pampered tree, revered as if through some speechless mode it could communicate the gist of the wonder that its parent witnessed.

Over lunch the professor had been discussing scientific evidence for rebirth. Trained in England, he esteems the principle of verification as highly as any other analytic positivist. A Buddhist by tradition and conviction, he insists that the testimony of paranormal experience be seriously considered.

In Colombo a high-ranking civil servant invites the visitor to a ceremony on the thirteenth anniversary of his father-in-law's death. The host's home is crowded with lay guests seated on mats. Eighteen saffron-robed monks file in, the host meeting each one and washing his feet at the door. The monks are seated, and the women of the house present them with gifts—towels, pillowcases, books—and serve them dinner. Monks of the Theravāda sect do not eat after midday, but this generous meal of rice, fish, vegetables, and fruit is adequate to last until next morning. The senior monk leads the laity in reciting the Three Refuges and the Five Precepts (see pp. 00, 00, 00). Then he delivers a short sermon in memory of the deceased, stressing that we live on through our children, that how we bring up our family decides what kind of moral legacy we leave. He chants the scripture for offerings to the departed. While the hostess and her mother pour water offerings from a pot into a bowl, after this ceremony, the monks take leave, and the laity eat.

At the ancient and sizable shrine of Kelaniya, outside Colombo, murals in the central chapel show Mahinda, Aśoka's son, bringing Buddhism to Ceylon, and Portuguese soldiers desecrating and destroying the Kelaniya Temple. A gilded image of the Buddha seated in meditation posture occupies the shrine chamber of the main chapel. The side chapel contains a huge Reclining Buddha, to whom crowds of women and children offer flowers. An adjacent building holds images of Hindu gods before which Buddhist worshippers pray for mundane favors. In the spacious courtyard stands a huge, magnificent old Bodhi Tree.

The meditation center at Kanduboda, almost an hour's drive from Colombo, is devoted to practicing the controversial "Burmese method." The visitors walk around the men's meditation building (there is another for women) and observe that the four-by-eight cells are rather depressing, and afford little auditory privacy. The monk in charge receives the visitors kindly in his cabin, offers them milk from a green coconut, and invites questions.

"Is this method successful?"

"Yes, look at the testimonials in the visitors' book."

The visitors scan the book. A Dutch hitchhiker says that he attained *samādhi* (concentration).

"Is it necessary to attain the four trances to achieve insight?"

"One passes quickly through the trances but does not stay in them."

Afterward, the two Sinhalese tell the Westerner that this sounds dubious. This method of cultivating insight apart from the trances has been denounced as heterodox by some of the most learned monks in Ceylon.

TIBET-IN-INDIA

The fourteenth Dalai Lama, legitimate spiritual and temporal ruler of Tibet, lives in exile in a mansion looking out over the lower hills toward the Punjab plains. The visitors climb fifteen minutes from the refugee-crowded bazaar of Upper Dharmaśāla, register with the Indian government checkpost just inside the barbwire fence, wait a few minutes in a well-carpeted and well-decorated room, and then are ushered into an ordinary-size sitting room where the Dalai Lama greets them with no more ceremony than a handshake. He is a tall, well-built man in his early thirties, with strong features, a mobile expression, and an aura of intelligence and sincerity unexpected in such an object of piety. The visitors have said they want to discuss Mādhyamika philosophy (see p. 00) with him. He asks, "Is this coffee table real?"

"From the relative standpoint, yes. From the absolute standpoint, no."

"But don't you perceive it?"

"Yes, but what we perceive is not what it seems to be."

After undergoing this examination, the visitor asks: "Does one need to have cultivated insight through the meditative trances in order to understand Mādhyamika?"

The Dalai Lama says: "There is a lower degree of understanding that non-saints can attain, and then there is a higher degree accessible only to accomplished contemplatives." He goes on to ask the visitors whether they think the doctrine of rebirth can be scientifically demonstrated. If so, this would compel even such materialists as the Communists to acknowledge the reality of the spiritual realm. In the light of this knowledge, worldly contention would cease and larger nations would allow smaller nations to be free.

At Dalhousie, farther east in the Punjab hills, the lamas of a Tibetan craft community are preparing for ritual dances to celebrate the festival of Guru

Rimpoche (Padma-sambhava, see p. 188), the legendary founder of Tibetan Buddhism. A procession of maroon-robed lamas walks around the ritual area, installing a multicolored picture of the appropriate Great King at each of the four directions. This is the first of many measures to protect the dance from demons.

Later, a *maṇḍala* (sacred diagram), with the divinities in their residences painted meticulously in colored sand, is placed in the middle of the space within a large tent. On top of the maṇḍala is set an altar table carrying several tiers of offering figurines modeled out of dough and brightly colored; two bowls containing, respectively, "long-life" pills and "long-life" water; an incense burner; and several large and splendid goblet-shaped silver butter lamps. Lamas come in, wearing their finest robes and large red mitres. They recite their worship service before the altar, and then go out.

As the dance proper begins, four lamas enter in sorcerers' costumes, with large-brimmed black hats and robes of heavy, bright-hued brocades. They dance in a ring around the stage-ground, planting ceremonial daggers at the corners, and gradually increasing their tempo until, as the robes fly out and the booted feet kick higher, the dance reaches a climax. When the stage has been purified in this way of evil forces, two long-haired *yogins* (practitioners of yoga) come out wearing large, brightly painted masks. They jump in the air, cross their legs in "lotus" position, and land cross-legged on the ground. Their presence shows the scene to be a cemetery, a favorite place for ascetics to meditate. Then Guru Rimpoche comes on stage, followed by his eight transformations, alias-forms that he is said to have been able to assume magically. The "real" Guru Rimpoche sits on a high seat, while his aliases, all wearing striking masks and gorgeous costumes made in this craft community, go through solo dances which do not tell a story but simply express the character of each personality. The performance is accompanied by a weird orchestra of trumpets, oboes, cymbals, and drums. The dances are at once a magical rite and a contemplative exercise. Ideally, each actor is supposed to concentrate on his role until he "becomes" it.[1]*

VIETNAM

When the visitor lies awake before dawn in a guest room in the Xa Loi Pagoda, Saigon, the nightlong noise of planes and helicopters is intermittently broken by distant explosions or drowned by the roar of army trucks along the tree-lined avenues. He dresses, hurries the few paces to the chapel, slips off his sandals, and squats on the colorful tiled floor just as an elderly monk begins to chant the first service of the day. The fast, fluting plainsong is punctuated occasionally with gong strokes. The monk, alternately standing and kneeling before a giant image of Gautama Buddha, is half hidden by a wide offering

*All notes appear at the end of the book, beginning on p. 211.

table lacquered with scenes in the distinctive Vietnamese style. The image is at once impressive and attractive, serene in manner, modern and international in its facial expression. After the service the visitor walks around to the alcove behind the image, where tables on either side hold rows of wooden memorial tablets inscribed with the names of the deceased. In the center, back to back with the large image, are photographs of the martyrs, the monks who underwent self-immolation during 1963 in the Buddhist struggle against the dictator Ngo Dinh Diem. These photos, like the paintings of the martyrs found in all the modern Saigon temples, are stark and jarring.

On Sunday morning the Xa Loi chapel is crowded with laymen participating in the chief congregational service of the week. They kneel and bow in rows on the bare floor, chanting responses from little manuals in roman-letter Vietnamese, men sitting to the left of the center aisle and women to the right. There are four or five uniformed Americans in the congretation. Two weeks later, one of them marries a Vietnamese girl in a Buddhist ceremony.

The Xa Loi temple has a good library of Buddhist books in Vietnamese, Chinese, French, and English. It and the classroom downstairs are used by the Buddhist University, pending completion of the new building. Fifty students come to hear the foreign speaker, and the chairman later apologizes for the small crowd. Only three months have passed since the Buddhist demonstrations were quelled by the government; dozens of youth leaders are still in jail, and many others are prudently avoiding public meetings. The talk is followed by a twilight dinner party in the temple garden. After the meal a singsong, featuring solo and group renditions of folk and popular songs, is held by lamplight in the temple portico. Boys and girls tease each other and laugh. The atmosphere is the worldwide one of the church social.

The elderly layman sits in the guest's room at the pagoda and discusses the state of Buddhism in Vietnam. The true Buddhist, he says in French, should be a nirvāṇa-seeker rather than a political activist. Without religious depth, such movements as the current one will wither away and leave Buddhism no better than before. The aim of the Buddhist Study Association, of which the speaker is president, has been to focus attention on the study of the scriptures and to encourage the individual layman to lead a good Buddhist life. But Vietnamese Buddhism is rent by jealousies and contention. The monks grudge influence to the laity, and even among the monks themselves there is discord between the modernizers and the traditionalists.

The car stops near the tombs of the former abbots of a Zen monastery on the outskirts of Saigon. The visitors meet the present abbot, an elderly ascetic in dark robes, who shows them first into the central corridor where portraits of his predecessors are arrayed in shrines. To the right is a large hall where the forty-eight monks eat, and sleep on long hardwood benches with only thin mats for bedding. The chapel, to the left, is small, dark, and crowded with images. Unlike the Xa Loi Pagoda, it is not a place for congregational worship. Along one wall are the ten judges of hell, a favorite Far Eastern cult sect. The images in the central shrine are darkened with age. The temple is three hundred years old, it is said. Elegant Chinese inscriptions adorn the wooden pillars.

As the car approaches the crossroads in front of the Cambodian Embassy, the young high school teacher says that this is where Thich Quang-duc performed self-immolation in June 1963. The seventy-three-year-old monk sat down on the pavement while an attendant poured gasoline over him. Then he lit a match, ignited himself, and burned to death with serene composure, evidently in a meditative trance. The visitor asks his guide what his reactions were at the time. First shock and horror. Then realization of the gulf between true selfless devotion and his own lukewarm commitment to Buddhism. Then pride that there were such men in Buddhism today. Some subsequent self-immolators, he says, were cranks seeking notoriety. But Quang-duc was a pure-minded saint.

JAPAN

The young Japanese scholar and his Western guest pay the entrance fee (usual at famous old Japanese temples), take off their shoes, and shuffle along the plank corridors to look at the sixteenth-century rock garden for which this temple is famed. Rocks and pieces of wood artfully lure the viewer's concentration. Before long, one imperceptibly becomes quieter, stops having associative fancies, and enjoys this microlandscape as a world in its own right. The visitor is mildly jolted when a robust, fortyish Zen monk in light-colored robes, with shaven head, quicksilver facial expression, and glowing eyes bounces in and offers to explain the garden.

"What is there to explain?"

"Well, nothing, but I have an explanation that I've made up for the tourists."

"Doesn't the garden explain itself?"

"Yes, it does. You speak Japanese extraordinarily well." (This being outrageously false.)

"You are flattering me." (A bass giggle, then the mischievous silence of the saints.)

After a few minutes of jocular sparring, the monk invites the two sightseers to join him for tea in a nearby room. There he starts talking straight and asks about the situation in Vietnam.

The young scholar tells the visitor afterward that the monk is the director of the University of Kyōto Zen Club. He has finished his Zen training and is a master. The Zen Club practices meditation regularly and sometimes holds retreats. As they go to a restaurant, the guide admits to the visitor that he finds meditation a refreshing respite from the grueling study of Sanskrit and Tibetan scholastic treatises. Unlike many scholars of Buddhism, he is not the son of a priest. He took to studying Buddhism in quest of a viable philosophy of life, an alternative to the facile hedonism now dominant in Japan. What has he found in Buddhist studies? It is hard to say, but he is still young, still looking, and well on his way to a noteworthy academic career.

At Tōji (the Eastern temple) south of Kyōto Station, old women in mushroom-shaped peasant hats circumambulate the statue of Kōbō Daishi (p. 000), who founded the temple in 823 A.D. They pick up and put down tally sticks at the end of each round, and mumble formulas as they walk. They are seeking relief from physical ailments.

Fifty miles south, in the precincts of Kōyasan Monastery, which he founded in 816, Kōbō Daishi's remains are enshrined at the end of a long mortuary glade lined with cedars, cypresses, and the illustrious dead of intervening centuries—saints and generals, emperors and poets. One plot is reserved for ashes of employees of the Osaka Life Insurance Company. Bands of aged pilgrims clutching their rosaries in bare hands struggle through the snow, reciting their offices at each station on their route. The visitor asks the student monk who accompanies him: "Have you practiced meditation?"

"Yes, I did a session of a couple months last year."

"What did you get out of it?"

"Nothing much."

"Did you enjoy it?"

"No."

"Then why did you do it?"

"Because our sect [Shingon] requires it as part of our training. I am going to take over the temple when my father retires."

A high gateway and a simple wooden signboard mark the entrance to the little Jōdo-shin-shū Temple (see p. 177) in a back street of Kyōto. Inside, the "minister's" family's quarters are on the left, and the small chapel is straight ahead across the courtyard. The congregation leave their shoes on the veranda, go in, and squat on the mat-covered floor. A large part of the chapel is taken up by the shrine, gilded and lacquered and hung with ornaments under an overall canopy. The central object in the shrine is a very old and beautiful statue of Amida Buddha (see p. 112). He is standing on a lotus, his right hand raised in the gesture of reassurance and his left outstretched, palm upward, in the gesture of gift-granting. A halo rises behind his head. On each side of the Buddha-image is a scroll painting, one of Shinran (the sect's founder), and the other of Hōnen, Shinran's teacher (see p. 176).

On New Year's morning, fifty or sixty people have gathered for the first public service of the year. Following the lead of the minister, they chant the Three Refuges in classical Japanese, then recite the Profession of Faith: "Forsaking all sundry practices and attitudes of self-power, we rely wholeheartedly upon Amida Buddha for salvation in the life to come. . . ." Then the congregation chants Shinran's "Hymn of Right Faith," a long poem in Chinese giving the history of the Pure Land teaching. The melody is involuted, the tempo is slow, and the effect is solemn and compelling. Afterward, they chant a stanza dedicating the merit (from reciting the hymn) to all sentient beings so that they may attain rebirth in Amida's Pure Land. The minister then delivers a short sermon. The service concludes with everyone reciting "Salutation to Amida Buddha."

An official of the Risshō Kōseikai (Society for Establishing the Right and Cooperative Self-fulfillment) is showing the visitor around the sect's large and busy premises in a western suburb of Tōkyō. He wears a black robe and carries a rosary, but carefully states that he is a layman, that their sect, founded in 1938, is entirely a lay movement. They take the *Lotus Sūtra* (see p. 110) as their chief scripture and find in it not only the essence of Mahāyāna Buddhism but a guide to life in a modern industrial society. As he talks flocks of pretty young women in traditional costume sail by. The official says that his sect does not believe in coercive proselytizing and political activism, like its rival Sōka Gakkai, nor does it practice faith healing, like some other new sects. It concentrates instead on solving life problems through application of Buddhist principles. He shows a large hall where numerous groups, each of about ten people, are engaging in discussion under guidance of a leader. The guide says that modern Japanese cities are filled with uprooted people who need friends and substitutes for traditional families and village communities.

They come to the sect's chief chapel, an enormous round building with a many-galleried interior like a European opera house. It can hold 10,000 people, the guide says. The visitor reminds himself that not all mass movements that hold gigantic rallies and revere charismatic leaders can justly be accused of fascist tendencies.

THE UNITED STATES

Three hundred members of the Young Buddhist Association are attending the annual seminar in a seaside park near Monterey. Of the forty in the advanced discussion section, thirty are Japanese Americans, the rest European Americans. The point in dispute is whether American Buddhists should be socially active, support integration, work for racial equality, and give aid to the Buddhists of Vietnam. The young minister, a recent immigrant from Japan, diffidently but staunchly presents the orthodox viewpoint of old-country Jōdoshinshū that, though Buddhists as individuals may participate in sociopolitical action, Buddhist institutions should neither participate in nor endorse such action. An American graduate student points out that in the sixteenth century this same sect led a mass revolt of peasants against their feudal lords and became a feudal power in its own right. Under pressure from the Americans, the minister finally admits that his own sympathies are with them rather than with the orthodox view of his sect.

ENGLAND

The three-story house is distinguished from others on the London street only by its yellow front door. Upstairs, an English Buddhist monk, home after fifteen years in India, sits on a Tibetan carpet under a Tibetan scroll painting. Every five minutes the phone rings, and the monk deals in a brisk office voice with another piece of business. The Saṅgha Association committee handles finances and administration, but the lecture program, meeting inquirers, and public relations leave him little time for study and meditation. The monk speaks enthusiastically about a meditation center his group is starting in an old mansion in the countryside. Beside him sit two novices who are preparing to go to India for full ordination and training.

INDIA AGAIN

Three Westerners—a musician turned contemplative, a Zionist in search of a meditation master, and an orientalist—sit talking in a hill town. All three are willing to call themselves Buddhists but are ill at ease when non-Buddhists do so. The musician has been practicing meditation daily for several months. His face has the special mobile radiance of the contemplative. He speaks spontaneously to the occasion, with implicit authenticity. The Zionist chronicles his career from law school dropout ("They kept giving me fellowships but I realized it would ruin my mind") to kibbutznik ("It's a wonderful way of life, but when you've got it, what are you going to do with it?") to itinerant seeker. The orientalist quietly cherishes his newly consolidated realization that he has finally reconciled his scholarship and his religion.

They speak of the general dissolution of old institutions and doctrines, of chaos as the beginning of new creation, of an imminent resurgence of intuitive wisdom, and of enlightenment as the cardinal source of justice. They sense a turning point in history when, after enduring for millenia, conventional wisdom crumbles and new world views stand revealed.

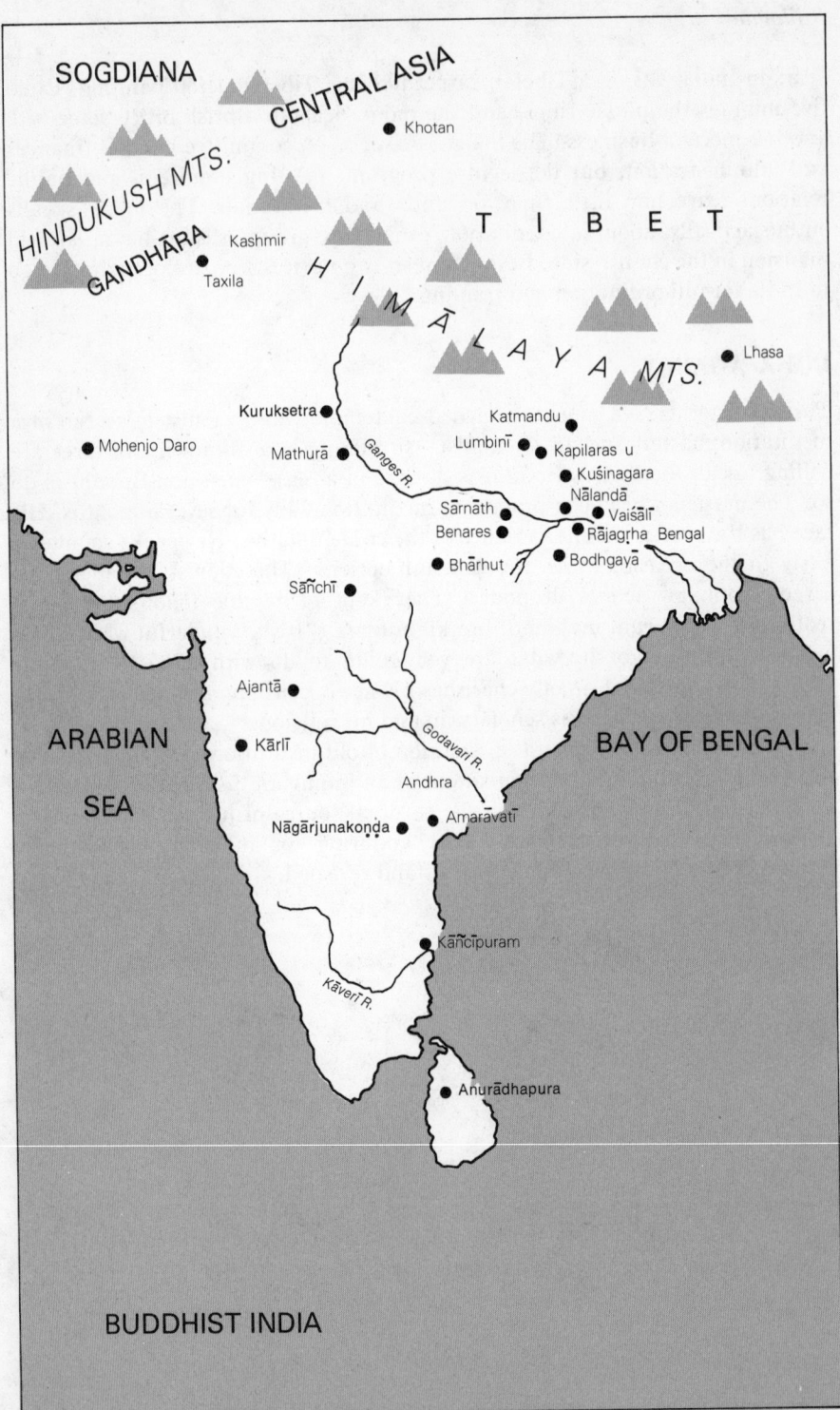

SOGDIANA

CENTRAL ASIA

Khotan

HINDUKUSH MTS.

GANDHĀRA

Kashmir

Taxila

TIBET

HIMĀLAYA MTS.

Lhasa

Kuruksetra

Mohenjo Daro

Mathurā

Ganges R.

Katmandu

Lumbinī

Kapilaras u

Kuśinagara

Nālandā

Sārnāth

Vaiśālī

Benares

Rājagrha

Bengal

Bhārhut

Bodhgayā

Sāñchī

Ajantā

ARABIAN

Kārlī

Godavari R.

BAY OF BENGAL

SEA

Andhra

Nāgārjunakoṇḍa

Amarāvatī

Kāñcīpuram

Kāverī R.

Anurādhapura

BUDDHIST INDIA

Part I

THE BUDDHISM
OF
SOUTH ASIA

1.
Antecedents of Buddhism

BACKGROUNDS: INDUS VALLEY AND INDO-ĀRYAN RELIGION

Indian civilization was cradled in the area of the Indus River Valley and the Punjab. The earliest members of the Indus Valley civilization occupied a considerable area of the northwest sometime between 3000 and 1800 B.C.[1] Unfortunately, we know tantalizingly little about the religious ideas and practices of these peoples.

A figurine from Mohenjo-daro, of the Indus Valley Harappan civilization. Perhaps a priest or holy man, he wears his robe across one shoulder similar to the way later Buddhist monks wore theirs. His eyes appear half-closed, as if in meditation.

This civilization was in decline when Indo-Āryan tribes, crossing high mountain passes in the far northwest, invaded and settled the Punjab between 1800 and 1500 B.C. The religion of the Indo-Āryans was a regional variant of Indo-European practices, called either Vedism or Brahmanism.[2] Unlike the relatively peaceful agrarians of the Indus Valley, these new peoples were rough Bronze Age cattle herders who over the centuries spread from the upper Indus into the sprawling, fertile Gangetic plain, clearing forests and taking increasingly to cereal culture. Within the tribe, political authority and military power rested with the warrior *(kṣatriya)*[3] class, whose leaders were not kings but rather first among equals. They appear to have appropriated women, peasants, herdsmen, menial servants, and perhaps even religious specialists quite freely from their conquered enemies. In this same process, the Āryans inevitably also absorbed from the earlier peoples of India many ideas and practices, ironically even the fear of pollution by alien contacts. This, and the closed-in honeycomb society of classical Hinduism, came only after more than a millenium of Indo-Āryan growth and expansion.

While it is doubtful whether the office of priest *(brāhmaṇa)* was hereditary among the early Indo-Āryans, by the time that the Buddha taught, only members of certain lineages were eligible. The Buddhist contention that personal merit, not birth, makes one an Āryan, pure and religiously fit, is as much a survival of older usage as a protest against later brahmin presumption. In the sixth century B.C., there were many peoples, such as the Vṛjis of Vaiśālī, who practiced Indo-Āryan cult without the services of the priestly guild. Certain rites such as marriage and offerings to deceased relatives seem to have been performed originally by people who were not officially priests; later, they were adapted and taken over by the brahmins in one way, and by the Buddhists in another. Brahmanism is thus one systematization, not the whole, of the diverse Indo-Āryan religion. Buddhism is another, somewhat later branch from the same stock that grew and flourished in the religiously diverse Indus and Ganges plains. Popular Hinduism, finally, was another.

The objective of Vedic sacrifice was to please the gods and so to obtain health, wealth, fertility, long life, and glorious victory. Vedism declared that the broad earth is a good place, on which one wishes to live a full portion of one hundred years. Hunger, disease, drought, and death are menaces, but the gods prevail over demons, and good men—the strong, the noble, and the generous—prevail over the bad. The Vedic hymns do not show much dread of the afterlife, seen as a ritually achieved destiny for the righteous in a heaven of the deceased fathers. While the gods to whom the sacred verses of the *Ṛg Veda* (circa 1500–1000 B.C.) are addressed did not become the objects of popular veneration, the early Vedic poets had provided north Indian thought with some powerful speculative images, particularly in the hymns composed in the Veda's latest period. One such image, for example, is the twelve-spoked wheel of time, or life *(Ṛg Veda* I.164, meaning Book I, Hymn 164). The image was later used by Buddhist artists to represent the doctrine of dependent co-arising, and formed the numerical basis of the Buddhist conception of creation.

The great battle at Kurukṣetra, where Āryan fought Āryan (described in the long epic poem, *Mahābhārata)* and datable around 900 B.C., marks the close of the Vedic period. It signaled the move of the invaders eastward and their occupation of the Gangetic plain. The introduction of iron about 700 B.C. facilitated clearing the jungle, leading to population increase and warfare, thus expediting concentration of political power. The brahmins responded to the new affluence of their princely clients by elaborating more costly and ostentatious rituals. The speculation tentatively begun in the late *Rg Veda* was greatly magnified in this period from 900 to about 600 B.C. New fundamental assumptions, such as the notion of recurrent death *(punar-mrtyu)*, made their fateful appearance, and responses to them greatly stimulated and broadened the religious horizons of north India. Immortality became an object of repeated speculation as an escape from the *samsāra* world system, no longer deemed as satisfying as in the Rg Vedic world view. The times were right for major changes.

The sixth century B.C. was one of the most pivotal in the history of India. It marked the shift from tribal oligarchies to monarchies and empires, the growth and multiplication of cities, the quickening of trade, increasing craft specialization, beginnings of a monetary sector in the economy, development of bureaucratic institutions, and emergence of two new classes, the rich merchants and the professional royal advisers. During this century there arose a welter of nonsacerdotal religious teachings which pushed the Vedic orthodoxy from dominance in the middle Ganges area, the very region where social change was most advanced. Incomparably the most successful of these sects was Buddhism, essentially because it combined appropriateness to its original time and place in its moderate responses to the age's spiritual needs with the capacity to spread and adapt to other situations.

THE IMMEDIATE CONTEXT OF THE BIRTH OF BUDDHISM

The Upaniṣads

Some Indian thinkers questioned the significance of performing ever bigger and more complex sacrifices, prompting them to seek the key to efficacious rites in knowledge of their "meaning." By the early sixth century B.C., Brahmanical thinkers in the Upaniṣads,[4] among other seers and ascetics, were deprecating ritual action and extolling the power of thought. They affirmed the older mythic idea that the Primordial Being created the world by thinking (or willing). Mind for these archaic Indians was objective, a subtle substance that is all-pervasive, that goes everywhere on its own ethereal plane. It is thus a sort of god, just as the senses are termed gods in the Upaniṣads because they are sentient, unseen powers. If this is the case, it seems reasonable that by taking thought one can not only increase one's stature (contrast Matthew 6:27) but transform one's entire state of being.

The early Upaniṣads identified the *ātman* (self) of the person with the indwelling world power *(Brahman).* One who knows the meaning of something, it was thought, has grasped its essence and controls it. So one who knows the identity of one's own essence and the cosmic power becomes divine and "is magnified in the world of Brahmā." An outstanding feature of the Brahmā-world is that beings there do not die and go to rebirth elsewhere.

Belief in rebirth was not Vedic but came into prominence about 600 B.C., deriving perhaps from attempts to explain the cycles of life in the natural world. The spirits of the dead go either on the path of the gods *(deva)* to the solar world of Brahmā, or on the path of the "fathers" to the moon, where they are eaten by the gods and descend again to become rain, which is absorbed by plants, which are eaten by men and animals and converted into semen, which engenders further animal life. The lunar path involves repeated dying, and so is undesirable not because life is miserable, but because death is painful. So the goal of early Upaniṣadic striving is to reach the world of Brahmā, from which people do not return. Early texts are vague as to whether the Brahmā-world is a paradise or a formless, inconceivable state, whether it is the top zone of space or a nonspatial realm. They agree that deserving souls go there after death, and that the decisive factors are one's deeds during life and the purpose that rules the mind at the moment of death. The practice that leads to the immortal realm is devout meditation *(upāsanā)* upon the immortal part of oneself, and the main philosophical problem is to identify this part and distinguish it from the other, perishable parts.

The Ascetic Movement

The Vedic priesthood and the Upaniṣadic sages were householders, observing celibacy only during their student years, and affirming the value of the procreative act. In the sixth century, the celibate ascetic or wandering mendicant *(śramaṇa)* appeared on the scene. These "strivers" abandoned family life, generally gave up normal work and lived by begging; they wandered around from village to village, dwelling in the forest and forming unstable congregations around masters who propounded a wild diversity of teachings. Some were materialists who taught that there is no afterlife, that when the four elements (earth, water, fire, and air) separate at death, the senses and mind dissolve into space. Some held that the highest happiness is to enjoy the pleasures of this world. Most, though, believed in transmigration and maintained that life is misery and liberation from the cycle of birth and death the supreme good. The materialists thought that the soul and the body were identical, while the others thought that soul and body are different. In general, though, the ascetics placed more emphasis on ascetic regimen than on knowledge as a means to liberation.

The old tales in the *Mahābhārata* describe austerities *(tapas)* undertaken to win the favor of deities, who when duly propitiated appear to the devotee and grant the boon—give offspring, or answer questions. The ascetics, though, were not worshippers of the deities but accumulators of merit, a spiritual currency as impersonal and public as gold. The post-Vedic brahmins had reduced sacrifice to a mechanical determinism such that the gods had no option but to comply. Since it was human action that made the rites efficacious, the gods became redundant, and the ascetics dispensed with them. To their minds, the sacrificing priests were crass mercenaries who collected fees and earned no merit, since merit is the spiritual compensation for material rewards foregone. The ascetics lived in poverty and strove for imperishable and inalienable riches. Among the chief fruits of their exertions were magic and spiritual powers.

The ascetics who believed in an individual soul distinct from the body considered austerity a means of purification. First the body was purged of dark, coarse, bad matter. Then the soul was cleansed of material stains and finally liberated from transmigrant bodies. This is the position of Jainism,[5] whose great master Mahāvīra was a contemporary of the Buddha. The Jains hold that *karman* (action) is a special kind of subtle matter that darkens and binds the naturally bright and free soul. Bad deeds are more adhesive and pollute the soul more than good deeds, which are easily dispelled. So the ascetic must overcome bad action with good action and then overcome good action through inaction. Austerity eliminates karman already incurred, and restraint prevents the influx of new karman. The *jina* (victors) or *arhant* (adepts) achieve liberation while in the body, but live out their last life through the force of residual karman. Mahāvīra, thirty years after becoming a jina, achieved final release from the body by fasting to death.

The Jains say that the pure soul is omniscient and perfectly blissful. Matter, then, is an obstacle to the exercise of paranormal powers. It veils perception and impedes motion. So, of course, austerity frees the innate magic faculties or psychic powers of the holy individual.

Austerity *(tapas,* literally "heat") was associated in archaic Indian thought with procreation, cosmic and animal. "That One was born through the power of heat [*tapas*]. In the beginning there arose desire [*kāma*], which was the first semen of mind/will [*manas*]" *(Ṛg Veda* 10.129, 3-4). It was believed that emission of semen depleted one's vital force, so the aspirant to paranormal attainments ought to conserve his energy by practicing continence. Moderation, though commended to the householder, would not suffice for the ascetic, who strove for perfection. Moreover, celibacy was convenient, since a man without a family could live and travel as he pleased, and a reputation for chastity assured the wandering stranger of a better welcome from householders.

Why did men want to become wizards and adepts? Only some were strongly impelled to achieve release from transmigration. The majority were professionals, happy to become "worthy of reverence, worthy of offerings." Householders gained merit by donation to a holy man, by feeding and ministering to him. Hospitality was a cardinal virtue among the Indo-Āryans. Any guest was to be treated as a god, and a holy man especially so. In return, adepts used their supernormal insight to solve the problems of petitioners.

They gave diagnoses and made predictions, advised on policy and warned of dangers. To this day, Buddhist monks and Hindu renunciants continue to practice these useful arts.

The quest for the ultimate lured an adventurous minority who were not content with merely deserving the alms they received. Conversely, the ordinary ascetic enjoyed greater prestige if his path had led famous saints to perfection. Competition and, consequently, transcendence were built right into the ascetic movement.

THE WORLD VIEW OF EARLY NORTH INDIAN THOUGHT

The large number of ascetics in the sixth century B.C. was occasioned not merely by the decline of sacrifice and the new vogue for austerity, though this change must have left many priests in search of a new vocation. The incorporation of tribes into kingdoms and the breakdown of the old patrician democracies sent many members of the warrior (kṣatriya) class "looking for jobs." Some entered commerce, some took service with strong kings, and quite a number entered the religious life, to which they brought the characteristic versatility of the refugee. At once uprooted and freed, they wandered around the new, wider world and fashioned a more universal world view.

The world view they elaborated was assumed by most of the new *religieux* of the sixth century B.C., the creators of both Buddhism and Hinduism. Distinctive and quite un-Vedic, this picture of the world made basic assumptions about five aspects of life.

(a) It assumed that time and space, once created, are endless. Time is measured in aeons *(kalpas)*, incomprehensibly long cycles which repeat themselves endlessly. The drama of human life and salvation takes place within this temporal frame.

(b) Further, this view assumed that death is recurrent, that personhood and identity extend beyond this lifetime, being continuous both from the past and into the future. Mortality does not mean that one dies once, but that one dies endlessly, or until one escapes into the deathless realm.

(c) A third set of hypotheses concerned individual identity. One's identity is morally determined by the influences of karman (action) taken in previous lives. These influences extend into this life, and potentially into subsequent lives unless stopped by counteractive measures. Everything that one is depends on the moral choices one made in previous lifetimes. Everything that one will become depends on the continuation of this process in the current lifetime. The individual is totally responsible.

(d) It was believed that the world system into which the individual is repeatedly reborn is transient and ever-changing, perilous like an ocean or a swiftly moving stream. Called saṃsāra, "that which turns around forever," it is the mortal realm into which karman-laden beings are reborn to experience endlessly transforming destinies determined totally by their prior choices and actions.

(e) Yet another underlying belief was the existence of <u>an alternative to</u> <u>saṃsāra, an escape from endlessly recurrent death and karman</u>. <u>This was</u> *nirvāṇa* or *mokṣa* <u>(release), the transcendent, deathless state, salvation, the</u> <u>ultimate goal, respite from suffering and the trials of mortality.</u> The ultimate goal *(artha)* of moral betterment in Indian thought, whatever the intervening stages, is this escape. Western readers should note that <u>heaven *(svarga)* is not,</u> <u>in the Indian world view, nirvāṇa, but a part of the saṃsāric world system.</u>

A peacock medallion from early Buddhist art.

2.
Gautama's Enlightenment

The extant versions of the complete life of the Buddha were all composed 500 or more years after his death. They draw on much earlier material from the canonical *Sūtras* (Discourses) and *Vinaya* (Discipline) for events after the Renunciation. Except for sporadic incidents, they give a legendary account of his earlier life, a fabric of myth and literary invention. The authors viewed the Buddha as an epic hero, and their purpose was to celebrate his deeds; they were not chroniclers but poets. Nonetheless, Aśvaghoṣa (first century A.D.), in his *Acts of the Buddha,* saw Gautama as a genuine human being; and even where the narrative is not historical, it is dramatically authentic. The hero is a man experiencing conflicts; undergoing genuine temptations; trying, and ultimately rejecting, false courses; at every point exercising choice and prevailing, not through fate or the intervention of other men or gods, but through his own action. He is motivated by compassion for suffering mankind; and he exhibits the martial virtues of courage, steadfastness, initiative, and self-discipline. Throughout his ordeals he sustains a delicate sensitivity and an unshakable dignity.

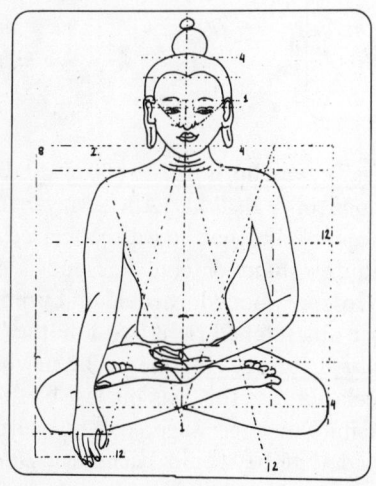

The enlightened Buddha, here sketched according to the Tibetan tradition to show the traditional proportions of the Buddha-image. His right hand touches the earth to recall the drama of Enlightenment. By this gesture he called Mother Earth to bear witness to his merit and thus to his power to defeat Māra and gain salvation from Māra's realm of recurrent birth and death.

How close is this attractive character to the historical person? Probably as close as Aśvaghoṣa could make it with the data and concepts at his disposal. The quest for the objective Gautama, like that for the historical Jesus, is foredoomed to a measure of failure. We cannot get behind the portraits that the early communities synthesized for their founders; their reports are all we have.

But though the *Saṅgha* (Community) created the image of the Buddha, the Buddha created the Saṅgha and in so doing impressed upon it his personality. The master exhorted his disciples to imitate him, and they formulated and transmitted an image of him, along with his teachings, as a model for later generations to imitate. Though the process of formulation entails distortion, the purpose of transmission ensures a measure of fidelity.

A,

BIRTH AND YOUTH OF THE BODHISATTVA

The Śākyas were a warrior *(kṣatriya)* tribe inhabiting a border district just below the Himālayan foothills. For some unknown reason, they used the brahmin clan name Gautama ("descendent of the sage Gotama"). The future Buddha's father, Śuddhodana, was a king of Kapilavastu, a town whose remains archeologists have not been able to find.

King Śuddhodana and Queen Māyā, the father and mother of the Bodhisattva. (From an Ajantā cave wall painting of the sixth century.)

Śākyamuni ("Sage of the Śākyas"), was born about 560 B.C.[1] Buddhists celebrate his nativity on the full moon of Vaiśākha (April-May), the fourth month in the Indian calendar. The legend says that he was conceived when his mother, Māyā, dreamed that a white elephant entered her body. When her time was approaching, she retired to the wooded garden of Lumbinī, near Kapilavastu, where, standing with her upstretched right hand on the branch of a tree, she gave birth to the *Bodhisattva* (future Buddha). The newborn child stood up, strode seven paces, and declared that this was his last birth—that he was destined for enlightenment. Asita, an aged sage, came, examined the marks on the infant, and prophesied that he would become a *Buddha* (an enlightened one). Other accounts specified that he would become such only if he chose to leave the palace to become a wandering ascetic; otherwise, he would become a world-ruling monarch. They called the boy Siddhārtha, "he who has achieved his goal."

The purpose of all the mythic elements in the nativity cycle is to show that the Bodhisattva was innately different from ordinary men. The view that

The dream of Queen Māyā. (From the Bhārhut stūpa, second century B.C.)

The birth of the Bodhisattva from his mother's side under the tree. (From an eleventh century palm leaf Sanskrit manuscript.)

normal procreation and birth are impure betrays a body image in sharp contrast to the Upaniṣads, which liken copulation to sacrifice.

Seven days after giving birth, Māyā died. Śuddhodana married her sister, Prajāpatī, who brought up the young Bodhisattva. When he came of age, he was married to a bride, usually called Yaśodharā, whom his father selected. The legend embellishes this phase with epic folklore motifs, saying that Śuddhodana tried to prevent his son from leaving the palace and becoming an ascetic by tying him down with sensual pleasures, not only arranging his marriage but surrounding him with song-and-dance girls and every delight a man could desire.

At left, the four encounters outside the palace walls. Beginning from the top, the Bodhisattva successively encounters an old man, a sick man, and one dead. At bottom, he sees a religious mendicant, who symbolizes the spiritual alternative to attachment to the world of impermanence and suffering. (After a ninth century Chinese silk painting from Tun-huang.)

In due course Yaśodharā bore Siddhārtha a son, whom they named Rāhula, "The Fetter," an indication that the young father's heart was already turning away from the household life.

THE GREAT RENUNCIATION[2]

The legend tells that Prince Siddhārtha, sheltered by his overprotective father from every hint of sorrow and suffering, went out for a chariot ride and for the first time saw a decrepit old man. Shocked, he asked his charioteer about the man's condition; the charioteer declared that such is the destiny of all men. The prince turned back to the palace and brooded in melancholy, taking no relish in the gaiety and pleasure around him. On a second ride, he saw his first diseased man, and reflected that people are foolish to revel under the constant threat of disease. On the third trip, he saw his first corpse; dismayed, he marveled that people could forget the fear of death and live heedlessly.

The life of princely pleasure provides effective counterpoint to the traumatic encounters with impermanence and suffering. Aśvaghoṣa exploits the theme skillfully; then, in the conventions of Sanskrit drama, he composes a dialog between his hero and a confidant, the king's counselor, who advises him to follow the example of bygone heroes and sages and pursue the pleasures of erotic love. The Bodhisattva's reply is an eloquent statement of the ascetic case against the sensual life. Sensual joys are fleeting; death casts its long shadow back over life and blights all transient happiness.

The brooding prince rode out again, observed the peasants plowing, and, unlike the ordinary patrician, was moved to grief at the suffering of toilers and oxen, and even at the slaughter of worms and insects by the plow. He sat under a tree, entered the first *dhyāna* (meditative trance), and found some peace of mind. He meditated on the truth of suffering. After a while he saw a religious mendicant and made up his mind to leave the household life.

The legend poignantly describes how in the depth of night the prince took a last look at his wife and infant son, mounted his horse, and rode out of the sleeping city, accompanied by his charioteer. Siddhārtha dismounted, sent his charioteer back to Śuddhodana with his ornaments and a message, then cut off his hair and exchanged clothes with a passing hunter.

The kernel of this episode, the Great Renunciation, is the conflict between the household and the ascetic ways of life. Far from encouraging his son to become a monk, Śuddhodana did everything in his power to prevent him. And at each point, Siddhārtha recognized his duty and expressed strong affection toward his father. Aśvaghoṣa puts into the Bodhisattva's mouth a speech

The prince's great going forth from the palace and the sleeping city of Kapilavastu. Attendant divinities muffle the sound of his horse's hooves while over him is the royal umbrella. (From a seventeenth century painting on silk from Thailand.)

justifying departure for the homeless life as fidelity to an even higher *dharma* (duty, norm).

THE BODHISATTVA'S STUDIES

The new mendicant, then twenty-nine years old, went first to a teacher called Ārāḍa Kālāma, who apparently taught a kind of meditation leading to "attainment of the state of nothing at all." His means were faith, energy, mindfulness, concentration, and wisdom. Gautama practiced the method and quickly attained the goal. Kālāma then set him up as his equal and coteacher. But Gautama concluded that this dharma (teaching and practice) did not lead to enlightenment and nirvāṇa and went away. He then studied under Udraka Rāmaputra, who taught the way to the "attainment of neither conception nor nonconception." Gautama mastered this dharma, was acclaimed a teacher, found it, too, unsatisfactory, and abandoned it.

The canonical account of Gautama's study under these two teachers is an old one, formulated in the concepts and literary modes of the early Buddhist church, but otherwise plausible. What the teachers and their illustrious disciple were pursuing was not contemplative identification of the soul and the world spirit (like the Upaniṣads), not starving out impurities through abstinence (like the Jains), but attainment of *bodhi* (enlightenment) and *nirvāṇa* through cultivation of meditative trances. This path is known in later Hinduism as *rāja-yoga,* "the royal discipline." But the earliest clear references in the Upaniṣads to this method are later than the Buddha, the fullest archaic Hindu description of it being found in the *Bhagavad Gītā* (circa 200 B.C.); and it became part of the systematization of yoga in the *Yoga Sūtras* of Patañjali (circa third or fourth century A.D.). Rāja-yoga came into Buddhism not from Brahmanism but from the ascetic wanderer sects of ancient India.

The fivefold path of Ārāḍa Kālāma—faith, energy, mindfulness, concentration and wisdom—occurs twice in the Buddhist list of thirty-seven elements "conducive to enlightenment." The individual items occur repeatedly in various Buddhist formulations. The account indicates the attainments of the two teachers with reference to another early Buddhist formula, the eight liberations *(vimokṣa).* It is expressed as the movement through stages that correlate with ever more subtle planes of existence. The meditator, passing beyond perceptions of visible form *(rūpa),* ceases to perceive diversity and abides in stage four, awareness of the infinity of consciousness. Subsequent stages are (5) awareness of nothing at all, (6) awareness of neither conception nor nonconception, and (7) the cessation of conception and feeling. Ārāḍa's attainment is stage six, and Uddraka's is stage seven. The author of the canonical account may have taken this means to express a hazy tradition that the Buddha's teachers had almost, but not quite, realized the highest trance attainment; or, on the other hand, the formula may have originated in the Buddha's systematization of his own experience.

The technique indicated is to contemplate things that have shape-and-color *(rūpa),* that is, visible form, until they become transparent. Solid objects and their corresponding sensory images dissolve; the meditator escapes from the confines of the solid body and in ecstasy abides in the mind-body. The four form-realm elements commonly experienced in the realm of form (earth, water, fire, and air) are transcended. Then as the consciousness of the yogin becomes subtler and more all-pervasive, awareness is transcended of the fifth element, space-ether *(ākāśa)* and then of the sixth element, consciousness. In this stage, the awareness of nothing at all, there is still consciousness but it is so subtle that no object corresponds to it. But conceptions and feelings evidently remain. The seventh stage is the upper limit of the formless realm, at the end point of existence; this end point is fittingly expressed in the pattern "neither *X* nor non-*X,*" which commonly indicates in Buddhist language a point at which the series is transcended and opposites merge.

Gautama forsook the dharma of the two teachers because it did not conduce to "aversion, dispassion, cessation, tranquility, superknowledge, enlightenment, and nirvāṇa," says the Sūtra. These seven quasi-synonyms taken together show the main features of the goal that Gautama sought:

pacification of mental turbulence, perfect direct knowledge, and attainment of the unconditioned realm.

HIS AUSTERITIES

The Bodhisattva then went eastward to Uruvelā near Gavā, where he found a pleasant spot and settled down to austerities.[1] He practiced stopping his breath to induce trances, and was not deterred by the violent headaches that resulted. He fasted and came as close as he could to eating nothing at all, becoming utterly emaciated. He was joined in his strivings by five ascetics, and continued

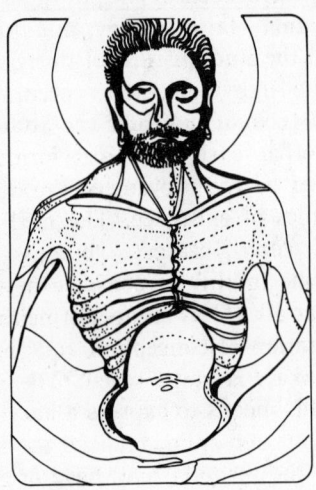

The Bodhisattva at the height of his austerities. (After a second to third century A.D. Gandhāra sculpture.)

in this painful course until six years after the Great Renunciation. Realizing that by this severe mortification he had not achieved sublime knowledge and insight, he tried to think of another way. He remembered an incident in his childhood when he sat under a shady tree while his father was plowing. His mind had happened on a dispassionate equilibrium and he had entered the first *dhyāna,* (level of meditative trance), a pleasant and zestful state. Perhaps this pointed to a fruitful method. But his body was too weak and lean, he realized, to gain this blissful exaltation.

The later legend says that Gautama then sat under another sacred tree. A woman named Sujātā had vowed a yearly offering to this tree if she bore a son. The wish was fulfilled, and she prepared as offering a fine bowl of rice milk. Her maid came upon the Bodhisattva sitting there, mistook him for the spirit of the tree, and reported the apparition to her mistress, who came and presented the food to Gautama. The earlier Pali[4] text says simply that Gautama took solid food, rice, and yogurt. The five mendicants then left him in disgust, saying that he had given up striving and was living in abundance.

   Gautama's rejection of extreme austerities hinged on a critical moment when he realized that in his childhood he had known a state of happiness free from sensual desires and immoral thoughts. It dawned on him that there was nothing wrong with being happy. He went on to recognize that a healthy body is necessary for the pursuit of wisdom. In so doing, he turned toward enlightenment and took the first step on the Middle Way, which became the central point of his Dharma. While rejecting both mortification of the flesh and sensual indulgence, he accepted happiness as good. Moreover, the act of breaking his fast affirmed that the person is not a soul-substance alien to the body, but an organic entity in which both physical and psychic factors participate. *(as opposed to the dualistic approach of Jainism.)*

TEMPTATION BY MĀRA[5]

According to the legend, on the fourteenth of Vaiśākha (April-May) Gautama dreamed five dreams indicating that he was about to become a Buddha. The next day he accepted the meal from Sujātā. He went and sat under the Bodhi Tree, facing east, and resolved not to arise until he attained enlightenment. Māra (Death) was alarmed at the prospect of the Bodhisattva's victory, which would allow him to escape from Death's realm, and came to assail him with an army of fearful demons. The Bodhisattva was protected, though, by his accumulated merit and his friendly love *(maitrī)*. After failing to shake him, the hosts of demons fled in defeat. Māra then invoked his own merit so as to convert it into magic power and overthrow the Bodhisattva. But Gautama invoked his own superior merit, amassed through many previous lives. Māra called on his retinue to witness his merit; and Śākyamuni, having no other witness on his side, touched the earth with his right hand (a pose often shown

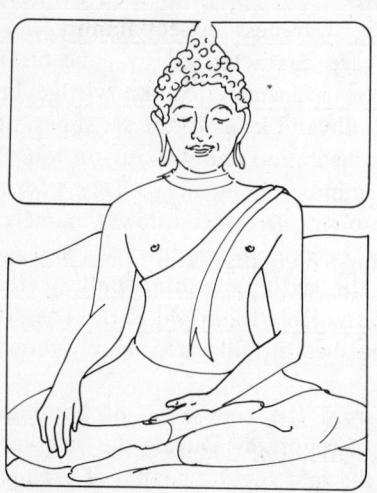

The defeat of Māra. (After a fourteenth century Thai sculpture.)

in Buddhist art), and called Mother Earth to testify to his merit. The earth quaked in response. Then Māra, having failed with intimidation and compulsion, turned to temptation. He sent his three daughters, Discontent, Delight, and Desire, to seduce the future Buddha, who remained as impervious to lust as he had to fear. As the sun set, Māra and his hosts gave up and withdrew.

This temptation episode is quite a late addition and entirely mythical. The myth, though, is a suitable expression of an experience common to most contemplatives. The seeker eventually is committed to an integral attempt, overcomes doubt and inertia, and sets to work. This conjures up the demons of fear from the unconscious. All the habit-hardened dispositions protest against their coming destruction. But good habits sustain the seeker's resolve. The waves of fear pass, and doubts arise as to whether the candidate is really equal to the challenge. If the seeker possesses genuine self-confidence, the doubts are vanquished. The last peril is of course the rosiest and the deadliest. Perfect love (maitrī) may cast out fear, but it all too easily changes into libido.

THE ENLIGHTENMENT[6]

On the night of the full moon, the Bodhisattva ascended the four stages of dhyāna (trance). The first trance is produced by detaching from sense objects and calming the passions. It is marked by zest and ease, and thinking in it is discursive, focusing and gazing at the mental images as they pass. Similar trances sometimes occur spontaneously when the mind is concentrated, stimulated, and focused steadily on one object by love or hate, intellectual discovery or artistic inspiration. The second trance is nondiscursive. There is one-pointedness of mind, serene faith, zest, and ease. The third trance is dispassionate rather than zestful; it is mindful and conscious, with a feeling of bliss in the body. The fourth trance is free from opposites such as pleasure and pain, elation and depression. It is pure awareness and equanimity.[7]

All of the dhyānas or trances are characterized by concentration and insight. The insight they facilitate is not theoretical knowledge but direct perception. Attainment of the fourth dhyāna leads to the six superknowledges (abhijñā[8]): (1) magic powers (such as levitation and walking on water); (2) the divine ear; (3) knowledge of others' minds; (4) memory of one's former lives; (5) the divine eye; (6) and extinction of the āsrava (outflows), namely, sensual desire, desire for continuous physical becoming, wrong views, and ignorance. The first five are mundane, while the sixth is realized only by the arhant (perfected saint) who has completed the Holy Eightfold Path. The attainment of the sixth superknowledge distinguishes the liberated adept from the mere wizard.

The progress toward release from the conditions of bondage is also described in terms of unusual kinds of cognition. During the first watch of the night (evening), Gautama acquired the first cognition, that of each of his own previous existences, seeing them one by one, just as they had been.

During the second watch (midnight) he acquired the divine eye (the fifth superknowledge and second cognition), with which he surveyed the decease and rebirth of living beings everywhere. The whole universe, it is said, appeared to him as in a mirror. He saw that good karman (acts) leads to a happy rebirth and evil karman to a miserable next life. *cf. Bhagavad Gita, Ch. II*

During the third watch (late night), he acquired the third cognition (and sixth superknowledge), that of the extinction of the outflows. He perceived the Four Holy Truths, noting, "This is suffering, this is the source of suffering, this is the cessation of suffering, and this is the path that leads to the cessation of suffering." According to Aśvaghoṣa, he realized the principle of *pratītya-samutpāda* (dependent co-arising), and meditated on the twelve preconditions *(nidāna)* for the arising of existence. His mind became free from the outflows, and as the Sūtra says, "In me emancipated arose knowledge of my emancipation. I realized that rebirth has been destroyed, the holy life has been lived, the job has been done, there is nothing after this."

The new day dawned on Gautama, now the Buddha. According to legend the animate and natural worlds celebrated the event with prodigies. The earth swayed, thunder rolled and rain fell from a cloudless sky, blossoms fell from the heavens. Gautama's ancestors, then sages in paradise, observed his victory and offered him reverence. The Buddha thus acquitted on a higher level the family obligation that, as a Bodhisattva, he had forsaken in the worldly sense.

B. INTERPRETATION OF THE ENLIGHTENMENT

What actually happened on the night of the Enlightenment? The oldest account is stylized and exhibits typical mythic features. It purports, though, to be autobiographical. First-person reporting of "peak experiences" was not a genre in pre-Buddhist Indian literature and flourished only sporadically in later centuries. Implicit in it is the affirmation that the particular experiences of a historical person are of outstanding value. The dignity, economy, and sobriety of the account not only highlight the magnitude of Gautama's claims, but also strongly suggest a remarkable man behind the style, self-assured and self-aware, assertive but not bombastic. If disciples put such words into the mouth of their master, then who put into their minds such an image of him?

Later doctrine elaborates the idea of "the silence of the saints" and holds that nirvāṇa is indescribable; but nowhere does the early Canon say that the content of the Enlightenment is nonintellectual, or that it is inexpressible. However splendid the visions and however exalted the mystic state of mind, the Enlightenment consisted of the discovery of communicable ideas. It is described as the realization in trance of the specific destinies of all living beings and of the general principles governing these destinies. The first cognition, memory of one's own former lives, is a shamanic power, documented even among the Amerindians. The second cognition, perception of living beings everywhere dying and being reborn, is likewise a variety of shamanic power—

unobstructed cosmic vision—widely attested in archaic cultures. It evidently involved seeing the past and future, as well as the present, condition of others, a power universally attributed to prophets. The specifically Buddhist feature is correlating good deeds with happy births and bad deeds with miserable ones. The third cognition is a philosophical theory (Greek *theōria,* "a seeing, a vision, a contemplation"). It is presented not as the fruits of speculation but as a direct perception, like the first two cognitions. The phrasing looks rather abstract to the modern reader, but clearly it was intended, for all its generality, to be experiential and concrete. The universals that Gautama saw were simply the aggregates of observable particulars. The content of enlightenment is thus two-thirds shamanism ethically transformed, and one-third philosophy, a feature that higher civilization does not share with the archaic and the primitive.

The sequence of nocturnal watches matched with the three cognitions, and the coincidence of daybreak and enlightenment, are mythic but not necessarily fictitious. Many a person has sat rapt in thought all night and, quickening to the new day, has seen a solution in a flood of light. The initiant into Mediterranean mystery cults sat in darkness until engulfed by a great light. Darkness is an objective aid to sensory withdrawal without which the inner light cannot burst into radiance. The Eskimo aspirant to shamanhood passes long hours in solitary meditation and, in the climactic moment feels aglow with a mysterious, brain-centered light which enables the meditator to see in the dark as well as to see the future and other occult things. The light in question, with shaman and *bhikṣu* (Buddhist monk), is not just a figure of speech but a physical experience of overwhelming radiance. The experience is described often and vividly in meditation manuals. It has obvious analogies with certain experiences under psychedelic drugs and may perhaps have a similar physiological basis. In any event greatly heightened sensitivity is a factor.

The full moon may be a ritual element in the story. The nights when the moon changes phase, especially the new and full moons, were considered ominous in ancient India and marked with fasts and rites. Other wanderer sects were celebrating these dates by assembling and preaching their doctrines, so at the instance of his followers the Buddha prescribed that his Community should do likewise. The ritual high point of the month, the night of the full moon, would have seemed most appropriate for the Enlightenment, and the event may in fact have taken place then. One can imagine the effect on Gautama's psyche of the cool, moonlit, tropical night scene.

As already remarked, the Enlightenment fused archaic shamanic attainments with an ethical and philosophical vision. The primitive elements are in service to the higher ones. The first and second cognitions, remembrance of former lives and cosmic vision, constitute an empirical verification of the doctrines of transmigration and retribution for deeds. In Gautama's view, the materialists who say that there is no afterlife and that there is no fruition of past deeds are as wrong as the dualists who hold that there is a soul separate from the body. What determines one's rebirth, though, is not sacrifice or mere knowledge, as in the Upaniṣads, but the quality of one's entire life. Those who do good in deed, word, and thought, who speak well of the saints and hold right views, are reborn in a happy state, in paradise. Those who do evil are reborn in a wretched state, in hell.

The idea of moral causality seems only in the sixth century B.C. to have become dissociated from notions of the efficacy of ritual and ascetic acts. There is no assurance that Upaniṣadic passages expressing the idea are pre-Buddhist. If, as is probable, Gautama discovered this comprehensive moral world view, it is no wonder that the vision burst upon him with relevatory force, that he saw the principle enacted in a cosmic panorama of doing, dying, and rebirth.

One novel feature of early Buddhist ethics is that it gives primacy to intention. Good and bad are not quasi-physical as in Jainism, but are assigned to a distinct moral dimension. Unintentional deeds have merely common-sense consequences, not karmic ones. The *Vinaya* (Discipline) regularly distinguishes deliberate from inadvertent violations of the rule. In contrast to later Hinduism, the physical act is of itself neither pure nor impure. Gautama's achievement in freeing ethics from ritual and tabu was as momentous as Paul's emancipation of Christianity from the Jewish Torah.

THE TWELVE PRECONDITIONS OF DEPENDENT CO-ARISING

The variant accounts of what Gautama realized during the third watch agree that he found the causes and the cure for miserable bondage to rebirth in saṃsāra (the round of existence). The twin causes are invariably *tṛṣṇā* (desire) and *avidyā* (ignorance), and the cure is knowledge.

The formula used to explain the origin and interdependent causes of this bondage to "old age, death, grief, lamentation, physical and mental pain, and despair" is *pratītya-samutpāda* (dependent co-arising). Insight into this, according to Aśvaghoṣa, immediately preceded Gautama's release from saṃsāra. Pratītya-samutpāda is equated with Dharma; whoever sees one, sees the other. It is thus a subject of paramount importance to Buddhists and a subject of constant meditation.

Dependent co-arising, or the Buddhist law of moral cause and effect, is expressed in its twelve preconditions *(nidāna)* leading to continued *duḥkha* (suffering) and bondage to rebirth. These are: (1) ignorance, (2) dispositions, (3) consciousness, (4) name-and-form, (5) the six sense fields, (6) contact, (7) feeling, (8) rebirth, (9) appropriation, (10) becoming, (11) rebirth, and (12) aging and dying.

Causation, a central problem throughout the history of Indian philosophy, first drew consideration in early archaic speculation about creation. The question was, simply and vaguely, how the world came into existence. Gautama's question, though, was not how the manifested world came to be projected or created from the unmanifest, but what suffering depends on and how it can be stopped. He began at the end of the chain and worked backward,[9] observing that:

(12) Aging and dying depend on rebirth (if there were no rebirth, then there would be no death).

(11) Rebirth depends on becoming (if life X did not die and come to be life Y, there would be no birth of Y).

(10) Becoming depends on appropriation (if the life process did not appropriate phenomenal (observable) materials just as a fire appropriates fuel, then there would be no transmigration).

(9) Appropriation depends on desire (if one did not thirst for sense objects, for coming to be after this life, and for ceasing to be after this life, then the transmigrant process would not appropriate fuel).

(8) Desire depends on feeling (if pleasant and painful feelings were not experienced, then one would not be conditioned to seek continuing experience of the pleasant or cessation of the unpleasant).

(7) Feeling depends on contact (the meeting of sense and object is necessary before pleasure or pain can be felt).

(6) Contact depends on the six sense fields (the six pairs of sense and datum, namely, eye-visible form, ear-sound, smelling-smell, tongue-taste, body-touchable, mind-dharma).

(5) The six sense fields depend on name-and-form (mind and body; as the sense fields are equivalent to name-and-form, some lists of preconditions omit the sense fields).

(4) Name-and-form, the whole living organism, depends on consciousness, which here means the spark of sentient life that enters the womb and animates the embryo.

(3) Consciousness depends on the dispositions accrued throughout life as karmic residues of deeds, words, and thoughts.

(2) The dispositions, or karmic legacy that produces rebirth, depends on ignorance of the Four Holy Truths.

(1) Ignorance.

Gautama's prescription is: When ignorance ceases, dispositions cease, and so on until aging and dying cease.

Each precondition depends on the one before it, and evidently ignorance is held to depend on aging and dying, so that the twelve preconditions form a circle, represented in Buddhist art as the Wheel of Life. The logical character of the chain is shown by the affirmative and negative forms: If B exists, then A has existed. If A does not exist, then B will not exist. The relation between the links is implication. As a theory of causation, this "dependent co-arising" concerns the formal concomitances among things rather than their material derivation from one another. It resembles a medical diagnosis in several ways. By showing that the ailment depends on a series of conditions, it indicates the point at which the series can be broken and so facilitates a cure. This counteracts the theory that the disease is a fortuitous happening, against which no remedy would be effective. It also opposes the view that the ultimate cause of the malady is some entity outside the process such as God or an immutable soul. Salvation from transmigration is to be found in the process of transmigration itself.

Two metaphorical readings of the twelve preconditions of dependent co-arising from later commentarial traditions will help to understand it. Buddhaghosa (circa fifth century A.D.) restated the twelve in similes which compare it to the course of a physical injury and its consequences. Ignorance (1) is a blind man who does not see what is before him; the dispositions (2) are that he stumbles; the resulting consciousness (3) is that he falls; name-and-form (4) is that he develops an abscess, which accumulates matter inside—the six sense fields (5); he presses against it, producing contact (6); and it begins to hurt, the feeling precondition (7). The man craves a cure, which is desire (8), uses the wrong medicine, appropriation (9), which, with the wrong ointment, becoming (10), results in the abscess swelling even more, rebirth (11) and bursting, the final precondition of aging and dying (12), which is the *duḥkha* (suffering) that results from the original avidyā (ignorance).

Another set of illustrations for the twelve preconditions comes from the Tibetan paintings of the Wheel of Life. Ignorance (1) is portrayed here too as a blind person, this one groping with a stick; the dispositions (2) are a potter with his pots. The potter's wheel in this image recalls the Wheel of Life, its movement initiated by the original ignorance; the pots are the impermanent consequences or formations that result. Consciousness (3) is illustrated by a monkey climbing a fruit tree; here the mind is compared to a wild monkey going this way and that after the objects of its desire. Name-and-form (4) is compared to a boat (the form *skandha* or personality aggregate) ferrying four passengers (the other four skandhas or personality aggregates) across the ocean (of saṃsāra). An empty house stands for the six sense fields (5), the house being the body whose windows on the world are the five senses and the mind;

Illustration of two links of the chain of causation from a Tibetan Wheel of Life, showing contact (condition 6) at the right leading to feeling (condition 7)—an arrow in the eye.

all are empty of any permanent self. Two lovers kissing and embracing illustrate contact (6), while a man with an arrow in his eye portrays the painful resultant precondition, feeling (7). Desire (8) is shown as a woman offering a drink to a man, or a man drinking wine, since *tṛṣṇā* (desire) literally means thirst; its concomitant, appropriation or grasping (9) is shown as a man gathering a large basketful of fruit from a tree. Becoming (10) is a pregnant woman, a mother in childbirth is rebirth (11), a corpse being carried off to the cemetery is aging and dying (12).

Both metaphorical readings of the life-chain emphasize the sufferings and misfortunes of bondage to rebirth. This chain of bondage can only be broken by counteracting the original ignorance with knowledge.

THE WHEEL OF LIFE AND THE HIERARCHY OF BEINGS

Just as Gautama realized the causal links in his third night watch, in the previous watch he observed with his "pure divine eye" the details of saṃsāra, or the world system. He saw, according to Aśvaghoṣa's account, "beings appear and pass away according to their karman." His vision, combined with the twelve preconditions, was systematized in later Buddhist art in the figure of

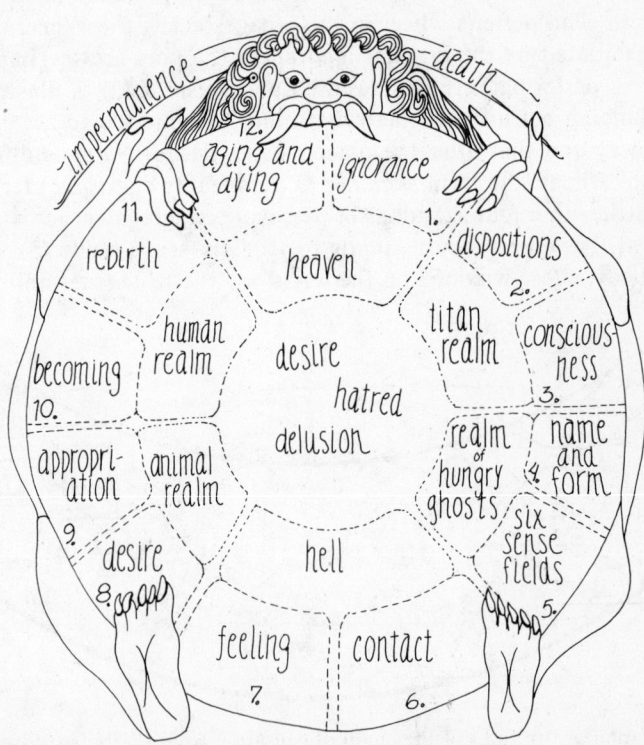

Figure 1. The Buddhist Wheel of Life

the Wheel of Life. This image (see Figure 1) is the map Buddhists use to make their existence intelligible.

Buddhist texts present no prominent account of creation. Rather, it is assumed that it is more important for the individual seeking release to understand the proximate causes of bondage and to take actions in this life that will alleviate *duḥkha* (suffering). The Wheel of Life is the Buddhist creation myth. Psychological in its basis, it is an attempt to account for a person's world experience; it presents the drama of personal choice and consequence.

One Buddhist text describes the Buddha instructing his disciples to paint this diagram over the gateway of a monastery. In Tibetan monasteries it was often conspicuously painted in the vestibule or on hanging scrolls for meditation, showing graphically how the individual is bound to saṃsāra, the endlessly turning Wheel of Life.

Māra as Impermanence, the ruler of the material world and the god of death, holding the Wheel of Life in his fangs. Below, center to right, the chain of causation begins with ignorance (first precondition), the blind leading the blind. At far left, the result (twelfth precondition) death—a person being carried off in a litter for disposal of the body. (From a Tibetan Wheel of Life.)

The whole wheel is held in the mouth and claws of the demon Death, or Impermanence, and its perimeter is ringed with the twelve preconditions. In its nave are three animals: the cock symbolizing desire; the snake, hatred; and the pig, delusion. They are the propelling forces of the cycle of existence in which karmic retribution determines where on the wheel each individual will be reborn.

The cock, the snake, and the pig, symbolizing, respectively, desire, hatred, and delusion, each of which leads to and reinforces the others. (From the center of a Tibetan Wheel of Life.)

There are six rebirth realms, or destinies, within the wheel.[10] The three lower destinies result from evil acts; the three upper reward good. The most degraded beings are the inhabitants of the hells, hot and cold subterranean places of age-long but not everlasting retribution. Buddhist hells are purgatorial: once the ripening of the karman (deeds) is complete, a process accomplished only through passage of time, the condemned individuals can ascend and reach the human realm, where again they must face moral responsibility for their future. Next lowest is the realm of hungry ghosts. These beings haunt the earth's surface, continually tormented by insatiable hunger. They stand outside walls and gates, mutely pleading to be fed. The realm of animals are considered to rank just above the hungry ghosts. Individuals reborn as animals have to suffer the cruelties to which dumb creatures are subjected.

The three upper, fortunate destinies reward good karman. Of these the human destiny is considered the lowest but also the most important since only here can virtue and wisdom be increased. All other realms are retributions or rewards for choices and actions taken in the human realm. Even when someone attains nirvāṇa while sojourning in a heaven, it is due to the ripening of merit won as a human being. Human beings stand in the middle of the animate hierarchy, not, as in the post-Darwinian world view, at the top.

The two highest rebirth realms are those of the gods and the demigods or titans (beings of a slightly lower order than gods). Both of these realms are inhabited by a diversity of beings, but all are there by virtue of their karman and, when traces of their actions run out, are subject to reincarnation. Thus, even the gods, those born in one of the heavens, suffer death and expulsion from their transient dominion. Their loss of pleasure is painful. Lacking sufficient merit, they may be reborn, even in realms lower than the human. Because of his superior merit, the Bodhisattva was reborn from a heavenly domain for his last rebirth as Gautama among humans, and attained there the completion of his samsaric destinies.

In Indian mythology, a demon devours the moon when an eclipse occurs. In this traditional Thai adaptation, the demon is Māra, who devours those (symbolized by the moon-disk) who remain attached to material life. This sort of picture was painted on the gates of Thai monasteries to remind passersby to strive to free themselves from their mortal fates.

All the realms of saṃsāra are transient and subject to recurrent death. Buddhism's final goal is release from the Wheel of Life entirely. Nirvāṇa is nowhere on the wheel but utterly transcends it.

The continual appearance of gods and spirits in early Buddhist texts is a fact to be seriously considered even though the texts insist that the Buddha and the *arhants* (perfected saints) are superior to all the gods since technically they have transcended saṃsāra. The existence of spirit species is taken for granted; their members frequently have transactions with human beings; and human beings, too, go to rebirth in these incorporeal destinies. All, even the highest gods, are included within the wheel's system of karmic retribution, and no being holds a rank forever. Even the great gods of the popular religion of the time, Indra and Brahmā, are not eternal persons but merely karmic individuals born into those positions. The spirit world is given an ethical basis and thus rendered rational and more benign. The frequent theme in Buddhist literature of the ogre's conversion expresses the conviction that human virtue can overcome even the most malignant nonhuman beings. Accordingly, the proper mode of transaction is to make food-offerings to a spirit just as if it were a human guest, a brahmin or a monk. If the being is malign, it should not be appeased with sacrifice but rather tamed through the power of a holy individual. Buddhists do not consider the spirit world especially sacred, and in fact treat it as a gaseous extension of the animate realm.

What is striking about the Wheel of Life's version of the moral drama of creation is the central place human volition holds in it. No one but the individual is the author of rebirth in a lower or higher realm, and no one else can bring about the individual's ultimate salvation. The human person stands at the center of creation with the assurance that whatever destiny is suffered or enjoyed is fully merited. The image accounts for every turn of one's life experience.

KARMAN AND PERSONAL RESPONSIBILITY

"According to their karman" beings appear, disappear, and reappear somewhere else on the ever-changing Wheel of Life. During the first night watch, Gautama remembered all his previous lives and understood his personal karman. In the second, he saw that karman was what determined this passage through saṃsāra's possible fates, and noted the correlation of good karman with favorable destinies and evil karman with unfavorable. During the third watch, he transcended karman entirely, winning salvation and escape from the Wheel. Karman contains the mystery of both bondage to saṃsāra and release from it.

Karman, meaning action or deed, is correlate with saṃsāra. All Buddhist ideas of human destiny, retribution, and salvation derive from it. Based on the prior Brahmanical sacrificial idea that ritually prescribed actions lead to desired consequences, the notion of karman asserts that every action leaves a trace which will inevitably bear fruit *(phala)* or have consequence *(vipāka)*. Buddhist moralists repeatedly insist that the consequence of karmic acts will inevitably come, in this or subsequent lives.[11] Once an act occurs, it cannot be denied or forgotten, but its consequence must either be counteracted or inevitably occur.

In many ways, the idea of karman is like the psychologist's notion of habit. Both have their inception in the prior acts of an individual and, once established, become a deep-seated predisposition to act in a certain way, for instance, to smoke cigarettes or overeat, or to act out of compulsive desire or neurotic hatred. These are extremely difficult to break. Also, the karman conception makes one responsible for what one is. It is not predetermined fate or irrevocable destiny; nor is it an absolute determinism. No matter how strong the force of one's previous karmic endowment is, it can always be counteracted and transformed.

Three dimensions of karman are important: acts that generate good consequences in the realm of saṃsāra, acts that produce bad consequences in this realm, and acts that lead to release from it. The first two aspects of karman lead to continuance of life in saṃsāra; they focus on moral betterment in saṃsāra rather than ultimate salvation from it. These are particularly relevant to lay Buddhists, who have not dedicated themselves to the earnest pursuit of total escape from the Wheel of Life. According to its intention and nature, karman is good and meritorious or bad and destructive. The latter is based on the three ignorant mental habits found at the center of the Wheel— desire, hatred, and delusion; they lead to killing, stealing, sexual transgression, and acts of vocal transgression such as lying and slander. These condemn one to rebirth in the lower saṃsāric destinies. Acts of merit, on the other hand, especially giving *(dāna)*, virtue *(śīla)*, and self-discipline result in happy rebirth, especially in blissful states or in heavenly realms.

Though contemporary evidence indicates that it is the goal of many Buddhists, even monks, this relative improvement of position within the Wheel of Life is not the ultimate goal. The highest goal of Buddhism is finally to become free from karman's consequences altogether. This is the third dimension of karman: acting in such a way as no longer to be subject to karmic retribution. It is accomplished through a complete retraining of the personality, counteracting its evil tendencies and increasing its mindfulness and knowledge until the sources of any karmic deeds are extenuated and finally extinguished. To achieve this goal takes years or decades, even lifetimes. Gautama himself spent six years in such training in his last lifetime alone, at the end of which he attained *bodhi* (a special knowledge) that released him from further rebirth. From that point on his actions generated no further consequences that bound him to saṃsāra. The effects of previous actions, presumably, had allowed this *bodhi,* and no other consequences remained that would keep him, at death, on the Wheel of Life.

Mind, Buddhists insist, creates the reality in which every person lives. Purified of karmic intentions, skilled in spiritual practice and compassionate, the Buddha expected no rebirth and understood every mortal trial. His karman after Enlightenment is the model for all Buddhists. It expressed the final fruit of Buddhist self-discipline and meditative self-transformation—active, insightful involvement in a world that continues to suffer the consequences of its own ignorance.

3.
The Buddha as Teacher

THE DECISION TO PROPAGATE THE DHARMA

Tradition says that the Buddha spent forty-nine days in the neighborhood of the Bodhi Tree. Then two merchants en route from Orissa passed close by and were advised by the spirit of a dead relative to make offerings to the new Buddha, who was sitting at the foot of a certain tree. They offered honey cakes and sugar cane and "took refuge" in (formally committed themselves to the authority of) the Buddha and his Dharma, thus becoming the first Buddhists and the first lay devotees in the world. In this case Gautama did not preach Dharma to the two men but merely received their reverence and offerings. Worship of holy persons is nonsectarian and does not involve subscribing to their ideas. Buddhist lay cult is here shown developing naturally out of pre-Buddhist practices.

The Buddha preaching to a group of monks and nobility including, on his left, some foreigners. (From an Ajantā cave wall painting, sixth century A.D.)

The canonical account says that the Buddha at first thought that humanity, addicted to its attachments, would find it hard to understand his Dharma. If he tried to propound his doctrines and they did not understand, this would weary and vex him. Brahmā, the highest god in the popular religion of the time, read the Buddha's mind, left the Brahmā-world, appeared before the Buddha, and pleaded, "May the Blessed One teach the Dharma. May the Well-gone One teach the Dharma. There are living beings with little dust in their eyes who fall away through not hearing the Dharma. They will be recognizers of the Dharma." Then, out of compassion for living beings, Śākyamuni surveyed the world with his Buddha-eye and saw that some beings had little impurity and some had much, that some had keen faculties and some had dull ones. Realizing that there was a suitable audience, he decided to proclaim the Dharma.

In the Buddhist myths Brahmā claims to see everything, so it is appropriate that he should tell the hesitant Gautama that there are living beings who are ready to recognize the Dharma. Then and only then did he use his Buddha-eye to confirm this fact. The Canon commonly presents inspiration as a message from a god.

Either Gautama actually experienced an apparition, or this tale is a fiction. In either case, it expresses a critical choice that he must have made. If he had not decided to return and act in the world, his withdrawal would have been insignificant for human history. The stated motive for his reconsideration was compassion. This virtue, the peer of wisdom and superior to all others, figures prominently in Mahāyāna Buddhist doctrine, but also is regularly ascribed to the Buddha earlier, in the Pali Canon. The Buddha, furthermore, observes the Āryan gentleman's etiquette. He does not thrust his doctrine on those who are unready to accept it; he waits for an invitation. Since he was to be the teacher of gods and men, who else but Great Brahmā was worthy to invite him?

THE FIRST SERMON

Having decided to proclaim his doctrine, Gautama thought first of telling his two former teachers; but a deity informed him that Ārāḍa had died a week before, and that Udraka had died the previous night. The Buddha confirmed this with his superknowledge, then thought of the five mendicants who had shared his austerities. With his divine eye he saw that they were staying near Benares, so he set out to enlighten them.

On the road Gautama met an ascetic who remarked on his clear eyes and radiant complexion and asked about his religion. The Buddha declared that he was a Victor, that he had no equal in the world of gods and men, that he had become omniscient and had reached nirvāṇa. The ascetic answered in one word which means either "it may be so" or "let it be so," shook his head, and walked away on another road. This curious encounter seems like historical fact rather than pious invention. Gautama's first proclamation of his Buddhahood was ignored.

The Blessed One walked by stages to Benares, about 130 miles from Gayā. Four miles north of the city, in the Deer Park at Sārnāth, the five ascetics saw him coming and resolved not to show more than the minimum

The Buddha preaching the first sermon at the Deer Park of Sārnāth, hands in the "turning the Wheel of the Law" posture. (From a fifth century A.D. Sārnāth sculpture.)

courtesy to the backslider who had taken to the easy life. But his charisma was too strong for them; and against their own resolve, they saluted him, took his bowl and robe, prepared his seat, and gave him implements with which to wash his feet. The impact of his spiritual presence preceded any word.

The five mendicants called him "Friend Gautama," but he told them not to do so, since he was now a *Tathāgata,* an arhant, a perfectly enlightened one. He declared that he had attained the immortal; that he was going to teach Dharma; and that if they practiced as he taught, they would quickly realize it for themselves. The five were dubious, protesting that one who quit striving could not have attained the superhuman Dharma. The Buddha denied that he had given up striving, and reasserted his claim. Eventually they admitted that he had never spoken to them in this way before and agreed to listen willingly and receptively.

Whether the Buddha actually preached on this occasion that discourse the Canon attributes to him is as moot as whether Jesus pronounced the Sermon on the Mount as one discourse on that occasion alleges. The doctrine of the Middle Way, though, is entirely appropriate to the task of persuading the five ascetics that one who had abandoned extreme austerities had not necessarily forsaken the ascetic quest.

The Blessed One condemned two extremes, saying that sensual indulgence is low, vulgar, worldly, unspiritual, and useless, while self-torture is painful and also unspiritual and useless. The Tathāgata had avoided these extremes and so had discovered the Middle Way which leads to enlightenment and nirvāṇa. This Middle Way is the Holy Eightfold Path: (1) right views, (2) right intention, (3) right speech, (4) right action, (5) right livelihood, (6) right effort, (7) right mindfulness, and (8) right concentration.

The Buddha then declared the Four Holy Truths. The first is the truth of *duḥkha,* or suffering, found in every aspect of existence. Birth, illness, decay, death, conjunction with the hated, and separation from the dear—in short, the experienced world made up of the five *skandhas* (groups of material and mental forces) is suffering. The second Holy Truth is the truth of the source of suffering. This is thirst or craving for sensual pleasure, for coming to be, and for ceasing to be. The third is the truth of the cessation of suffering. When craving ceases entirely through dispassion, renunciation, and nondependence, then suffering ceases. The fourth is the truth of the path leading to cessation of suffering, the Holy Eightfold Path. Suffering must be thoroughly understood. The source of suffering must be forsaken. Cessation must be realized, made actual. The Eightfold Path must be cultivated.

Gautama testified that he attained supreme, perfect Enlightenment when, and only when, he had acquired purified true knowledge and vision of these Four Truths. He had understood suffering, forsaken its cause, realized its cessation, and cultivated the path.

The five monks welcomed the discourse; and during it, one of them, Kauṇḍinya, acquired the pure Dharma-eye and saw that whatever is subject to arising is subject to cessation. Then the Buddha declared, "Kauṇḍinya has caught on! Kauṇḍinya has caught on!" Kauṇḍinya asked the Buddha for full ordination, which he received with the simple formula, "Come, bhikṣu, the Dharma is well proclaimed. Walk the holy course to the perfect termination of suffering." Thus he became the first member of the Order of Monks. The Buddha, having already experienced such an awakening, could thus recognize it in another and publicly indicated Kauṇḍinya's new state of mind before the others.

The other four mendicants took turns begging alms for the group and listening to the Buddha's instruction. Very soon all four attained the Dharma-eye and received admission to the Order.

The Buddha then preached a discourse on the five skandhas, briefly mentioned earlier under the First Truth. Form, feeling, conception, dispositions, and consciousness are each *anātman* (devoid of self). They are impermanent, and so are subject to suffering. Hearing this exposition, the five monks overcame their infatuation for the five skandhas and were freed from the outflows; thus they, too, became arhants, or saints.

COMMENTARY ON THE FIRST SERMON

It is noteworthy that Gautama proclaimed and insisted on his own status. He used two terms current among the ascetic sects—*Victor* and *Tathāgata* ("he who has gone thus, or he who has reached what is really so"). The claim of a hairless ape in bare feet and saffron rags to be omniscient and immortal is virtually incredible to the post-Darwinian world. It was scarcely less preposterous to professional ascetics in the sixth century B.C. Unable to convince the stranger whom he met on the road, Gautama eventually prevailed with his old friends only by appealing to their knowledge of his responsible character.

Gautama's apparent motive in self-proclamation was not vanity but to prepare the listener to receive the doctrine. He did not proceed to instruct the five mendicants until they acknowledged his authority and were disposed to assent. His style in the first sermon, as in many later discourses, was didactic rather than demonstrative—elaborating the points but not attempting to prove them. The chief guarantee of their truth is that they are the testimony of an Enlightened One. It is assumed that men with keen faculties will find them self-evident. The tone is earnest and exalted, free from sentimentality and hyperbole. Gautama's manifest desire to convince his hearers never shakes his gravity.

Faith in the Buddha as revealer of the Dharma is a first step on the Path. Faith is not a substitute for knowledge but is the seed which grows into confirmatory realization. It is willingness to take statements provisionally on trust, confidence in the integrity of a witness, and determination to practice according to instructions. It is not a mental state of boiling zeal but rather of serenity and lucidity. Śāriputra, one of the great disciples, explained that the confidence, like that of a lion, with which he proclaimed the Doctrine came not from his own superknowledge but from the faith inspired in him by hearing Gautama teach. "I, understanding that Dharma, perfected the quality of faith in the Teacher. And I confessed in my heart: The Blessed One is supremely awakened; the Dharma is well proclaimed by him; the Saṅgha (Buddhist Community) has followed it well."

The fruit of faith is not just progress in wisdom. The saintly disciples who possess faith in the Three Jewels (Buddha, Dharma, and Saṅgha) may predict for themselves that they will never go to rebirth in hell, as animals, among the ghosts, or in any state of woe. They are "stream-winners," lowest of the four grades of saint, and they are confirmed in the course of enlightenment. The objects of faith are not credal statements (faith is not belief), but holy persons (the Buddha and the Saṅgha) and the Truth (Dharma), of which their statements are just expressions. The decisive efficacy of faith is not that it stimulates its objects to act supernaturally but that it transforms the subject.

The ideas of prediction and confirmation played a conspicuous part even in early Buddhism, as it was propounded in the Pali texts, and then underwent progressive embellishment after the rise of Mahāyāna, or later Buddhism. The Pali texts often show the Buddha declaring that such-and-such a disciple has become an arhant, or has become a "nonreturner" who will sojourn in the highest heavens until attaining nirvāṇa, or has become a "once-returner" who will attain arhant-ship on rebirth as a human being, or has become a stream-winner who is assured of not relapsing until attaining enlightenment. Confirmation is not an externally imposed predestination but an irrevocable change in the karmic endowment of the subject. The Buddha, or any arhant, can predict a person's destiny by reading the dispositions in the person's mind, a feat that is possible through the superknowledge.

Closely related to pre   ation of attainment. The Buddha's declaration "Kauṇḍinya h   e first instance of this formal act. Identifying the saints ha   rtant for the Buddhist devotee, whose chief religious aut   n Enlightened One. Enlightenment is recognized by a ṭeacher,   hieved it, in another, who is striving for it. Once the sainthood of the Buddha is granted, as it is when one professes the Buddhist faith, it is a convenience to have the Buddha's or an arhant's certification that so-and-so is a saint of such-and-such a degree. Like many other early Buddhist institutions, this is a legal solution to a spiritual problem.

THE MIDDLE WAY

THE FOUR HOLY
    TRUTHS
1. Of suffering
2. Of the source of — *pratitya samutpadha*
   suffering
3. Of the cessation of
   suffering
4. Of the path
   leading to the
   cessation of
   suffering

THE HOLY EIGHT-FOLD PATH	THE THREEFOLD TRAINING
1. Right views	Wisdom-Prajñā
2. Right intention	
3. Right speech	Morality-Śīla
4. Right action	
5. Right livelihood	
6. Right effort	Concentration-Samādhi
7. Right mindfulness	
8. Right concentration	

Figure 2

What is the Middle Path proclaimed in the First Sermon? (See Figure 2.) It is, like the Greek and Chinese Middle Way or Golden Mean, a course of moderation in which the bodily appetites are fed sufficiently for health rather than indulged or starved. But it comprises much more than this. The Eightfold Path is equivalent to a shorter formula, the Threefold Training: namely, morality (right speech, action, and livelihood), wisdom (right views and intention), and concentration (right effort, mindfulness, and concentration). We have already seen all three as strands in the Enlightenment. Morality goes beyond mere self-mortification because it involves intention and the effects of one's acts on others. Wisdom here means intellectual understanding of the Doctrine, of the kind obtained through thinking, study, and meditation. To discipline the intellect is a higher asceticism than merely to hold the breath and keep fasts. Concentration is achieved through specific techniques apparently known to Gautama's two teachers but not favored by the five mendicants. It requires not the mortification of the body but the cultivation of psychic skills. The Three Trainings are dependent on one another. A Pali text *(Dīgha Nikāya 16)* says: "Concentration suffused with morality becomes very fruitful; wisdom suffused with concentration becomes very fruitful; the mind suffused with wisdom is quite freed from the outflows." The Middle Way is not only moderate but comprehensive, engaging the whole person. It is nonetheless a stringent discipline, a yoga, going against the current of worldly life.

In the Eightfold Path, right action means abstaining from the three bodily wrong deeds: taking life, taking what is not given, and sexual misconduct. Right speech means abstaining from lying, slander, abuse, and idle talk, the four vocal wrong deeds. Right livelihood is abstention from occupations that harm living beings: for example, selling weapons, liquor, poison, slaves, or livestock; butchering, hunting, fishing; soldiering; fraud, soothsaying, and usury. Right intention is marked by dispassion, benevolence, and aversion to injuring others. Right views means knowledge of the Four Truths. This explains the otherwise abrupt transition in the First Sermon from the Path to the Truths. Another implicit connection is that the Path is the Fourth Truth.

We have already seen that ignorance of the Four Truths is the first of the twelve preconditions, and that knowledge of them is the antidote to transmigratory misery (suffering or *duḥkha).* By realizing them during the third watch, Gautama extinguished the *āsrava* (outflows): sensual desire, desire for continuing becoming, wrong (or speculative) views, and ignorance; he understood that he had overcome rebirth. Just hearing them, Kauṇḍinya "caught on," had an opening of his religious vision. The Word of the Buddha was no ordinary word, and his Four Truths were no mere worldly theses. These statements were proclaimed to people many of whom believed that the Primal Being produced Speech out of himself, then copulated with her to produce all other creatures. Human speech was considered objectively effective, too; *mantras* (incantations) were the chief stock in trade of the brahmin ritualist. The propositions of archaic Indian philosophy were just one step removed from mantras. The Holy Truths, like the Great Statements of the Upaniṣads, were not premises for a deductive system but enunciations of *gnōsis* (saving knowledge), to be meditated upon until the hearer "catches on" and breaks through to another plane of being.

For such meditation the Buddha declared that the five skandhas, that is, the phenomenal world-and-person, are duḥkha. His first Holy Truth states essentially that all conditioned states involve this duḥkha, experienced either as actual physical or psychological pain or as the various concomitants of attachment to conditioned states that result from the five skandhas making up the fiction of a "real self." These concomitants include all human insecurities and anxieties which are present even during states of so-called happiness. It is difficult to select any single word to translate the term duḥkha because it means all the unsatisfactoriness of existence in the material realm. Suffering is one of several acceptable near-equivalents.

In this first Holy Truth, the Buddha specified the crucial attribute of the five skandhas, duḥkha, for meditation, which was designed to achieve eventual mastery over them. Why, though, did Gautama single out suffering? One of the mendicant teachers held that there are several eternal substances, including happiness, suffering, and the self. But Gautama did not say that suffering is a substance, much less that it is everlasting. This would have expressed true pessimism. The point is that attainment to worldly pleasures is the cause for rebirth; it blocks attainment of the immortal. So meditation on suffering is a therapeutic exercise to counteract tṛṣṇā (desire), which, with avidyā (ignorance), is the source of attachment and rebirth.

The frequent charge that Buddhism is pessimistic because it declares life to be suffering is inaccurate. An early text glowingly praises the blessings of the good householder's life—the company of the wise, honoring the honorable, living in a congenial country, erudition and skill, good manners and speech, looking after one's family, having a peaceful profession, giving alms, doing good deeds, practicing the religion, and becoming immune to worldly sorrow and defilement. The delights of life among the gods are also praised highly, and it is never denied that there is much happiness in the world. It is only asserted that sooner or later one must suffer through separation from dear things, that worldly happiness is yoked to suffering. This observation is a preacher's commonplace, but its acceptance in one form or another is inescapable when bereavement occurs.

The study of comparative religion suggests two reasons why Gautama gave such prominence to a personal recognition of suffering. The first is that suffering is the hallmark of that condition from which salvation is sought. It (1) results from sin (deeds committed out of craving and ignorance, not disobedience as in the Judeo-Christian myth of the Fall), and until the results are seen for what they are, the remedy will not be welcomed. The second reason is that suffering is the essential component of the chief primitive rites of initiation into (2) adulthood. The warrior brotherhood (in many traditional societies) tests the initiant by ordeal to see whether he is worthy and to stimulate his martial powers. Among the nonliterate peoples of Northeast Asia, the shaman guild initiates the neophyte with a ritual dismemberment and other austerities to solemnize the newcomer's change of status, but even more to effect a transformation of personality and to endow the initiate with powers. Suffering kills the old self and induces "the second birth." The Buddhist way partakes of both martial and shamanic elements. It is a state of prolonged self-transformation,

lasting until nirvāṇa is attained. The Buddha rejected extreme physical mortification, but in its place he put mental mortification, the contemplation of
universal suffering.

Meditation on suffering should result in longing to escape from it, but not
through alienation. One ought to cultivate awareness of the suffering of
others; doing so arouses compassion. Unable to bear others' misery, one tries
to lead them out of it. One sees their helplessness and is moved to help. As
compassion grows, the desire to harm others withers away. We have noted that
during the Enlightenment Gautama observed the sufferings of all beings, and
that is was the ensuing compassion that moved him to accept the god Brahmā's
request to preach.

The way out of suffering leads, paradoxically and homeopathically,
through asceticism, sane and consequential but still painful and hard to
accept. One must cut off the roots of suffering, which according to the Second
Truth are libidinous drives or _trṣṇā_ of all sorts—craving for sensual gratifica-
tion, hankering for survival, even the wish for extinction. But how can anyone
stop seeking pleasure and continued existence except by desiring death? In
Buddhist doctrine death is not release but merely the prelude to rebirth. So
the longing to escape from this life through dying (dis-becoming) is as fatuous
as the yearning for another life in suffering.

The Third Truth affirms that there is a happy state free from suffering.
When craving ceases, suffering ceases. But is this not tantamount to saying
that happiness is a purely negative state consequent upon the extinction of life,
an absolute death? And is it not better to live and suffer than to escape at the
price of total annihilation? How can there possibly be positive happiness if all
desire is destroyed?

In Buddhism, as in Hindu Vedānta, the pairs of opposites are not exhaustive. They are contraries rather than true contradictories. To be or become
means to be or become in the realm of saṃsāra. To "dis-become" or "not be"
means to pass out of one form (and on to another) within the phenomenal world.
In the earliest Indian thought, "being" was the solid, reified state of things, and
"nonbeing" was their subtle, unmanifested state. The meaning of the terms
changed shortly before the Buddha's time, and "being" came to mean that which
endures as against that which changes, the ground or essence in contrast to its
modifications. The Buddha is reported to have denied the two widespread extremes of eternalism and annihilation, saying that the Enlightened One, seeing
how the world arises, rejects the idea of its nonbeing, and seeing how it perishes,
rejects the idea of its being. The Middle Path that avoids these extremes is
"dependent co-arising": "When _A_ exists, _B_ comes to be." The formula of the
twelve preconditions is the usual elaboration of this principle. It is the Middle
Way in metaphysics just as the Eightfold Path is the Middle Way in ethics.

The term "exist" has been used here in two senses: (1) to occur at one
time after arising and before ceasing, and (2) to exist at all times without

beginning or end. The second sense is impossible given the Buddhist position that no substance exists apart from its modifications. The Upaniṣad says that the clay is real and the pots are mere modifications created by "naming." The Buddhist says that no clay ever exists apart from particular forms, so the unchanging substratum is unattested and does not exist. Existence in the first sense means manifested existence, and no form of Buddhism has ever denied that commonsense things exist in this relative way, though there has been continual apprehension lest this admission lead people to believe in the second, absolute kind of being.

A wanderer is said to have approached the Buddha and asked a series of questions about ultimate matters. Are the world and souls eternal, noneternal, both, or neither? Are the world and souls infinite in space, finite, both or neither? Are the soul and the body the same or different? Does the Tathāgata exist after death, not exist, both, or neither? The Buddha in some versions is said to have remained silent (though explaining his silence afterward to a disciple), but in most of the Sūtras he answers definitely that the questions do not fit the case, are not true to fact. But how can it be denied that someone exists without affirming that the person does not exist? Perhaps one exists in some ways and in others does not exist. But this, too, is denied, and it would seem to follow then that one neither exists nor does not exist, except that this fourth alternative is denied, too. The answer is that the categories of existence and nonexistence are applicable only in the realm of the conditioned. Nirvāṇa, the unconditioned, transcends them. The fire which "goes out" does not go north, south, east, or west, but home to its unmanifested source. When the fuel (ignorance of impermanence) of the skandhas is exhausted, the arhant goes home to the unconditioned. The perfected one is deep, immeasurable, unfathomable, like the great ocean.

Cessation, it is plain, is transcendence rather than annihilation. Early Buddhism accepted the axiom that being cannot come from nonbeing and cannot go to nonbeing. Thus it ruled out genuine annihilation. Transcendence, though, would not seem to accommodate happiness in any mundane sense. This is congruent with the basic pattern of early Indian negation. Suffering and happiness are paired opposites of finite extension, so to achieve perfect felicity one must rise not only beyond misery but beyond ordinary bliss as well. The notion of "positive happiness" is a finite, contingent one. But so long as the five skandhas have not dissolved, the arhant lives, and between his or her enlightenment and death certainly is happy. The Canon pictures the Buddha and his liberated disciples vividly as calm, cheerful, spontaneous, even humorous, free from strife, and humane: "Let us live happily, hating none in the midst of men who hate. Let us live happily, then, free from disease. Let us live happily, then, free from care. Let us live happily, then, we who possess nothing. Let us dwell feeding on joy like the Radiant Gods" *(Dhammapada,* verses 197-200).

NIRVĀṆA, EARLY BUDDHIST MEDITATION, AND THE DHARMAS

The Buddha taught that the Holy Eightfold Path would lead the aspirant to nirvāṇa. The single, ultimate goal of all Buddhist religious life is nirvāṇa. How are we to conceive it?

A person achieves nirvāṇa by counteracting ignorance. Nirvāṇa allows escape from saṃsāra, the turning Wheel of Life. The problem of continuing attachment to states of existence that are miserable, impermanent, and without substantiality ends when a person reaches nirvāṇa. One can see nirvāṇa, come to, acquire, and delight in it, according to verbs used in Pali in connection with the noun nirvāṇa.

It is axiomatic in Buddhism that nirvāṇa results from wisdom, as it did for Gautama on the night of his Enlightenment. Wisdom, in its turn, depends on the conditions of purity and meditation, both of which precede and are requisite for the saving vision. Wisdom destroys or cuts the obsessional attachments (desire, hatred, and confusion) which bind a person or transmigrating entity to the process of recurrent birth and death and suffering. From the dissolution of these obsessional attachments results a truly spiritual happiness, not one dependent on states of mind and things produced by causes and conditions. This is nirvāṇa.

Nirvāṇa can be achieved while still living. Two conditions of nirvāṇa can be distinguished. One, "with basis still remaining," means that obsessional attachments have been cut off but the person still experiences the world through the five senses. The Buddha lived in this state from the time of his Enlightenment until death. The second, "without basis," indicates the state of nirvāṇa at the moment of death, when liberation from all conditions and any further process of becoming occurs.

This state guarantees the cessation of additional rebirth and any further suffering that would result. Nirvāṇa does not save a person from experiencing old age and physical death in this rebirth, but in all new births that would otherwise come. To understand the impact of the notion of nirvāṇa, we must thus see it as an event that occurs within the meaning structure of the general Indian presuppositions concerning life and death. The attainment of nirvāṇa finally resolves the dilemma of humankind as conceived by the Indian world view: that people are all condemned to recurrent rebirth into an impermanent, insubstantial world process that will continue without end. Such rebirth always involves suffering. Nirvāṇa puts an end to this.

The Pali texts assert clearly that nirvāṇa is a transcendent alternative to saṃsāra and the process of repeated becoming. It is altogether beyond the compounded, causally produced phenomenal world seen in the Wheel of Life. The goal of the Buddhist lies in crossing over the "ocean of becoming" to this alternate, uncreated and unchanging nirvāṇa. Everything within the Wheel is born, becomes, is compounded causally, and thus is subject to decay and ultimate disappearance. The earliest canonical reference to the Wheel of Life

Nirvāṇa, three experiences, as shown in a traditional Thai manuscript. Above, a monk lies wakefully on his right side smiling amid the flowers. Below, left, a layman investigates the world. Right, a monk meditates.

directs that an image of the Buddha be made "pointing out the circle of nirvāṇa," which presumably is altogether other than the Wheel, clearly transcending it.

The most common early metaphor for nirvāṇa's attainment confirms its nature as an alternative state of being. In his "Fire Sermon," the Buddha likened the world of the Wheel of Life to a fire burning with the flames of desire, hatred, and confusion. When one extinguishes these three, the fire engulfing the individual is put out, the person is "cool, like the waters of a lake," quieted among the surrounding flames. This accords with the etymology of the term nirvāṇa, which is composed of the verbal root *vā,* "to blow," to which is added the negative prefix *nir,* meaning "out." The person who has attained nirvāṇa experiences the same Wheel and the same conditions but responds not as others do but rather in a detached, uninvolving manner.

Such a person has solved the problem of the ignorance that misconceives self and world. Ignorance leads to mistakes; mistakes spawn regrets and suffering. The process must continue, life after life, until the individual interrupts it by new intentions or choices leading to its alternative. Wisdom makes possible this change by permitting choices that break karmic chains and attachment to the burning (i.e., that is forever changing) Wheel of Life. Nirvāṇa's achievement comes when the Buddhist accomplishes a meditative transformation of mind *(citta).* The Buddha, as his title indicates, was one who had "understood." He freed his mind by dissolving its obsessional attachments, desires and hatred (in modern psychology, approach and avoidance), and confusion.

Reaching nirvāṇa depends therefore on meditation. The last three members of the Holy Eightfold Path—right effort, right mindfulness, and right concentration—direct the process of the transformation of mind. Early

concen-
tra-
tion

Buddhist meditation sought to make these three elements of the Path effective in a person's spiritual life, thus allowing the wisdom requisite for nirvāṇa. Right effort concerned itself with the preliminary clearing of the mind necessary for advanced meditative practice. It sought to develop the mind, purifying it of evil and nurturing its wholesome states. Right mindfulness *(smṛti)* then became crucial to the attainment of proper meditative states. It pertained to becoming aware of one's habitual activities *(karman):* everything done with the body; feelings; mind and its thoughts, conceptions, and ideas. Something cannot be changed and extinguished until a person is aware of it; this is accomplished in mindfulness meditations. The third, right concentration *(samādhi),* resulted in the state requisite for wisdom itself, being the cultivation of the meditative trances *(dhyānas).*

The importance of Buddhist meditation for the attainment of nirvāṇa becomes clear. Without meditation, the wisdom needed to reach nirvāṇa would not be forthcoming. Drawing from the many techniques described in the Pali Canon, the Commentator Buddhaghosa systematized Theravāda (earlier) Buddhist meditation in his classic *Path of Purity* (Pali *Visuddhimagga)* into the following elements. He distinguished two practices, the first concerned with meditative calming of the mind, the second with its gaining wisdom.

Within the calming stage (śamatha), reflective techniques first prepared the meditator for the special states of consciousness of the trances through a series of preliminary, purifying contemplations. This avoided the arising of ill-thoughts later during the extremely delicate states of meditative ecstasy. Meditators at this stage were given exercises by their teachers intended to

Monks pointing to corpses for counteractive meditations. The one at the top is "gnawed," a good counteractive against lust for flesh. The corpse below is "scattered," counteractive to greed "for grace of limbs." (From a traditional Thai manuscript.)

counteract their karman-producing habits—desire, hatred, and confusion. To counteract desire monks meditated on examples of ugliness, such as decomposing corpses or on the filthiness of their body functions. The meditative counteractive of hatred consisted of the four immeasurable contemplations, in which the nirvāṇa-seekers attended to love, compassion, sympathetic joy, and equanimity. Against confusion, monks and nuns practiced mindfulness of breath, becoming aware of their breathing and thus calming both confusion and excessive excitement. Meditators were also instructed to call to mind other things conducive to advancement on the Path, including the virtues of the Buddhist Path and the peace at its end. Finally, as counteractive to attachment, they also practiced contemplation on the loathesomeness of food and on the four elements (earth, water, fire, and air) of all compounded things, as well as mindfulness of death.

All these techniques led to the point where the meditators could begin to use meditation to induce the trances. They began with an external support for contemplation, such as a circle of earth, water, or colored cloth. In a place free of disturbance, the contemplative sat with legs crossed (the lotus position) before the circle and focused all five senses upon it, trying to form a clear mental image of it. Concentration was sustained until the image became mental and independent of the external support. The process took time, since one had to overcome the hindrances to the concentration required to maintain the mental image. When able to retain the image for a sufficient time, the meditator then learned to transform it at will and was ready to enter the first trance.

After achieving complete control over the four trances, the contemplative was ready to begin the practice of wisdom *(vipaśyanā)* that would lead to nirvāṇa. Meditation makes the mind supple and receptive, preparing it for the difficult achievement of knowing oneself and the world as they really are, unaffected by subjective preoccupation. In this practice, the person perfects the two most important aspects of the Eightfold Path, right intention and right views. Since, in the Buddhist view, everything that happens depends on the mind, these hold the key to release. Right intention entails an attitude of dispassion and freedom from ill-will and violence since these result in evil consequences. Right views involve understanding the basic Buddhist formulation of wisdom as stated in the Four Holy Truths and seeing everything as it really is.

Having achieved a meditative calm and its consequent dispassionate objectivity, the meditator then considered understanding. Self-examination of the person, the body, the senses and their objects, and the five skandhas, brought the realization that they are but causally interrelated phenomena, dependent all on each other. The monk or nun perceived that no reality underlies them corresponding to the idea of "I" or "my self." He or she investigated the causes of body and mind as well as of things and events in the world, seeing that they arise and disappear entirely dependent on causes and conditions. None exist by themselves independent of the world process. The contemplative specifically saw that nowhere in the conditioned world of the Wheel of Life could something permanent or truly satisfying be found and concluded that all things are transitory, insubstantial, and afflicted by suffering. In true Buddhist fashion, the seekers used this exercise of insight to bring them to the doorway of nirvāṇa, cutting off their obsessive attachment to becoming, so that at death they would be assured of final release.

The Buddhist goal of wisdom, or of "seeing things as they really are," must be adjudged difficult indeed. Many thinkers have distinguished the surface appearance of things from their actual reality. The assumption that appearance and reality are different is the basis of most metaphysics. Practically speaking, Buddhist wisdom seeks to extricate a person's knowledge from the mass of confusing elements that usually hides the true nature of reality behind the curtain of subjectivity (desires, fears, and confusions). The curtain's fundamental cause is ignorance, lack of self-insight. This ignorance is deep-seated, part of a person's total personality structure; it includes such elements as conscious and unconscious desires, predispositions, motivations, and defense mechanisms. The practice of insight is intended to lead the person beyond these limitations on knowledge to gaze upon the self and the world as the Buddha did under the Tree of Awakening—with infinite clarity.

Buddhaghosa defined wisdom as the "penetration into dharmas as they are in themselves." This simple definition contains the Buddhist strategy for freeing a person's knowledge from the complex webs of its delusions. Much insight meditation focused on the dharmas as its object. When they contemplated the dharmas, meditators tried to transform the way they understood everything about themselves and the world. By reducing their view of everything to a meditative dharma-analysis, they peered below the commonsense surface of objects and experiences to see their true, causal nature, uncomplicated by subjective ideas and feelings about the surface patterns in which the dharmas occur. Ordinarily, for example, we label the collections of dharmas that make up our experience our "self," just as we call wheels and axle and bed an "ox-cart." Buddhists say there simply is nothing in reality that corresponds to the linguistic designators "self" and "ox-cart." This can be a very liberating insight indeed.

What does the term dharmas mean in this context? Notice first that it occurs mostly in the plural while other uses of the word are usually singular. Dharmas are the smallest units of all phenomena, their basic elements. Dharmas are the momentary constituents of everything phenomenal or created, the ultimate building blocks of all that is within the Wheel of Life. This includes what we and the world are, as well as our experiences (feelings, sensory data). The advantage of such a description is that it eliminates reference to any underlying substance or object corresponding to the names and conceptions we place on perceived patterns of dharmas, such as 'event,' 'thing', 'person', and 'self'. The reason patterns of dharmas appear to be objects, persons, or events is that they progress on their way to disappearance and transformation in causally organized series *(saṃtāna)*, but in reality such objects, persons, or events are only made up of their component dharmas.

The dharmas arise and are destroyed each moment. They appear to be substantial and to have continuing being but actually are only coordinated complexes of constantly changing phenomena—in proper temporal perspective, mountains change and continents shift across the face of the earth—so that ultimately, commonsense reality to the Buddhist is something of a false appearance. For example, one does not realize most of the time that one is mortal and going to die, even though headed for inescapable death at every moment. One "knows" that one owns possessions but fails to realize that there is no "I" to possess anything, even if what is possessed were more than it actually is, just linked series of dharmas like the "I." When a person has an intensely pleasurable or painful experience, he or she is happy or dejected but fails to realize there is no "self" to experience the pleasure or pain. There is only a fictive "I" conception imposed on the skandhas (personality aggregate) but ultimately nonexistent.

The contemplation of dharmas was thus the object of much early Buddhist Psychology meditation. Dharma meditation gave birth to one of the first, if not the first, sophisticated systems of psychology in the ancient and premodern world, and resulted in an entire section of Buddhist literature called *Abhidharma*. In the Pali Canon, one entire "basket" was devoted to the texts of Adhidharma analysis. The term might be interpreted to mean "psychological metaphysics" since 'abhi' means "over," corresponding to 'meta'. This literature grew precisely out of mindfulness and insight meditation that focused on the contemplator's subjective experiences, the flow of body and mental factors that appear to make up a "self" that experiences "things" in a "world." Abhidharma literature tried to classify into discrete categories the totality of a person's experience, whether meditative or not, to lead the individual out of delusion. In the process, Buddhist thinkers elaborated a striking psychology of dependence and freedom that perhaps has never been equalled. This contrasts with the early Greek thinkers, who paid little attention to psychology and the psychological factors that influence and distort knowledge. By ignoring such a psychology, Greek thinkers failed to develop concrete personal steps to lead persons out of the ignorance that they deemed, as did Buddhists, a fundamental obstacle in the pursuit of human happiness.

One of Buddhism's greatest strengths as a soteriology (doctrine of salvation) derives from its sophisticated psychology, which assumes that subjective elements can considerably distort accurate cognition of reality. Psychologists today have ample confirmation that this assumption is correct and study its mechanisms experimentally. Early Buddhists chose meditation as the way to release themselves from ignorance, for it was through contemplation of the inner world of the self and its psychology that nirvāṇa was to be won. Given the Indian world view, the nirvāṇa gained through this wisdom offered final escape, not from the death that will terminate this life but from all other lives and deaths to come. The concept of nirvāṇa thus might be seen as another of the many religious ideas promising escape from death. Primitive religions, as well as shamanism and the historical religions of both East and West, have all been concerned with what happens to a person at death. In its concern with death, the Buddhist religion is no different from any other.

FOUNDING THE SAṄGHA (THE BUDDHIST COMMUNITY)

After the Second Sermon, there were six arhants in the world, counting Gautama himself. Soon Yasa, son of a rich merchant of Benares, waking up during the night in a state of anxiety, went out to Sārnāth, where the Buddha comforted him and taught him the Dharma suitable for laymen, namely, the merit of donation, the moral precepts, heaven, the wretchedness of sensual desires, and the blessings of forsaking them. Then he preached the higher Dharma, the Four Truths, to the young man, who attained arhant-ship and then took full ordination as a monk. Later, Yasa's father took the Three Refuges (rites of entry) and thus became the first lay devotee *(upāsaka)* in the strict sense; the two merchants who had brought offerings to Gautama at Bodh-gayā had not been able to take refuge in the Saṅgha since it did not yet exist. Yasa's mother and sisters took the Three Refuges and became the first female devotees *(upāsikā)*. The young man's friends came, listened to the Buddha, took ordination, and became free from the outflows until there were sixty-one arhants, enlightened ones, in the world.

Throughout its history, Buddhism has appealed particularly to the merchant class, especially those engaged in the caravan trade and in large-scale finance. Mercantile ideas of accountability and responsibility underlie the doctrines of merit and karman. A world view in which fortune is rational, the regular result of specific acts, appeals to entrepreneurs who would rather shape their destiny than just let fate happen to them. And the doctrine of the conservation of virtue reassures them that even if they fail in business they can succeed in religion.

The Buddhist Saṅgha consists of four assemblies: monks, nuns, laymen, and laywomen. The rites of entry into these assemblies are both legal and sacramental in character, hence the great importance that the Vinaya (books on moral discipline) attaches to their institution. Going for refuge is a formal act of submitting to the authority and claiming the protection of a powerful patron, whether a man or a god. The formula is uttered three times to make it solemn and magico-legally binding. Those, and only those, who take refuge in Buddha, Dharma, and Saṅgha are Buddhists. Though it has been said that the monastics are the only true Buddhists, this is not the case. All who have taken the Refuges belong. The commitment is formal and definite. Though it does not require credal assent to tenets such as the Four Truths, it does constitute a profession of faith in the Buddha's wisdom, the truth of his teaching, and the worthiness of the Sangha.

When the cadre of sixty enlightened monks was consolidated, the Buddha sent them out as missionaries, charging them to travel and proclaim the Dharma for the benefit of the many, out of compassion for the world, for the welfare of gods and humans. Beings with keen faculties would attain liberation if, and only if, they heard the doctrine.

The historic success of Buddhism stems from its concern for the many, regardless of race, caste, class, or sex. Compassion is not just feeling the suffering of others, but acting to alleviate it, and the foremost act is "Dharma-donation." The Brahmanical schools kept their teachings as secret as possible, and their teachers retained personal control over the students. In contrast the Buddhists broadcast their message to the multitudes, aiming it specifically, though, to those most ready to receive it. Good Dharma-preachers use their divine eye (or lacking that, the science of character analysis) to discern whether people are dull, ordinary, or keen minded, and to adapt the teaching to the hearer's capacity. In the Quaker phrase, they "speak to the condition" of their audience. The Buddhist missionaries aim not only to proclaim their doctrine but to communicate it.

Only Buddhas attain enlightenment without receiving the gift of Dharma from another, and even they, according to later theory, heard it many lives ago from a former Buddha. (There have been many Buddhas in the past and another is expected in the future.) Thus no one works out personal salvation unaided: "You yourself must make an effort. The Buddhas, for their part, are the revealers" *(Dhammapada 276)*. The later disputes over self-power versus other-power concern the price of salvation and do not deny that it takes two parties for anyone to achieve it. Every form of Buddhism has held that guides are necessary; and though the Buddhas are the highest guides, the other saints and even some worldlings perform the office.

The sixty missionaries were soon so successful that many converts came long distances to receive ordination. The Buddha noted the hardship this caused them, and so granted his monks permission to confer ordination themselves wherever they went. This made the Sangha self-propagating and enabled it to spread far beyond the area within which the Buddha or any pontiff could have exercised personal control. Even during his lifetime, Gautama entrusted his Community with management of its own affairs, serving as lawmaker when his disciples consulted him on problems but otherwise not imposing his authority. By the time of his decease, the Sangha was consolidated as a republican society, a loose federation of little democracies bound together by a common code, a common oral tradition, and the constant coming and going of itinerant monks.

Sakyamuni spent the first three-month rainy season after his enlightenment at Sarnath, near Benares. This summer monsoon retreat became an institution and is observed to the present day in Theravāda countries (Ceylon, Burma, Thailand, Cambodia, and Laos). After the rains he returned to Uruvelā, where he had practiced austerities. The Vinaya relates that there he encountered and converted three brothers of the Kāśyapa clan who, with their hundreds of disciples, belonged to the Jaṭila sect of Brahmanic ascetics.

This tale shows how Buddhism grew not merely through individual conversions but by incorporating whole sects. It is remarkable that all the early converts speedily became arhants. In later centuries Buddhists attributed this to the superior capacities of people born in the auspicious age when a Buddha was alive. The arhant-ship of individual famous disciples is uncontested in the tradition even though the attainment is sensed only by the person and others who had achieved it. Doubtless Gautama's personal charisma enormously facilitated realization. Furthermore, his good news burst like a sudden light in a milieu thronging with expectant seekers. The fuel was dry and ready for the spark.

The Buddha went on to Rājagṛha, capital of Magadha, where he was greeted by King Bimbisāra and a large crowd. The king entertained him and donated the Bamboo Grove park just outside the northern gates of the city. Soon Śāriputra of Nālandā, about ten miles north of Rājagṛha, and his friend Maudgalyāyana were converted. They became the two chief disciples, Śāriputra being foremost in wisdom, and Maudgalyāyana foremost in magic powers. They died before the Buddha did, and relics said to be theirs are now enshrined in a new temple on the ancient site at Sāñcī. Among other famous disciples there was Mahākāśyapa, foremost of those who keep the ascetic rules, who shortly after the Buddha's decease convened the Council of Rājagṛha and superintended standardization of the recitation of the Sūtras. Subhūti, foremost among those who dwell in peace, supreme in practicing the samādhi (concentration) of emptiness and paramount among those worthy of offerings, attained arhant-ship by meditating on friendly love (maitrī). Kātyāyana, a brahmin and court priest from Avantī in western India, was sent by his king on a mission to the Buddha, who sent him back as a bhikṣu (monk) and arhant to spread the Dharma in Avantī. He was the father of Buddhist exegesis, known as "foremost of those who analyze at length what the Buddha has stated concisely." Upāli, the barber of Kapilavastu, became "foremost among those who keep the Vinaya," which he recited at the First Council. Tradition says that Gautama's own son, Rāhula, received ordination and became an arhant. He was considered unrivaled among those who love to train.

Gautama's cousin Ānanda became a monk and was his favorite disciple and constant attendant for the last twenty years of his life. He figures often in the account of the Buddha's last weeks and was present at his death. Ānanda alone among the great disciples had not become an arhant, so Mahākāśyapa excluded him from the First Council, admitting him after he had retired and overnight achieved extinction of the outflows. His exceptional memory enabled

The inscription reads, "Anāthapiṇḍika [a rich merchant] dedicates Jeta Grove, purchased with a layer of gold." The merchant bought Prince Jeta's grove with as much gold as would cover the ground (the gold is being unloaded from carts at right). At the center the merchant formally presents the grove by pouring water over a tree symbolizing the Buddha. Thus the Saṅgha quickly became a corporate landowner. (From a second century B.C. Bhārhut stūpa medallion.)

him, it is said, to recite accurately the dialogs of the Buddha which then composed the *Sūtra Piṭaka*.

The Order of Nuns is said to have been instituted by the Buddha at Ānanda's repeated plea. Gautama's foster mother, Prajāpatī, and her attendants became its first members. Queen Kṣemā, wife of King Bimbisāra, was converted and became a prominent nun. Despite the example of such wise and saintly women, the female order never became nearly so important as the male one.

The early lay converts included a good array of kings, princes, and rich merchants. Of the latter, Anāthapiṇḍika donated the land for the famous Jetavana monastery at Śrāvastī. Two wealthy laywomen also donated to the Saṅgha, the courtesan Amrapālī giving her garden at Vaiśālī and the matron

The Buddha teaching in the house of a layman. (From an Ajantā cave wall painting, sixth century A.D.)

Viśākhā giving land for a monastery in Śrāvastī. Thus even during the Buddha's lifetime, his Saṅgha became a wealthy landowner.

THE DEATH OF THE BUDDHA (ATTAINMENT OF PARINIRVĀṆA)

For forty-five years the Buddha journeyed around the central Gangetic plain, staying in the Saṅgha's parks, receiving all callers—ascetics, brahmins, princes, and commoners—and answering their questions, converting the unconverted, and instructing the proselytes.

In his seventy-ninth year, Gautama set out on his last journey. He left Rājagṛha and moved by stages north and west until he reached Vaiśālī, where he fell seriously ill. The *Sūtra of the Great Decease* says that he told Ānanda that through magic powers he could stay alive for an aeon *(kalpa)*, but Ānanda failed to request him to do so. Then Māra approached and told Gautama that it was time for him to attain final nirvāṇa. The Buddha agreed, saying, "Trouble not, Evil One. Very soon the Tathāgata's parinirvāṇa will take place. After three months he will enter parinirvāṇa."

These episodes betray the notions of a later age puzzled by the seeming failure of the dying master to avert his own death. Control of one's life span is a yogic power, and even today India and the Buddhist world are full of reports about holy men who have lived well beyond a hundred years. Great holy men similarly can predict or determine the date of their death.

The Tathāgata's last meal was at the home of Cunda the smith. After eating a quantity of pork (later commentators say mushrooms), he became very sick, blood flowed, and he suffered sharp dysentery pains. He bore it calmly, arose and went to Kuśinagara, where he lay down between two śāla trees. There he received the wanderer Subhadra, to whom he recommended the Holy Eightfold Path. Ānanda then received this last of Gautama's converts into the Saṅgha.

The dying Buddha asked the assembled monks three times whether they had any last doubts or questions, but all kept silent. So the Blessed One delivered his last exhortation: "Conditioned things are perishable by nature. Diligently seek realization." Then he entered the first dhyāna and ascended the trance states up to the fourth, from which he passed into parinirvāṇa. The Buddha thus died in meditation.

The legend says that earthquakes and thunder marked the moment of death. Brahmā and Śakra recited stanzas, and the monks (except the arhants) burst into lamentation until Anuruddha reminded them that doing so was not in keeping with the Buddha's teaching.

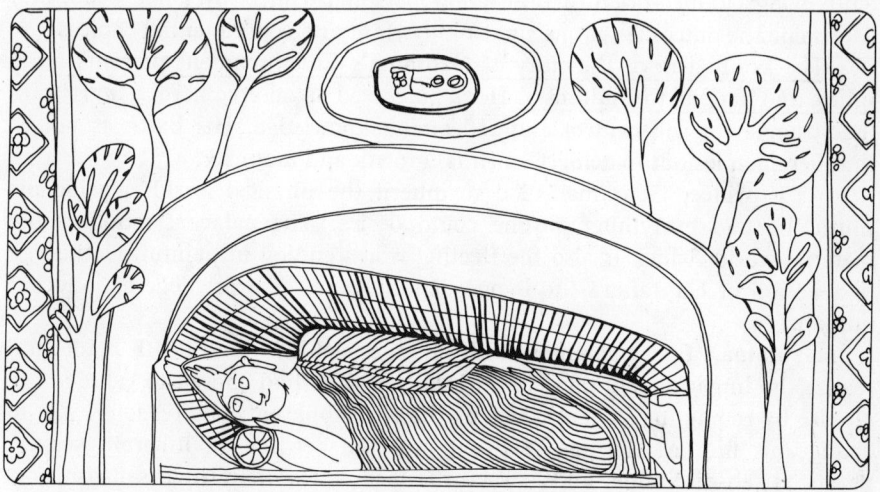

The death of the Buddha. Though his body died, his Word survives, indicated by the footprint symbolizing the path to salvation he taught. (After a Southeast Asian painting.)

The people of Kuśinagara came the next day and held a six-day wake for the Blessed One. They danced, sang, made music, and offered garlands and scents. The body was wrapped in alternate layers of cloth and cotton wool. On the seventh day, eight chiefs of the Mallas carried the bier in through the north gate and out the east gate of the town to a tribal shrine. There they cremated the body.

When they asked Ānanda how the remains of the Tathāgata should be treated, he replied, "Like those of a king of kings. Cremate the body and build a stūpa (memorial mound) at the crossroads to enshrine the relics."

Simple worshippers believe that the physical relics radiate a spiritual force. In fact the sense of physical continuity evokes such a power in the devotee's mind. But Gautama is reported to have said, "What is there in seeing this wretched body? Whoever sees Dharma sees me; whoever sees me sees Dharma." The immortality of the Buddha is that he is immanent in his Word.

INTERPRETING THE LIFE OF THE BUDDHA

The story of the Buddha's life is the cornerstone of the Buddhist religion. All else is organized around this ideal biography. As with the life of Christ, an example for Christians everywhere to imitate, it is the model life. The Buddha found in an ignorant world a comprehensive vision allowing a way out of saṃsāra's sufferings.

A religion is a means of ultimate transformation.[2] It asserts values, placing higher worth on one or another outcome of the actions that fill one's daily living. Values orient action, allow personal control over one's life, and determine the outcomes of one's most important and consequential choices.

The symbolism of the story of Gautama's Enlightenment presents these values and actions to Buddhists. He is portrayed as an epic hero, a warrior in the struggle for self-control and redeeming knowledge. His battle is not to conquer enemies but to achieve spiritual growth and maturity.

As a prince, Gautama stood to inherit the physical world. During his youth, he had everything anyone could desire. The palace symbolizes the material world, which is also the fleeting world ending in painful death. The first period of Gautama's life is one of indulgence, the privilege of innocent immaturity.

Gautama's first encounters with old age, sickness, and death made him realize the impermanent character of the world he had chosen to value above all else by remaining in the palace as the heir apparent. His response was to change his life. At the age of twenty-nine he became an itinerant seeker, practiced self-discipline, and learned the techniques of spiritual self-transformation current in his time, particularly meditation and asceticism.

In the context of his entire life, this period of six years was a therapeutic process, a time for learning and self-reflection during which Gautama transformed himself. It allowed him to take responsibility for his values and actions. It was a time of spiritual maturation, leading to his Enlightenment when, again making choices (against extreme asceticism, for the Middle Way), he decided on the values that would orient his life's actions. Based on his Enlightenment visions, his life was ultimately transformed by the culminating experience of his therapy.

He returned to the world, to his companions, family, and countrymen to share these new values and to exemplify the spiritually mature and humanly responsible actions they recommended. After a fulfilling forty-five years, he faced death with impressive composure. Unlike the painful death of one still immaturely bound to what must inevitably be lost, it was calm and dispassionately meditative.

The life of the Buddha exemplifies the threefold structure of the Buddhist Path. Everyone is born into a family and culture (the palace) and makes accommodations and adjustments, often defensive and stereotyped, to it. Life experiences result in a karman, a propensity to act in a certain habitual way.

The Buddha's life shows how one must come to terms with this heritage, becoming aware of it and counteracting it. Otherwise, there can be no spiritual maturity and no free individual.

The ideal Buddhist way of dealing with one's karman is patterned directly on the Buddha's experience. It begins with śīla, a set of moral rules to purify, and begin the transformation of, one's nature. Śīla increases the individual's self-insight and mindfulness *(smṛti)*,[3] essential since karman cannot be counteracted without its being brought to full consciousness. Then, samādhi, the cultivation of meditative calm *(śamatha)*, and finally one-pointedness of concentration, comes. Only from this state of mental control can the final step, prajñā (wisdom), be attained. Then, correct insight *(vipaśyanā)* can properly fathom the correctness of Buddhist truths (Dharma) and affirm trust in Buddhist life values. The ideal Buddhist course, for laity and monk alike, follows this progression modeled on the life of Gautama, the only difference being that the layperson's progress to the ultimate goal will take longer.

4.
Development of Indian Buddhism

FORMATION OF THE CANON

Just before the Buddha died, he reportedly told his followers that thereafter the Dharma would be their leader. The early arhants considered Gautama's words the primary source of Dharma (doctrine, teaching) and Vinaya (rules of discipline and community living), and took great pains to formulate and transmit his teachings accurately. Nonetheless, no ungarnished collection of his sayings has survived. The versions of the Canon (accepted scripture) preserved in Pali, Sanskrit, Chinese, and Tibetan are sectarian variants of a corpus that grew and crystallized during three centuries of oral transmission.

The Buddhist chronicles present an anachronistic and idealized story of the First Council, held at Rājagṛha during the three-month monsoon retreat after the Parinirvāṇa. Mahākāśyapa, it is said, first questioned Upāli, who stated when and under what circumstances the Buddha promulgated each rule of the Vinaya. Textual analysis, though, shows that while some of the material in the Vinayas of the various Hīnayāna (Small Vehicle or Course) sects may go back to the first generation of disciples, the literary form and much of the content had their origins centuries later.

Ānanda is said to have recited in order each of the five Nikāyas (collection of Sūtras, also called Āgamas) in the Sūtra Piṭaka ("Basket of Discourses"). Four Nikāyas are recognized by all the early sects: the Long (Dīgha), the Medium (Majjhima), the Connected (Saṃyutta), and the Item-More (Aṅguttara) Nikāya. But the Little (Khuddaka) Nikāya as a collection is found only in Pali and not in the Chinese translations, even though many of its texts (such as the Dhammapada) exist in Chinese as separate works or parts of other Āgamas.

The canonical texts are chiefly in prose, except for stanzas interspersed through the first four Nikāyas and the anthologies of verse (Dhammapada, Sutta-nipāta, and so on) in the fifth Nikāya. In the prose texts, the early disciples seem to have been concerned with the substantive content rather than with the exact words. Individuals were allowed to recite the scriptures in their own dialect. We do not know precisely what language the Buddha spoke, but it was probably the precursor of the Māgadhī dialect in which most of Aśoka's inscriptions are couched. The complete Canon of the Theravāda sect has been preserved in Pali, a vernacular descended from Sanskrit and most likely spoken in west India whence it was taken to Ceylon. Tradition says that the Pali Canon was written down in Ceylon during the first century B.C. Probably the Canon was reduced to writing in north India during the second century B.C.

Sectarian bias undoubtedly has occasioned distortions, additions, and omissions. Nevertheless, a large fund is common to all versions, and the Saṅgha seems from the first to have striven to exclude spurious texts and to maintain purity of transmission.

Strictness in preserving the essential kernel, and liberty to expand, vary, and embellish the expression, characterize Buddhist attitudes through the ages toward not only texts but also art, ritual, discipline, and doctrine. The perennial difficulty lies in distinguishing the kernel from its embodiment. The Buddha is said to have told Ānanda that, if the Saṅgha wished, it might revoke the minor rules; but Ānanda forgot to ask which rules were minor, so the First Council, it is said, decided to retain everything in the Vinaya.

Prodigious amounts of energy have gone into preserving and reproducing the Canon. In the early centuries, certain monks specialized in reciting a particular collection. But to memorize only one, such as the *Majjhima Nikāya,* which casts off to 1100 pages of modern printed text, is not merely an exercise but a vocation. And to copy such a collection by hand demanded ample donations to support the scribes. Short summaries of the Dharma have been available from the earliest times, nor does its essence require voluminous expression. But the very bulk of the Canon conveys the prestige of the Dharma. Hearing, learning, reciting, and copying the scriptures are a religious exercise for which the longer the Canon the greater the benefit. And the diversity of teachings, while frustrating the desire for unanimity, affords interest and options to the seeker. The Buddhist Canon, like the American system of government and the Japanese script, generates a surplus of energy through its fascinating unwieldiness. Buddhists have always been solicitous of their Canon, providing amply for the copying (or printing) and storage in monastic libraries of their precious texts.

The third collection in the Pali Canon is the *Abhidhamma* (Sanskrit, *Abhidharma) Piṭaka,* consisting of seven scholastic works. Among these are the *Enumeration of Dharmas,* which analyzes mental and bodily dharmas (constituents), the *Divisions,* which discusses the skandhas, dependent co-arising, the fetters, and meditation, and the *Subjects of Discussion,* which is a polemical treatise discussing the theses in dispute among Hīnayāna schools. Other segments of the *Abhidamma Piṭaka* list the dharmas; investigate causal relations; classify personality in terms of the preponderance of desire, hatred, and confusion; and give fuller explanations of matters left imprecise in the other collections.

We have already noted the importance of dharma analysis in early Buddhism (see "Nirvāṇa, Early Buddhist Meditation, and the Dharmas," pp. 50–56). Abhidharma literature, though composed by scholars of later centuries (beginning circa 350 B.C.) and not the word of the Buddha, is an important part of the Buddhist Canon. The term Abhidharma implies "that which is above or about the Dharma," or the teaching of the Buddha. Thus, it explains and orders the key ideas of the Buddhist religion in a systematic, more authoritative fashion. Couched in technical language, Abhidharma literature defines and explains both materials presented in ordinary language in the other texts as well as the experiences generated in meditations on the dharmas. In this sense, it provides an essential means for understanding Buddhist thought.

The Abhidharma literature of the Theravāda school was composed and preserved in Pali. Later, especially in the fifth century A.D. in Ceylon, commentaries were written on the Pali Abhidharma which came to define the orthodox Theravāda position on Buddhist doctrine. The famous south Indian, Buddhaghosa, went to Ceylon and wrote commentaries on all seven works. Today the Pali Abhidharma remains a living literature, especially among Buddhist scholars in Burma and Ceylon. Many early Buddhist sects composed their own Abhidharma literatures in Sanskrit. Most of these were lost over the centuries; only two survive in entirety because they were translated into Chinese.

EARLY SCHISMS AND SECTS

Tradition says that a hundred years after the Parinirvāṇa, (that is, about 380 B.C.), the monks of Vaiśālī proclaimed ten theses concerning discipline, some trivial (for example, storing salt in a horn vessel is permissible) and some significant (a monk may make use of gold and silver). When these monks went so far as to take up a collection of money from the laity on Observance Day, one monk protested and advised the laypeople not to donate. The Council assembly censured him and required him to apologize. He did so, but continued to assert his opinion until the laity of Vaiśālī were convinced, whereupon the monks suspended him for preaching without permission. He fled to the west, and lobbied his case until an impressive group of eminent monks convened in Vaiśālī, vindicated him, and censured the monks who had accepted money and had punished him. The importance of this Council lies in the indication it gives that there were differences among the early followers of the Buddha. It made apparent some of the conflicts and tensions that were beginning to split the Community. Many consider that the first great schism in Buddhism began there, dividing the Buddhist tradition into two groups who differed on points relating to discipline and the separation of monastic and lay matters.

The early teaching admits that laypersons can attain the first three degrees of sainthood (stream-winner, once-returner, and nonreturner); but whether they could become arhants was a disputed point. The Buddha reportedly declared that he took no categorical stand, that with the laity as with the monks, it is conduct that counts. The Sūtras list twenty lay followers who attained the highest goal without ever becoming monks. Their case, though, is rarer than that of monks becoming arhants, and the household life is not considered propitious for the highest attainment.

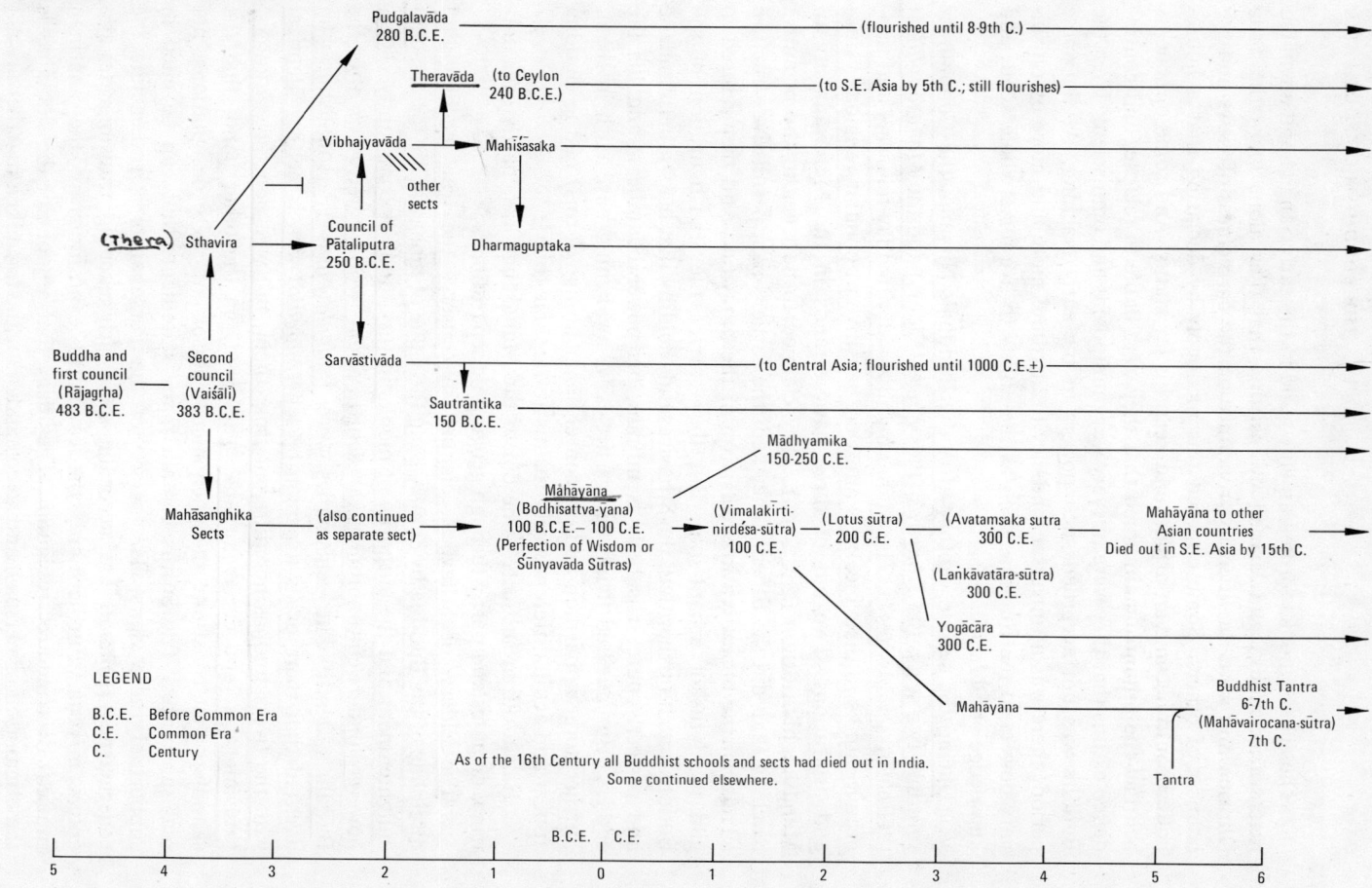

MAJOR BUDDHIST SECTS IN INDIA, 500 B.C.E.–600 C.E.

Pudgalavāda
280 B.C.E. ──────────────────────────────── (flourished until 8-9th C.) ───────────→

Theravāda   (to Ceylon ──────────── (to S.E. Asia by 5th C.; still flourishes) ──────→
240 B.C.E.)

Vibhajyavāda ──── Mahīśāsaka ───→

other
sects

(Thera) ── Sthavira ──→ Council of   Dharmaguptaka ──────────────────────────────────→
Pātaliputra
250 B.C.E.

Buddha and   Second   Sarvāstivāda ─────────── (to Central Asia; flourished until 1000 C.E.±) ──→
first council council
(Rājagṛha)   (Vaiśālī)   Sautrāntika ──→
483 B.C.E.   383 B.C.E.   150 B.C.E.

Mādhyamika
150-250 C.E. ──────────────────────────────→

Mahāsaṅghika   (also continued   Mahāyāna   (Vimalakīrti-   (Lotus sūtra)   (Avatamsaka sutra)   Mahāyāna to other
Sects   as separate sect)   (Bodhisattva-yana) nirdeśa-sūtra)   200 C.E.   300 C.E.   Asian countries
                                   100 B.C.E.– 100 C.E. 100 C.E.   Died out in S.E. Asia by 15th C.
                                   (Perfection of Wisdom or
                                   Śūnyavāda Sūtras)   (Laṅkāvatāra-sūtra)
                                                                                        300 C.E.

                                                                                        Yogācāra ───────────────────→
                                                                                        300 C.E.

LEGEND
                                                                                        Mahāyāna ──────   Buddhist Tantra
B.C.E.   Before Common Era   6-7th C.
C.E.   Common Era   (Mahāvairocana-sūtra)
C.   Century   7th C.

                                                                                        Tantra

As of the 16th Century all Buddhist schools and sects had died out in India.
Some continued elsewhere.

                                        B.C.E. C.E.

5   4   3   2   1   0   1   2   3   4   5   6

The arhant monks formed an elite guild in the early Saṅgha and alienated many other monks and laymen by insisting that they alone knew the True Dharma and were qualified to pronounce on the correctness of views and the holiness of others. Some opposed this monopoly by declaring that a householder could become an arhant and keep his lay status. And some opponents belittled the arhants, maintained that they were liable to relapse, and contradicted claims that they were in every way omnipotent and omniscient. Even the Buddha was not accorded such powers in the early teaching. At the same period, there was a universal tendency to attribute more and more extraordinary powers to the Buddha, such as the ability to live for a whole aeon, and knowledge of all facts.

During the second century after the Buddha's Nirvāṇa, the Community split into two sects, the Sthaviras (Pali Thera, Elders) and the Mahāsāṅghikas ("Great Assembly-ites"). The Mahāsāṅghikas admitted lay followers and non-arhant monks to their meetings and were sensitive to popular religious values and aspirations. Two out of three basic strands in the Mahāyāna are of Mahāsāṅghika origin (see p. 86). They claimed to be truer to the primitive teaching than did the Elders. They kept the earlier open, permissive structure as against the bureaucratic exclusivism of the Sthaviras. And they refused to gild the lotus of arhant-ship. But they carried the transfiguration of the Buddha much further than the Sthaviras did, holding that he is supermundane and perfectly pure. His body is infinite, his power boundless, and his life endless. He educated living beings tirelessly, awakening pure faith in them. Furthermore, apparition-bodies (conventional human forms) of the Buddha appear and act in different world-realms at the same time.

Half a dozen subsects came out of the Mahāsāṅghikas, partly over doctrinal disputes and partly through geographic separation.

The Elders, or Sthaviras, claimed to conserve the true teaching and discipline of the Buddha by emphasizing the value of monastic life for personal enlightenment and the authority of monks in the Buddhist community. They, however, underwent another major schism about two hundred years after the Buddha's death. The schismatics were Pudgalavādins (Personalists), who asserted that there exists a person or self (pudgala) who is neither identical with the five skandhas nor different from them, but who nonetheless knows, transmigrates, and enters nirvāṇa. They said, on the other hand, that the skandhas that constitute the phenomenal person are mere designations, not real substances. The Sūtras contain many statements that can be cited in support of these views. The person of the Personalists is rather like the consciousness (vijñāna) that, according to an early teaching, transmigrates and enters nirvāṇa. Furthermore, the canonical expositions of the anātman (no-self) doctrine are ambiguous. They deny that any one of the skandhas is the ātman (self or person), and so conclude that the five taken together are not the ātman.

The Personalists said that the person is to the skandhas as fire is to the fuel, neither identical nor different. If it were other than the skandhas, it would be eternal and unconditional, which is a heretical view. If it were the same as the skandhas, it would undergo annihilation, also a heretical view. The Abhidharma masters of the Sthavira schools declared that the *dharmas* (elements) are real things *(vastu)* or substances *(dravya),* while the person is just a designation. The Personalists denied that either *dharmas* or persons are real things, while affirming that both exist as designations, that is, as objects of commonsense knowledge and statements. It is also the position that Mahāyāna later took.

The Personalists maintained that nirvāṇa is neither really the same as, nor really distinct from, *dharmas* (phenomena). If the person is neither the same as, nor other than, its elements, then its cessation must be neither the same nor different. Saṃsāra, also, is to nirvāṇa as the fuel is to the fire. It would be going rather far to make an active principle out of nirvāṇa, even for the Personalists, but this is just what the Mahāyāna sect called *Yogācāra* (see p. (00) later did. The Sthavira tradition emphasized the utter transcendence of nirvāṇa and refused to concede that it is immanent in saṃsāra even when the Sūtras used worldly symbols for immanence such as the fire and the ocean. The Tathāgata who dies is like the fire that goes out. Gautama's hearers believed that fire is an indestructible element latent in every bright or warm thing, but especially in fuel. It alternates between manifestation and "going home" to its occult source. In the Brahmanical literature, the ocean is the reservoir from which the streams of differentiated existence proceed and to which they revert when the liberated one merges back. So the Tathāgata, residing in this nirvāṇa-realm, is subtler than the subtlest (like fire) and greater than the greatest (like the ocean). These are precisely the predicates of the ātman (self) and brahman (cosmic essence) in the Upaniṣads. The Personalists were more cautious than the Upaniṣads in asserting immanence, but they kept alive this aspect of the early ontology and prepared the way for Mahāyāna doctrines such as that all living beings are endowed with suchness and with Buddha-nature. As a sect the Personalists thrived for over a thousand years.

This seemingly obscure philosophical dispute really has vital relevance to a cardinal religious issue: the value to be placed upon this world. Buddhism, like Christianity, has passed its centuries in a continual quandary on this point. If a spiritual reality dwells in and suffuses this world, then worldy and secular activities such as raising a family and scientific research have inherent worth. But if the worldly and the spiritual realms are mutually alien and exclusive, then profane things and activities have no intrinsic value and are significant only insofar as they contribute to escape from the profane realm into the spiritual. Christianity sided wholeheartedly neither with the orthodox Jewish affirmation nor with the Gnostic rejection of this world. Buddhism similarly preferred an enigmatic Middle Way against the easy-to-understand dead-end extremes of mere worldiness and mere otherworldliness.

A third schism further rent the Elders' school at the Council of Pāṭaliputra about 250 B.C. The two factions were called Distinctionists *(Vibhajyavādins)* and All-is-ists *(Sarvāstivādins);* the latter's chief thesis is that past and future things really exist, as do present things. It is doubtful whether their theories about time and being are religiously important, but this Sarvāstivādin school did nourish a doctrine that became one cornerstone of the Mahāyāna: the *pāramitās* (perfections). A bodhisattva, they said, fulfills six pāramitās: giving, morality, patience, vigor, meditation, and wisdom. Each of these virtues is frequently commended in the Sūtras, but they become "perfections" only when carried to the utmost extreme. The Council of Pāṭaliputra decided against the view of the Sarvāstivādins, some of whom migrated north and west. These dissidents established a strong center in Kashmir which flourished for a thousand years. The *Tales of the Previous Lives of the Buddha* (Jātaka), attested in the art of the second century B.C., relate how Gautama in his former lives accomplished each pāramitā.[1] Reborn as a hare, he resolved to practice giving *(dāna),* especially on Observance Day. Disguising himself as a brahmin, the god Indra decided to test the Bodhisattva hare and requested food. The hare realized that he could not offer grass as food to people, so he instructed the brahmin to make a fire, roast him, and eat him. Indra lit the fire, but when the hare jumped into it, the flame did not singe a single hair. Indra revealed himself and praised the hare. Reborn as a mariner, the Bodhisattva became blind but achieved great feats of navigation through the practice of prajñā (wisdom). Reincarnated as a caravan leader, he exemplified vigor *(vīrya)* by persisting in the search for underground water when his caravan ran dry in the desert.

Living one of his former lives as an ascetic, the Bodhisattva was staying in the pleasure-grove of a dissolute king of Benares. The king entered with a flock of dancing girls, and when he fell into a drunken sleep, the girls wandered off and discovered the ascetic. On awakening, the ruler was enraged to find his girls gathered round the mendicant and listening to his sermon. He asked the Bodhisattva what doctrine he professed and was told patience *(kṣānti).* So the king summoned his executioner, had the Bodhisattva severely flogged, then asked, "What do you profess?" The answer was still "patience." So the king had his victim's hands and feet cut off, then his nose and ears. To the end, the Bodhisattva professed patience and felt no anger whatsoever. The Earth, however, ran out of patience. As the tyrant was leaving his pleasure grove, the Earth opened up beneath his feet and toppled him to the lowest hell. These popular tales urged the listeners to imitate the Bodhisattva, but did not tell them to become a bodhisattva, a step that was taken by early Mahāyāna doctrine.

RELIGIOUS LIFE IN THE EARLY CENTURIES

The Canon furnishes evidence for the practices of the Community, lay as well as monastic, during the second century B.C.[2] The Pali Vinaya (which is still in theory the rule in Theravāda monasteries, though large parts of it have fallen into disuse) prescribes the correct life for the monk and describes, in telling the origin of each rule, the colorful abuses against which the Order had to protect itself. Areas in which the Saṅgha was well established were divided into districts, each approximately twenty miles square. Each district had one observance *(uposatha)* hall, at which all monks resident within the district were required to assemble on the last day of each half-month for recitation of the Rules of Discipline (Pali: *Pātimokkha)*. This code defines five classes of offense, prescribes rules of deportment, and establishes some procedural principles. Four offenses warrant permanent expulsion: fornication, theft, killing a human being, and falsely claiming spiritual attainments. Similar rules, appropriately modified for the subordinate role of women in Indian society of that period, governed the lives of nuns.

Thirteen offenses require a formal meeting of the Saṅgha chapter, with a quorum of at least twenty monks, and are punished with probation. The first five of these concern sex: intentional ejaculation,[3] touching a woman or speaking suggestively to her, urging a woman to earn merit by yielding to a man of religion, and serving as a go-between. Two rules deal with the prescribed size and the approved site of monks' dwellings. Six rules pertain to concord in the Order. For example, it is an offense to harass a fellow monk by false accusations of an offense that merits expulsion, or to support such an accusation with misleading testimony. And it is an offense to persist in fomenting discord within the Saṅgha after the assembly has three times formally warned the culprit to desist. Likewise it is a misdeed for other monks to persist in supporting a schismatic, and for a monk to persist after the third warning in being obtuse and ignoring what the assembly tells him. An evil-living monk whose influence is pernicious to the laity is to be requested to leave the district. If, after the third request, he has not reformed his ways or taken leave, he is guilty of an offense that requires probation.

The probationer forfeits many privileges: he must not allow monks in good standing to offer salutation, provide seats for him, carry his robe or bowl, or shampoo him. He must not walk or sit in front of a rule-abiding bhikṣu. He must announce that he is on probation to newcomers, when he enters a new residence, on Observance Day, and at the ceremony terminating the rainy season retreat. His residence is restricted, he has few options for changing it. He is required always to take the lowest seat, the worst bed, the worst room.

A monk must not take a seat with a woman, either in private or in public. If he does so, the assembly may decide whether the offense requires probation or merely confession.

Thirty of the enumerated offenses require expiation and forfeiture of the article involved. They deal mainly with robes, alms bowls, and seat-rugs. The obedient monk must not have more than one of each of these at a time. He must not allow a nun to do his laundry, give him a robe, or prepare wool for a rug. When his begging bowl is broken in five places, he can exchange it for a new one. He may only store medicinal foods for seven days. He may not receive gold or silver, buy, sell, or barter.

Ninety-two of the designated (monk's) offenses require expiation. The list is quite miscellaneous: lying, abuse, slander, stealing another bhikṣu's (monk's) sleeping space, taking more than one meal at a public rest house, sporting in the water, or eavesdropping while other monks quarrel. It is prohibited to dig the ground, destroy any vegetable, or sprinkle water with living creatures in it. Thus the monk could not practice agriculture. These rules, ostensibly to protect worms and bugs, also safeguarded the religious against lapsing into peasanthood and neglecting the Dharma. Another group of rules prohibits the monk (except for good cause) from going near an army drawn up for battle, staying with an army more than two or three nights, and watching the troops on parade. The idea seems to be that the monk should not be an accessory to bloodshed. The prohibitions were doubtless also intended to prevent him from engaging in espionage or diplomatic intrigue.

Unlike killing a human being, taking animal life deliberately does not warrant expulsion, but merely expiation. The monk must not even drink water that contains living things. But eating meat is not forbidden in the Rules of Discipline, though drinking liquor is an offense to be expiated.

A monk who tells a layperson or another monk that he has extraordinary spiritual powers, even when it is true, commits an expiable offense, and so does one who tells a nonmonk that a bhikṣu has committed a grave offense. On the other hand, every monk is duty-bound to inform the assembly of any serious transgression committed by a fellow monk. Since the Vinaya provides formal procedures for judging the accused and prescribing penance, and since an unconfessed and unexpiated sin is considered an affliction that is aggravated the longer it goes unabsolved, the informer is doing the accused a kindness. On the other hand, the code treats false accusation as a serious offense, and forbids harrying another with insinuations that he is transgressing. These rules taken together demand that the Saṅgha keep its own counsel; shun both the adulation and reproach of outsiders; and compel honesty, conformity, and goodwill from its members.

Some of the seventy-five rules of deportment regulate the conduct of the monk while going on his begging rounds among the homes of the laity, receiving alms, eating, and excreting. He must at all times be properly clothed, keep his eyes downcast, not sway his limbs or body, not loll or slouch, refrain from loud laughter and noise, and observe good table manners—neither stuffing his mouth, smacking his lips, talking with his mouth full, nor tossing the food into his mouth. He must not excrete while standing up, onto growing grass, or into water. Sixteen rules forbid the monk to preach Dharma to a monk or layperson whose deportment is disrespectful: carrying a parasol, staff, sword, or weapon in the hand; wearing slippers or sandals, a turban or other head-covering; occupying a higher seat than a monk, sitting while the monk is standing, or walking on a path either in front of or beside the monk are all considered irreverent.

The overall purpose of the rules of deportment is to render the monk worthy of reverence and of offerings, and to ensure that he receives the formal respect to which he is entitled. The bhikṣu must himself maintain impeccable conduct and allow the laity to choose their response. If they revile him, he suffers it with gentle dignity. If they behave like pigs, he withholds the pearls of the Dharma. The good monk is indifferent to success and failure, gain and loss. But he does the things that are most conducive to success in fulfilling the Dharma, and sticks to his principles even when so doing places his life in danger. Monks, and presumably nuns too, have starved; died of disease; been killed by robbers, tyrants, and ferocious beasts; and been mocked and humiliated by hostile unbelievers. But wherever the Vinaya has been observed in spirit and in letter, the Saṅgha as a whole has earned respect, and has prevailed.

In themselves the rules of deportment seem trivial and quaint. The Saṅgha, it must be remembered, accepts recruits from all social classes and peoples. It has to refine vulgar boys and civilize uncouth barbarians. Etiquette alone does not suffice, of course, but it is a necessary part of the complete discipline through which character is shaped, good habits built, and external observances converted into inner discipline.

A noteworthy feature of the Vinaya rules is that they are utterly free from prerational tabus of the sort so common in the Brahmanical and Near Eastern lawbooks. There is no idea that certain foods are impure, that bodily wastes pollute spiritually, or that certain acts or objects are lucky or unlucky. The authors of the Vinaya certainly thought that spirits and gods exist, yet no place is given to tabu plants and animals associated with particular divinities, a department in which Classical Hinduism rivals the cults of the ancient Near East. Nevertheless, the two dominant ethical concerns of the code—not taking life and continence—are carried to extremes not justifiable on humanistic and pragmatic grounds. The implicit premises are that life breath (or lifeblood) and semen are tabu. Animal sacrifice offers up the sacred life substance, while nonviolence *(ahiṃsā)* earns merit by saving life and then devotes the merit to holy objectives, while ascetic continence saves the force of Eros and applies it to spiritual goals.

The Vinaya does not see the monk as working out his own salvation unaided, like the self-made man of nineteenth-century capitalist folklore. Each monk is his brother's keeper; and, when the ordinand joins the Saṅgha, he surrenders some liberties and submits to the collective authority of the Community. Several disciplinary procedures are laid down for reducing the obstinate and the wayward to conformity. A strife-maker may be placed under an act of rebuke, which excludes him from participating in ordinations, guiding novices, exhorting nuns, censuring monks, commanding a junior, or associating with the other bhikṣus. An ignorant or foolish monk may be put under an act of subordination that suspends the same privileges as an act of rebuke and, in addition, places him in the care of a tutor until he has learned the Dharma. Acts of banishment are directed against those who cause scandal to the Saṅgha. A monk who offends the laity may be made to submit to an act of reconciliation, under which he forfeits privileges until he has asked and obtained the pardon of the layperson whom he has wronged. An act of suspension is directed against the monk who refuses to renounce a pernicious doctrine. He is not allowed to eat or dwell with the Saṅgha and notice of his banishment is sent to neighboring districts in which he is likewise to be denied food and shelter. All these acts remain in force only until their object has mended his ways.

A few features of the Vinaya, or Discipline, merit comment. It insists throughout on due process of law. The offender is warned, reminded of the rules, and, if the unacceptable behavior persists, is formally charged and duly tried by a jury consisting of the whole chapter. A transgressor cannot be tried while absent, may speak in his or her own defense, but must accept the sentence once it has been passed. The code, like the Talmud and the New Testament exhortations, is designed to compel expiation of sins and reconciliation of conflicts. However, the Vinaya's insistence on confessing one's misdeeds is inimical to most present-day Hindu and Buddhist cultures, in which preserving appearances rates higher than solving the problem. One last point: the punishments prescribed in the Vinaya, while stringent, constitute a middle way between laxity and cruelty.

The Discipline presupposes a high degree of earnestness and integrity. It will work only if most candidates enter voluntarily and in good faith. For this reason, full ordination (upasampadā) is not granted to anyone under twenty years of age. Eight years, though, is the minimum age for the novitiate ordination, which even adult candidates must undergo before proceeding to full ordination. In the "going forth" ceremony, the ordinand is invested with the saffron robes, head shaven, and takes the Three Refuges and the ten precepts. The Ten Precepts for a moral life are to abstain from: (1) taking life; (2) taking what is not given; (3) sexual misconduct; (4) lying; (5) drinking liquor; (6) eating after noon; (7) watching dancing, singing, and shows; (8) adorning oneself with garlands, perfumes, and ointments; (9) using a high bed; and (10) receiving gold and silver. The ordinand is then a novice; and has left the household life.[11] If under twenty, the novice must live with a preceptor until of age. The preceptor must have passed ten years since full ordination and must be of good character and competent. The novice also receives instruction from a tutor.

Ordination is conferred by an assembly of at least ten bhikṣus. The candidate accompanied by one of his tutors comes before the president of the assembly, whom he petitions for admission to the Saṅgha. Then he retires to the foot of the assembly, his alms bowl strapped onto his back, and his two tutors examine him to ascertain that he has his bowl, under robe, upper robe, and mantle. Then one of the tutors asks him in the hearing of the whole assembly whether he is free from certain diseases and whether he is a free human male, debtless, exempt from military service, furnished with his parents' permission, and at least twenty years of age. The candidate is then made to go forward, kneel, and ask the assembly for ordination. The assembly signifies assent by silence, so the candidate stands up, and the tutors put him through the interrogation again. One of the tutors reports that the candidate desires ordination, is free from disqualifications, has a bowl and a set of robes, asks for ordination, and that the assembly grants ordination. The public proclamation is made: "If any approve, let them be silent. If anyone objects, let him speak." When the assembly keeps silent through the third repetition of this proclamation, the two tutors announce to the president that the candidate has received ordination. The date and the hour are then noted, since seniority in the Order commences from the time of ordination. The new monk is given an exhortation, in which he is told that henceforth his four reliances are to be on alms for food, on old rags for clothing, on the shade of a tree for shelter, and on cow's urine for medicine. Actual monastic life is usually much less austere; the laity prepare good food for the monks and donate new robes annually, just after the rainy season retreat. A Buddhist nun's ordination is similar in most respects to a Buddhist monk's.

The Buddhist monk owned nothing but his clothes, which consisted of an undergarment, an outer garment, a cloak, waist-cloth, and belt and buckle. The robes, donated by the laity, were red or ochre. He also wore sandals and carried a begging bowl, a razor, tweezers, nail clippers, ear- and toothpicks, some gauze for filtering water, a needle, a walking stick, and a bag of medicines. He was also allowed an umbrella against the sun and a fan against the heat. Every other month the monk shaved his hair without using a mirror, forbidden to him, as were adornments, cosmetics, and perfumes, along with profane music and song. The Buddhist nun's personal possessions were equally meager.

Originally, the Buddhist monk was a wanderer, having no fixed domicile. He lived under a tree or in a natural mountain grotto, on a hillside or in a glen or forest glade, even in the open air or on a haystack. Naturally, he stayed near some village or town to beg, sometimes living in a thatched hut or some other humble temporary dwelling. For three months out of the year, the rainy season made travel impossible and very soon recluses and monks tended to group their dwellings together. The Canon reports that on occasion the Buddha accepted groups of dwellings and parks from local merchants to house monks during the rain retreat. There they could pursue their spiritual development and conduct communal ceremonies relatively undisturbed. The site selected for such resting places had to be secluded to ensure a proper atmosphere for meditation but also close enough to a village or town so that the monks could go on their begging rounds.

About 200 B.C., they began to receive from wealthy donors rock-cut residences *(vihāra),* in which the features of the wooden prototypes—pillars, joists, and rafters—were imitated in stone. Around the same time, residences of fired brick came into general use. Doubtless humble dwellings of wood and thatch, like the typical village residence in modern Ceylon, continued to outnumber the imposing brick and stone ones that survive for archaeological study. The remains of the brick residences at Sāñcī, Sārnāth, and Nālandā, and their rock-cut counterparts at Kārlī and Ajantā, exhibit a common plan.

Four rows of cells, each eight to ten feet square, a half dozen or more cells to a row, surround a central courtyard which was part of the cave in the rock-cut residences and was probably enclosed with thatch or a canopy in the brick ones. The cells each contained one or two brick or stone benches, which were covered with rugs and used both as seats and as beds like modern Indian benches. Apparently only elders and perhaps their personal attendants lived in the cells; the junior monks and novices slept in the central courtyard, which also served as a classroom and a refectory.

At Ajantā (fifth to sixth century A.D.) walls surrounding the rock-cut monastery courtyards were covered with brightly colored paintings of Jātaka stories *(Tales of the Previous Lives of the Buddha),* donors, foreign visitors, celestial beings, beautiful princes and princesses, and formal designs. The monks who lived amid this aesthetic splendor were forbidden by their rule to discuss women, chariots, elephants, kings, and battles, but were permitted to see all these subjects exquisitely painted on their dwelling walls. They were exhorted to avoid even the thought of sexual love, yet the doorways to their residences were carved with consummately voluptuous loving couples. The paradox of the beauty of the walls and the austerity of the monks who found refuge within them remains today to puzzle the observer. Whatever its valuation of sensual things, Buddhism has never allowed its distrust of attachment to beautiful things to intrude and prevent the beautification of sacred premises. Buddhists used other sorts of pictures didactically. Paintings of hell, where the wicked suffer punishment for their evil deeds, were painted on the walls of monastery bathrooms and sweat baths. A picture of the Wheel of Life was sometimes painted over the monastery door or in a hall where passersby could see it, and a monk was appointed to explain it.

Some bhikṣus evidently lived alone in huts, either near a village or deep in the jungle. The Vinaya specifies the maximum size for such huts. Solitary residence was more favorable for meditation and the practice of austerities than

An anchorite, judging from his hairstyle not a Buddhist, in front of his solitary hut. Symbolic of harmony, he reaches out to a dove, a crow, a doe, and a snake. (From Mathurā, first century B.C.)

was the communal life of the larger residences, where the daily routine comprised many activities other than meditation, and where most bhikṣus did not practice more than the mild austerity required by the Vinaya.

Another important structure associated with early Buddhist monastic residences was the hall housing a stūpa *(caitya-gṛha)*. The stūpa is the principal object of worship for Buddhists, especially when it enshrines relics of the Buddha or of an important or locally revered monk. Stūpa worship includes circumambulation in the auspicious clockwise direction around the monument, prostrations, and offerings of flowers. When housed in a special structure, the stūpa was placed at the end of a long hall, with a nave in front in which worshippers could gather and an apse containing the stūpa itself. Outside aisles demarcated by a colonnade made circumambulation possible. In addition to stūpas, monastic residences, and such stūpa halls, Buddhists also built temples, few of which have survived in India.

The main outlines of the daily monastic routine seem to have varied little through the centuries in India, and to have undergone no major changes in China. The Ceylonese commentator Buddhaghosa in the fourth century A.D. based his account of the Buddha's daily habits on the standard monastic routine. The Buddha, he says, got up at daybreak, rinsed his mouth and went to the toilet; then he sat quietly until it was time to go on the begging rounds (about 8 or 9 A.M. nowadays in Theravāda countries), when he put on his robes, took his bowl, and entered the village or town for alms. The bhikṣu's residence was supposed to be near enough to a village that he could easily go there to beg, and far enough away that he would not be distracted by noise and company. The Buddha, says Buddhaghosa, was usually received with honor by householders, who vied to invite him and his companions to lunch. They would seat him, and place food reverently in his bowl. Then when he had eaten, he would discourse on Dharma to his hosts. Returning to the monastery, he sat in the refectory pavilion while the monks who had not been invited to dine in their donors' homes finished eating. Then he withdrew to his cell, called "the perfumed chamber," washed his feet, and rested. Following the siesta period he came out and preached to the monks who had gathered outside his cell. Then he responded to individual requests for guidance in meditation, after which the monks dispersed to their dwellings. The Buddha took another rest in the late afternoon, then preached to the lay donors and worshippers who came to call on him. Afterward he went to the bathhouse for a cool bath, then paced back and forth in the courtyard or garden and meditated. He concluded the evening (first watch of night) by granting interviews to individual monks. During the second watch of night, he received deities who came for instruction; during the third, he rested.

This schedule alternates rest and activity, retirement and sociability, covering a long and busy day at a leisurely pace. It is with good reason that the Vinaya and the elders in charge of the monasteries have consistently emphasized the daily routine and guarded its observance. Buddhism as a way of life is concretely realized in the monastic routine, with its provisions for cultivating morality, wisdom, meditation, and worship; with its scrupulous attention to the correct performance of everyday acts; and with its faith that in the still of the night the gods come down and converse with holy monks in the Saṅgha's moonlit groves.

The yearly monastic routine followed the rhythm of the seasons. During the monsoons (June/July to October/November), the monks retreated to their monasteries for study and meditation. Some were assigned specific functions to ensure efficient operation of the monastery. A senior member supervised the details of the structure's physical survival, and a layman acted as a liaison agent between the Community and the outside world. The dry season's return was marked by ceremonies which preceded the departure of the monks for their wandering and preaching. The laity presented gifts of cloth to the assembled monks, invited them to midday meals, and participated in processions. Only a few monks remained behind to maintain the monastery.

The Order of Nuns *(bhikṣuṇī-saṅgha)* was said to have been instituted reluctantly by the Buddha at the request of his aunt and foster mother, Prajāpatī, and upon the intercession of Ānanda. The Blessed One conceded that women are able to attain arhant-ship but laid eight special regulations on the nuns, subordinating them strictly to the Order of Monks. It is perhaps not surprising that an order founded so reluctantly should not have flourished. After the first generation few distinguished nuns are mentioned.

Female donors. (From a central Asian wall painting, circa eighth century A.D.)

We have already noted that the first two worshippers of the new Buddha were laymen (p. 40). We have also observed (p. 66) that all sects agreed that the laity could attain the first three degrees of sainthood and remain in the household life; the Sūtras and some Hīnayāna sects, however, affirmed that arhantship was open to the laity, though some insisted that immediately after attainment they must either die or become a monk or nun.

In ancient India, the layman dressed in white, as opposed to the colored robes of the monk, and lived as a married householder. Though he followed the Buddhist way of life, taking refuge in it and supporting the monastic community, he was not compelled to forego other religious practices common among members of his social class. He was required to follow the ethical code of the Buddhist layman, but his chief virtue was generosity in giving to the monks. Since he remained involved in the world, he was not expected to excel in meditation or wisdom. He could enhance the practice of his lay virtues by fasting six days every month, that is, eating nothing after his one prenoontime meal. These special days would be devoted to recitations, reading of the scriptures, and preaching sermons. The layman was also expected to be without personal luxury, which meant giving up fine furniture; flowers and perfumes; singing, dancing, and going to dramatic performances. For further spiritual advance, he could abstain from sex and generally follow the practice of novices and monks. Finally, he could take the ultimate step and join the Order, trading his white robes for those of the novice monk.

The laity in early Buddhism were thus assigned arduous functions and promised ample rewards in this life and subsequent ones. The monastic orders depended on their donations, and in return they instructed them in Dharma, especially in giving, morality, heaven, the wretchedness of sense-desire, and the benefits of overcoming sense-desire. By keeping the Five Precepts and having profound faith in Buddha, Dharma, and Saṅgha,[5] the layman and laywoman were sure to become *srotāpanna* (stream-winners), have only happy rebirths, and speedily attain full enlightenment. The virtuous householder was assured increase of wealth because of his zeal, a fine reputation, confidence in handling public affairs, a calm and unbewildered death, and after death, rebirth in a heaven. Girls were told to become good wives, to be willing and sweet tempered, to honor their husbands' relatives and guests, to be skillful at homecrafts, to manage the servants well, and to protect their husbands' valuables. As a reward, after death they would be born among the Gods of Lovely Form.

In the Saṅgha today as in antiquity, males are segregated from females and monastics from laity, resulting in a fourfold organization. Relations among members of the four orders are restricted so that they will not corrupt one another. The relations are expressed in formal gestures like bowing and proper address so that due honor and seniority will be observed. Though the individual layman may well be more moral and more spiritual than any given monk, the former must give precedence to the latter because the yellow-robed orders are superior to the white-clad laity. The nun must look up to the monk, and the laywoman to the layman, because the male sex per se is considered superior to the female regardless of whether particular women are better than any individual man. The scriptures do not present much of a case for male superiority, and their case for the ceremonial precedence of the monastics is fragmentary and weak. The homeless life is more favorable for attaining sainthood, because it is free from the distractions, temptations, and worries of family life. Hence it is presumed that, in general, monks are more moderate in eating and drinking and more zealous in following the moral precepts than the laity.

The householder is encouraged to take the first five of the ten *śīla* (precepts) undertaken by the novice (see p. 74). *Śīla* is defined as suppressing sins of body and speech in pursuance of a resolution made either in private or before witnesses. The first precept is to refrain from killing living beings *(prāṇin*, having life, breath). Animals of all sorts are intended, but plants are not. The sin is to know that something is a living being, to intend to kill it, attempt to do so, and to succeed. Unintentional killing is not a sin as killing, though it may constitute sinful negligence. The layman cannot avoid inadvertently killing small creatures while practicing agriculture, but if he undertakes this precept, he is supposed to minimize the destruction of small lives.

The second precept is to refrain from taking what has not been given. The sin consists in taking the property of another by force or by stealth. The offense is committed when one knows that the thing belongs to another, and intentionally attempts and successfully executes the act of taking it. If the ownership of an object is unknown, there is an obligation to try to find out whether it is the property of another before taking it.

The third precept is to refrain from misconduct in erotic matters. It concerns intercourse with a forbidden woman (the wife of another, a woman under the care of a guardian, a betrothed woman, a nun, a woman under a vow of chastity), as well as intercourse with one's own wife "by a forbidden passage," in an unsuitable place (that is, a public place or a shrine), at an unsuitable time (that is, when the woman is pregnant, is nursing, or has taken a vow of abstinence). Factors considered here are the rights and obligations of others, the wishes of the woman herself, her health, and that of her child. The elaborate commentaries on this precept do not consider intercourse with a courtesan forbidden unless she has become betrothed to another. Notice that the entire discussion on sexual matters pertains to a man's actions. Ancient India commonly assumed that women were by nature wanton and that, consequently, the responsibility for keeping them out of trouble sexually lay with their guardians.

The fourth precept is to refrain from lying speech. The sin consists of intentionally concealing the truth, or stating what is known not to be so, in order to deceive another person.

The fifth precept is to refrain from drinking liquor. The reasons given are that liquor does the body little good and much harm, and that by weakening self-control it occasions other sins.

Some Sūtras indicate that the laity were not usually given instruction on the more technical aspects of wisdom and meditation. Abhidharma scholasticism and the more abstruse contents of the Sūtras were reserved for monks. One ostensible reason is that the ordinary layperson does not have time to understand, let alone practice, such deep and difficult doctrines. But what of the extraordinary householder? Most of the Greek philosophers, the Talmudic sages, the philosophers of classical and imperial China, and the masters of the Hindu Nyāya-Vaiśeṣika and Mīmāṃsā schools were householders. Probably the monks feared that householders would rival them if they became too proficient in the deeper Dharma. Such self-interest belies the claim that the monastic orders surpassed the laity in detachment.

We know next to nothing about the life-cycle ceremonials of the Indian Buddhist laity. There were apparently Buddhist funeral and memorial rites, but there is no evidence of a Buddhist wedding ceremony. The Buddhist monk, even today, is not a caterer to mundane liturgical needs, like the brahmin. Weddings and other rites of passage may have been purely social ceremonies without participation of religious specialists, or brahmins may have been employed, or there may have been non-brahmin specialists. In the official Buddhist view, such matters were not religious.

We can infer from modern Theravāda customs that at some period Indian Hīnayāna (early Buddhist sects) must have celebrated calendrical festivals like New Year's (mid-March) and Offering to the Ancestors (fifteenth of the seventh month, that is, the beginning of October). The dates and many features of the festivals are close to the corresponding Hindu celebrations. But we do not have direct evidence that such festivals were in vogue in the second century B.C. They are just not the sort of thing that Hīnayāna monks wrote about, as can be seen from the works of modern Theravāda bhikṣus. A Tibetan student of Christianity would have equal trouble learning how Americans celebrate Christmas, New Year's, and Easter from the writings of contemporary theologians.

As the early extracanonical accounts of the lives of the Buddha regularly place both his Birth and Enlightenment on the full moon night of Vaiśākha (April-May), describing how the population of the whole cosmos worshipped and rejoiced with hymns and flower-offerings at both events, it is likely that the festival to celebrate these events was already celebrated in the last centuries before Christ. This festival is the greatest in the modern Theravāda calendar.

We do know something of ancient Buddhism's sacred places, forms of worship, and symbols, especially from its early art. Evidence indicates that at the popular level, Buddhism integrated local religious forms and the cults present in its environment. These had a long ancestry, extending in part back to the Indus civilization and other levels of Indian prehistory, in part deriving from Vedic and Brahmanical customs and lore. Buddhists and the followers of the Brahmanical religion shared the same world view and both conceived the world system on the model of the Wheel of Life. Cults of trees and tree spirits, serpents, fertility goddesses, and reliquary mounds all entered early Buddhism from the preexisting religious tradition. These became part of Buddhist cult practice and lore. For example, in the myth of the Buddha, Queen Māyā gave birth to her son under a sacred tree. In art, she is shown standing under it in a posture traditionally associated with female fertility.

In cult practice and holy places, Buddhism adopted much of the popular village religion. The considerable veneration paid to the sacred Bodhi Tree derived from ancient fertility cults and before that perhaps from shamanism. Characteristically, a sacred tree stood in every village; it became for followers of the Buddhist religion the Bodhi Tree under which the great hero was enlightened. (Notice that he was born under a tree and died resting between two trees). At the base of the tree was an altar, usually surrounded by a fence or railing of wood and stone. This Bodhi Tree (a type of fig, *Ficus religiosa*, *pīpal* or *aśvattha* in Sanskrit) has since the earliest times been a major object

Worshippers at a sacred Bodhi Tree, with garlands and offerings of leaves and lotus flowers, seen on the altar in front of it. Some stand with folded hands, others kneel at its foot. (From the Bhārhut stūpa, second century B.C.)

of veneration for Buddhists throughout Asia. Aśoka, tradition says, paid such inordinate attention to the tree at Bodh-gayā that his queen out of jealousy tried to have it destroyed. By virtue of Aśoka's devotion, Bodh-gayā was improved physically and became a major Buddhist shrine and place of pilgrimage. Also at this sacred site, in front of the tree, is a carved stone seat, the "diamond seat" *(vajrāsana,* so-called because here Gautama achieved stability) which, though empty, symbolizes his concrete presence.

We have already mentioned two most important sacred Buddhist monuments, the cave temple and the stūpa. People met and prayed in the cave temples, faithfully performing the ceremonial clockwise circumambulation *(pradakṣinā)* around the reliquary stūpa in the central nave at the back of the cave. Stūpas were also erected in the open air. In countries practicing the Buddhist religion, the stūpa remains today the most venerated of all its monuments. Deriving from funerary origins, stūpas were traditionally set up over the ashes of holy men, as in the case of the Buddha; or over relics belonging to them (the cult of relics being important in itself); or to commemorate a miracle, mark a sacred spot, or gain merit from sponsoring the construction. Its dome rests on a square or circular base. From its top rises a stone umbrella, symbol of the Buddha's spiritual royalty. Unfortunately, the iron pillar supporting the umbrella serves as a lightning rod, and has resulted in the destruction of many monuments. During the ceremonies consecrating

Two miniature stūpas of metal, the one on the left from the Southeastern-most Indian coast.

the shrine, the relics or holy articles were placed in the stūpa's interior in a specially constructed box, the tunnel leading to the box then being sealed permanently. The symbolism of the stūpa is complex, but ultimately it represents the body of the Buddha, his actual presence. Even though, technically, he has left saṃsāra, it is a concrete reminder of him. The dome is called the "egg" *(aṇḍa)*, thus suggesting that the stūpa commemorates not only his death, but his second, spiritual, birth into final nirvāṇa, too.

From early Buddhist sculpture we gain some idea of the religion's worship forms. We see people (and even serpents and celestial spirits) gathered around a sacred tree or a stūpa, their hands reverentially folded before them in Indian fashion, either standing or kneeling. Often they have placed garlands of flowers (especially lotus petals) on the stūpa, or hung them on the tree, and laid flowers or other offerings on the shrine before it. A fervent religious mentality ran deep in traditional India's consciousness. Perhaps the presupposition that every act, however minor, necessarily led to good or bad consequences encouraged this ardent religiosity. It expressed itself in bending, adoring, venerating, serving, and sacrificing (flowers and offerings) before the holy shrine. These acts acknowledge or "remember" the sacred presence manifested by the shrine. The Bodhi Tree, revered because the Buddha was enlightened under it, also functioned as the pan-Indian "wish-fulfilling tree," bringer of all desires, fruits, and essences of life.

In these early representations of Buddhist worship, we see many symbols used instead of actual figures of the Buddha, which came into general use only after 100 A.D., probably in response to devotionalism fostered by Mahāyāna,

Humans and celestial beings worship a stūpa with garlands of lotus flowers. (From the Bhārhut stūpa of the second century B.C.)

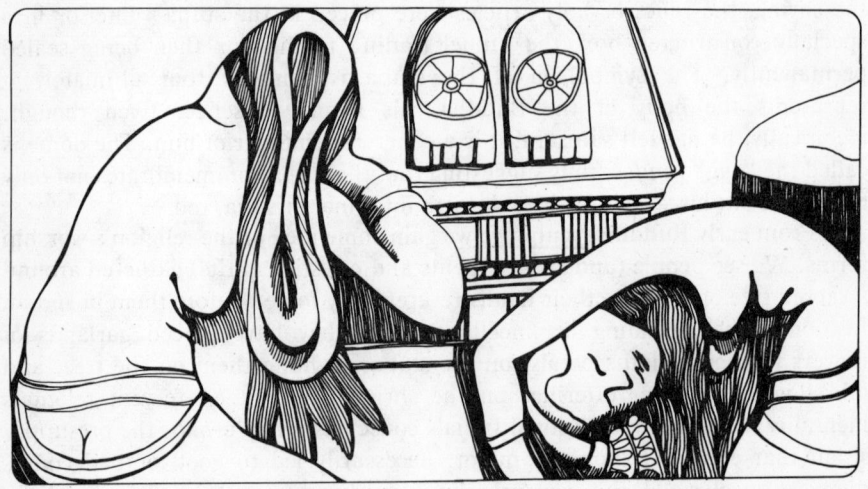

Two women venerating the footprints of the Buddha.

a later form of Buddhism. The objects for worship included the empty throne, a pair of footprints, a wheel or lotus, a shrine with a turban on it, or even a circle under a tree. The empty throne recalled the spot on which the Buddha attained Enlightenment; the pair of footprints reminded worshippers that he walked among people and, despite the attainment of nirvāṇa, left his Path and

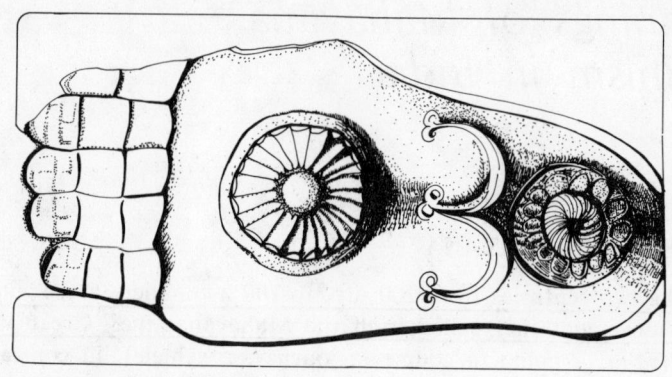

Symbols on an early representation of the Buddha's footprint, including svastikas (meaning "well-being" in Sanskrit) on his toes, a wheel, a symbol of the three jewels (Buddha, Dharma, and Saṅgha) and a lotus.

his continuing presence in the world. The turban symbolized what he had renounced, his royal worldly inheritance; the wheel stood for his First Sermon as well as the Wheel of Life. The lotus, probably the most frequent symbol, has a complex symbolism all its own. It grows from the mud of material existence yet transcends it in its purity—its leaves and beautiful petals appear not even to touch the waters (of becoming). Thus, the lotus, like Buddhahood, is self-created out of the defilements of existence. Frequently, we see lotus flowers on the altar before an enshrined Bodhi Tree, or in garlands draped over the dome of a stūpa or the branches of the tree. We can only speculate why the Buddha was not depicted in human form for almost 500 years after his nirvāṇa. Perhaps prior to that time, symbols were sufficient to recall his memory and establish his presence for the worshipper; or, perhaps respect for his attainment of nirvāṇa, a state entirely beyond representation, motivated the use of alternate symbols. Much of this cult practice and symbolism survives in Buddhist religious life today throughout Asia.

5.
Beginnings of Mahāyāna Buddhism in India

THE RISE OF MAHĀYĀNA

During the two centuries from 100 B.C. to 100 A.D., there arose within Buddhism a movement that called itself the Mahāyāna, the "Great Vehicle or Course" (yāna: a going, a course, a journey, a vehicle), in contrast to the Hīnayāna,[1] the "Inferior Vehicle." The Great Course, said its adherents, was that of the bodhisattva, which leads to Buddhahood (supreme, perfect enlightenment), while the Inferior Course leads only to arhant-ship. It appears that the Mahāyāna arose within the Mahāsāṅghika sects, which from the first had disparaged the arhant and had championed doctrines later typical of the Great Course, such as that phenomena are māyā[2] (illusory) and śūnya (empty), that the true Buddha is transmundane, and that the historical Buddha is a mere apparition of him (see p. 68). The idea of the bodhisattva, the future Buddha, was accepted by all the early sects. The Mahāyāna innovation was to proclaim that the bodhisattva course is open to all, to lay out a path for aspiring bodhisattvas to follow, and to create a new pantheon and cult of superhuman bodhisattvas and cosmic Buddhas who respond to the pleas of devotees.

The hallmark of Mahāyāna is its Sūtra literature rather than any one doctrine or practice. All Buddhists accept the authenticity of the Pali Suttas. When the early Canon was committed to writing in the second century B.C., it more or less fixed the corpus of the Sūtras (Pali: Suttas) but did not extinguish the preachers' old habits of embellishing the kernel of a Dharma-theme with their own innovations. These embellishments began the development of a new Buddhist literature that was accepted by some and rejected by others as normative for life and thought in the Buddha's Way. They are continuous with the last phases in the formation of the Hīnayāna Canon. The new Sūtras, written in Sanskrit rather than Pali, like the old claimed to report dialogs of the Buddha; and in the earliest extant "expanded Sūtras," the discussants are well-known figures of early Buddhism. Those who deny that the Mahāyāna Sūtras are the word of the Buddha are Hīnayānists. Those who accept them are Mahāyānists. As there is no special Mahāyāna Vinaya, a monk could follow the advice for spiritual training and morality in the new Sūtras without drastic change in his mode of life. If he happened to be a Mahāsāṅghika, he could accept the new literature without much alteration of his doctrinal convictions. The very earliest Mahāyāna Sūtras—for example, *The Small Perfection of*

Wisdom—do not disparage Hīnayāna, and in fact place the teachings of the bodhisattva course in the mouths of the great arhants. Eventually a wider rift developed between Mahāyānist attitudes and those of Buddhists who did not accept the new Sūtras as normative. For example, the *Vimalakīrti-Nirdeśa,* a somewhat later Sūtra, ridicules the arhants and says that even the worst sinner still has a chance to become a Buddha, while the arhant is at a dead end in an inferior nirvāṇa. The still later *Lotus Sūtra* is even more vehemently hostile to Hīnayāna, but adopts a seemingly conciliatory posture, affirming that the arhant is not really condemned to an inferior goal since there is in reality just one nirvāṇa, that of a Buddha, which even arhants will reach in due course. There could not have been much conflict beween the two Courses in 100 B.C. However, the rift between them widened more and more until, in 200 A.D., the *Lotus Sūtra* betrays an irrevocable schism.

The composition of Mahāyāna Sūtras continued from 100 B.C. until 400 A.D., reflecting changes in doctrine and religious life, regional and sectarian differences, and sociocultural factors, some of which can be identified from the evidence of the Sūtras themselves. There are no firsthand historical sources on this literature and the movement which produced it.

In the second century A.D., Mahāyāna authors started publishing treaties *(śāstras)* in their own names. Although they cited the Sūtras as proofs, they also relied substantially on experience and rational inference. These treatises served to present the Buddhist case to non-Buddhists who rejected the testimony of the Sūtras, and the newer Buddhist doctrine to Hīnayānists who denied the authenticity of the Mahāyāna Sūtras. The new respect for human authors stemmed from a crucial change in Indian elite culture—the emergence of a secular literature (fiction, poetry, and nonfiction), individual authorship, advances in science and knowledge, improvements in techniques of debate and logic, and greater confidence in people's ability to achieve knowledge without the aid of gods or superhuman saints. But the middlebrows and lowbrows continued to crave revelations and stimulate the composition of new Sūtras. The Hindus, likewise, went on writing Upaniṣads, Purāṇas, and Āgamas and attributing them to gods and ancient sages. Shortly after the Buddhists stopped writing Sūtras, they started composing Tantras (manuals of ritual observances and meditations), likewise anonymous and somewhat casually attributed to the Buddha.

There is a Mahāyāna theory of revelation which covertly justifies attribution of these discourses to Śākyamuni. Whatever the enlightened disciples teach is to be considered as Buddha's own teaching, because they have themselves realized his Dharma and nothing that they teach deviates from it. Early Buddhism, too, had maintained that the words of the arhants agree with those of the Buddha, a confidence somewhat shaken by the frequent falling-out of arhants. The Mahāyānists introduced the notion of the Buddha's inspiration or charisma *(adhiṣṭhāna, anubhāva),* through which he infuses thoughts into

the minds of men and sustains the advocates of his Dharma. Since the
Mahāyāna Buddha is eternal, omnipresent, and omniscient, it seemed reasonable that his influence would pervade the thoughts of men in the centuries after
the Parinirvāṇa, and that their inspirations would have the value of scripture.
Early Buddhism had a definite notion of Gautama's charisma (see p. 42), and
inasmuch as the Buddha and other arhants can read each other's minds (the
third superknowledge, see p. 28), it was not a big step to the idea that the
Buddha can implant thoughts in the mind of another. This theory, though,
was never openly used to defend the Mahāyāna Sūtras because to do so would
have meant giving up the false historical claim the Mahāyānists had foolishly
made—that their Sūtras were from the mouth of the Buddha.

Much obscurity surrounds the origins of Mahāyāna. We do not know
where it first arose, but the most likely areas are those where the Mahāsāṅghikas were strong, Andhra and Gandhāra. Scholars who think Iranian and
Hellenistic influences played a major part in engendering the Great Vehicle
favor northwest India as its birthplace. Considering, though, that bhikṣus
wandered the length and breadth of India and stayed freely as guests in the
monasteries of all sects, early Mahāyāna ideas doubtless spread rapidly
throughout the whole country. The laity, furthermore, were mostly nonsectarian, and as the Great Course developed among them, as well as among the
monks, the evolution likely took place in many areas far removed from the
spot where it first arose.

Wherever it originated, the Great Vehicle first flourished notably in northwest India, where it exhibited its greatest strength even at 400 A.D., when the
Chinese pilgrim Fa-hsien passed through.

The northwest was inhabited by many peoples, Iranian and Greek as well
as Indo-Āryan, Zoroastrian and Brahmanical as well as Buddhist. Buddhism
appealed more strongly to non-Indians than did Brahmanism, though one
inscription records the devotion of a Greek to Krishna. Several Hīnayāna sects
had achieved missionary successes long before Mahāyāna appeared on the
scene. Nevertheless, the contact of peoples and cultures seems to have affected
the complexion of Buddhism, to have favored ideas and cults closer to the
previous religions of Greece and Persia, and to have loosened the bonds of
conservative tradition.

THE TEACHING OF EMPTINESS

The *Prajñā-pāramitā* (Perfection of Wisdom) *Sūtras* are dialogs between saints
who are said to be "coursing in the Perfection of Wisdom," a state of samādhi
(concentration) which in some phases permits discourse. The perfection of
wisdom consists in the direct realization that all the dharmas, whether
conditioned or unconditioned, are *śūnya* (empty). Saṃsāra is empty and
nirvāṇa is empty; the Buddhas are empty, as are the beings whom they guide.
Thus there is no essential difference between the relative and the absolute. But

what is *śūnyatā* (emptiness), the common predicate of all things? It is absence of *svabhāva* (own-being), a term that means something (1) existing through its own power rather than that of another, (2) possessing an invariant and inalienable mark, and (3) having an immutable essence.

Early Buddhism had ascribed to all conditioned dharmas three universal marks: suffering, impermanence, and no-self (duḥkha, anitya, and anātman). Early Mahāyāna added a fourth, emptiness. The addition is not really an innovation since the effort to describe the personality-in-existence as a composite of dharmas was to indicate the emptiness of *ātman* (self). Its importance lies more in the value-tone of the word "empty" than in its formal doctrinal content. The early Buddhist emphasis on suffering and impermanence is intended to arouse aversion to worldly life. The Mahāyāna advocates of emptiness (Śūnyavādins) insisted on emptiness in order to summon the hearer to reevaluate transmigration and achieve release within it rather than fleeing it while still considering it real and important. Intellectually, svabhāvas (own-beings) are false reifications, conceptual figments. Emotionally, they are the foci of obsessions, the illusory idols that enslave the passions. The contemplation of śūnyatā is an intellectual and emotional therapy. The aim is not to deny commonsense reality to things as experienced in the commonsense world, but to cleanse one's vision of false views, and so to see the world "as it really is," that is, to see its "suchness" *(tathatā)*.

Empty entities are neither existent nor inexistent. Either extreme would be heretical, in Śunyavāda as in Early Buddhism (see p. 48). So emptiness is not an absolute substance, not a stuff out of which all things are made, like the Upaniṣadic Absolute *(Brahman)*. Rather, it is the fact that no immutable substance exists and none underlies phenomena. Śūnyatā is equivalent to pratītya-samutpāda, the principle which Gautama enunciated as the Middle Way between being and nonbeing (see p. 48).

Pratītya-samutpāda, though, is a descriptive law rather than a substantial entity. Ancient India was especially puzzled over the ontological status of abstractions, descriptions, and relational laws. Realists kept trying to reduce them to things, whereas the Buddhists consistently analyzed things into relations and principles. One of the chief obstacles for modern people trying to understand śūnyatā is that science discarded the substance-and-attribute mode of explanation centuries ago; and, thanks to popular science, we are all Śūnyavādins nowadays in our serious metaphysics, while often remaining naïve svabhāva-vādins in our theology and self-image. On the one hand, emptiness seems too obvious to be intellectually significant. On the other, it gives offense by attacking the emotional props that uphold the ordinary, unenlightened personality.

Throughout the ages people, alarmed and repelled by the idea of emptiness, have equated it with nothingness, an error against which the Sūtras and treatises warn repeatedly. Emptiness is the expeller of wrong views, but emptiness wrongly apprehended is as dangerous as a snake wrongly grasped or a spell wrongly recited. It is as wrong to crave obliteration into nothingness as to cling to, and long for, eternal existence.

The teaching of emptiness repudiates dualities: between the conditioned and the unconditioned, between subject and object, between the pure and the impure, between the relative and the absolute. It cannot be called monism, however, because it denies that reality is either a plurality or a unity; it is simply beyond individuation and numbers, both of which are fictive concepts *(vikalpa)* and mere designations *(prajñapti)*. What, then, is reality? It is called the Dharma-realm *(dharmadhātu)*, Dharma-nature *(dharmatā)*, the Dharma-body *(dharmakāya)*, the acme of the real *(bhūtakoṭi)*, suchness *(tathatā)*, reality *(bhūtatā, tattva)* and the highest entity or absolute *(paramārtha)*. But it is saṃsāra seen as it really is by the vision of the saints—nondifferent from nirvāṇa.

This doctrine comes to terms with the early Buddhist quandary about the relationship between the Nirvāṇa-realm and the world. Not only is nirvāṇa immanent in the world, but neither exists apart from the other. The world is a phantom conjured up by karmic action, the magician. But the phantom-maker is himself *māyā* (a phantom). These phantoms exist inasmuch as they appear and act, but inexist insofar as they are insubstantial and impermanent. To cause such a māyā-world and to reside in it does not degrade nirvāṇa to the level of a commonsense thing, nor does it construe it as a separate absolute.

Nirvāṇa is by definition changeless,[3] while pratītya-samutpāda (dependent co-arising) is the process of change or saṃsāra. Śūnyavādins say, though, that dependent co-arising is noncinematic. When seen from the absolute standpoint past, present, and future are all observed simultaneously, like a painting; while from the conventional standpoint, they appear as a series, like a motion picture. The contrast between the two truths (conventional and absolute) is the basic principle of the *Prajñā-pāramitā Sūtras,* and all their apparent paradoxes merely insist that what is true from one standpoint is false from the other. This epistemological dualism is the price that Śūnyavāda pays for ontological nondualism.

Emptiness has far-reaching consequences for the religious life. Monks in training who are ridden with feelings of guilt and shame because they have infringed the Vinaya are told to appease their guilt by meditation on its emptiness. This does not give them license to sin, but it liberates them from the burden of evil. The bodhisattva can work and play in the secular world without fear of contamination from sense objects, because he knows that intrinsically they are neither pure nor impure. He associates with merchants, kings, harlots, and drunkards without falling into avarice, arrogance, lust, or dissipation. He accepts and excels in the arts and sciences, welcoming them as good means to benefit and edify living beings. He recognizes the religious capacities of women, listening respectfully when they preach the Dharma, because he knows that maleness and femaleness are both empty. A rich man can be a good bodhisattva if, realizing that his wealth is empty, he is humble and generous.

A poor person who recognizes that poverty is empty and does not let it impair self-respect can also excel in holiness. It is all right to be a monk or nun, but a layperson often has better opportunities to practice skill in good means if he or she remembers that everything is empty. ✓

The Sūtras that claim all things are empty assert and illustrate but do not prove their theses. They employ much persuasive rhetoric, and very little inference and formal argument. Nevertheless, some proponents of the emptiness-teaching used logical arguments to convince those who did not accept the emptiness Sūtras. A notable example is Nāgārjuna (circa 150–250 A.D.) who was the founder of the Mādhyamika or Madhyamaka school, so-called because it claims to maintain the Middle Path *(Madhyamā Pratipad)* between being and nonbeing which the Buddha declared in his sermon to Kaccāna (see p. 48). Nāgārjuna grieved that the Hindu philosophical schools, employing the Nyāya (logical) methods of argumentation, were outclassing the Buddhists in the fashionable interschool debates, so he set out to argue the Śūnyavādin case against both Hīnayānists and non-Buddhists, using the standard rules of debate and certain special forms of argument. While taking his main concepts and definitions from the Sūtras, he tried to refute his opponents on their own grounds rather than on the authority of scriptures that they did not accept.

Nāgārjuna wrote two didactic works preaching morality and the way to nirvāṇa in straightforward, conventional, and positive language.[4] He is also the reputed author of several Mahāyāna hymns. But his best-known work is the *Middle Stanzas (Madhyamaka-kārikās),*[5] a polemical treatise of about 450 verses in which he refutes a wide range of "wrong views." He uses a kind of reduction-to-absurdity argument *(prasaṅga)* in which he shows that all the implications of the opponent's thesis are unacceptable in light of the opponent's own assumptions. The general pattern is much like this: If you assert that A and B are related, then they must be either identical or different. But since you maintain that the two terms of a relation cannot be identical, A and B are not identical. And because you hold that a real entity is not dependent on another, you must concede that A and B are not different. Thus you are wrong in asserting that A and B are related.

This refutation only works against an opponent who is affirming svabhāva (own-being). It works because the concept of svabhāva is self-contradictory. To be real, a thing must always exist, which means that it cannot change. Yet to exist means to change.

The opponent objects: If śūnyatā (emptiness) is not real, then your whole system is baseless. Nāgārjuna replies: If emptiness were real-in-itself, then things would not be empty, and my system would be baseless. But emptiness, too, is empty. My system is without foundation, because nothing has any ultimate resting-place. But the claim "all things are empty" is with me not an absolute claim on which to build a systematic philosophy; it expresses the highest truth only if one does not assume that it expresses some "thing" called "emptiness" having own-being (svabhāva). It, too, is a fictive concept; it is useful spiritually only if it serves to release a person from the false expectation of designating something with own-being.

Nāgārjuna did not deny that reason is valid for mundane purposes, but he condemned the rationalist project of "salting the tail of the Absolute," of arriving at metaphysical truth by wringing the essential meanings out of commonsense words and sentences. For him, utterances are just designations (prajñapti), complex actions like fingers pointing at the moon. One must look beyond the finger to the moon, and not confuse the naïve concreteness of the indicator with the dependent co-arising nature of existence. The meaning is not found in the utterance itself—as in an oath or magical formula—nor in some supposed referent corresponding to words. The goal is realized when thinking no longer binds a person to thought-construction, when nameables are not assumed to be more real than nonnameables and the cinema of thought-constructs ceases. Nāgārjuna's philosophy, like several others, achieves its goal when the thinker is no longer grasped by thought.

Nāgārjuna's immediate disciple, Āryadeva, carried on the polemic tradition, but he was inferior to his master in style and intelligence. Mādhyamika became quite popular but did not make qualitative advances until about 500 A.D., when Bhāvaviveka adopted the epistemology and logic of the logician Dignāga, and tackled a host of problems that his school had previously ignored. Candrakīrti (sixth century A.D.) then attacked Bhāvaviveka, severely criticizing his use of logic, and going back to the position of the earlier Mādhyamika commentators. Bhāvaviveka wrote one of the first handbooks of the Indian philosophical systems, and Candrakīrti composed an excellent compendium of the bodhisattva path, the *Introduction to Madhyamaka*. Both authors display a superb style and rigorous thought.

THE DOCTRINE OF MIND ONLY

We have seen that mind *(citta, manas)* and consciousness *(vijñāna)* occupied a unique place in early Buddhism. It was vijñāna that transmigrated, it was in a mind-made body that the adept traveled through the heavens, and the gods in the highest heavens had bodies made of mind only. The power of mind was proverbial.[6] "All dharmas are forerun by mind, chieftained by mind, consist of mind" *(Dhammapada 1)*. "Those who restrain mind, which is far-ranging, walks alone, is bodiless, and sits in the cave of the heart, will be freed from the bonds of death" *(Dhammapada 37)*. This concept of mind is much closer to the ātman of the Upaniṣads than to the six consciousnesses *(vijñāna)*, each specialized to one sense, into which early Buddhist doctrine fragmented the mind. It is sometimes said to be intrinsically pure: "This mind (citta) is luminous, but it is soiled by adventitious defilements," says the Pali Sūtra.

The Śūnyavādins were not concerned with the phenomenology of mind, but in asserting that all phenomena are māyā (illusion), cinematic fictions, and dreamlike, they accorded the mind a major role in creating the seeming world.

Conventional things, they said, are not purely objective entities but concepts or discriminations constructed by the mind under the limitations of ignorance. This raises several questions that the Śūnyavādins did not answer. What, in worldly scientific terms, is the process by which the mind creates and objectifies fictions? What is the real nature of error? If the sense-consciousnesses arise and perish moment by moment following their evanescent objects, which of them imagines the objects, and how is the process of world construction passed on from moment to moment? How do memories take place? And what is it that experiences the absolute truth free from discrimination?

The attempt to answer such questions gave rise to a new school called Yogācāra (Yoga Practice) or Vijñānanvāda (Teaching of [Fundamental] Consciousness). Its doctrines appeared first in several Sūtras about 300 A.D.: the *Avataṃsaka,* the *Sandhinirmocana,* and the *Laṅkāvatāra.* The earliest Vijñānavādin treatises are attributed to Maitreyanātha, who may have been either a human philosopher or the Bodhisattva. He inspired the two brothers Asaṅga and Vasubandhu (circa fourth century), who commented on his treatises and brought the school to its definitive form.

The Sautrāntikas, an early Buddhist sect, maintained that the effects of deeds are transmitted as a series of "seeds" until they ripen. The Yogācāra school named this stream of "seeds" the store or foundation consciousness *(ālaya-vijñāna).* They treated the mind *(manas,* the witness-consciousness responsible for sense or ego or "I" and "mine") as a defiled consciousness intermediate between the store-consciousness and the six sense-consciousnesses, and thus established a set of eight consciousnesses (vijñānas).

The store-consciousness is inactive, but the other seven consciousnesses are active. The store-consciousness is unconscious, while the other seven are conscious—that is, aware of objects. The store-consciousness is not a substance like the Upaniṣadic ātman (self), though. It is simply a series of seeds, each momentary, each giving rise to its successor. It contains not only defiled seeds, but also pure dharmas (conditioning elements of existence) which somewhat mysteriously emanate from the pure Dharma-realm to imbue living things with virtue. As the person progresses toward enlightenment, the defilements are gradually eliminated and displaced by untainted dharmas until finally there occurs a revolution of the personality-base *(āśraya-parāvṛtti).* As the *Laṅkāvatāra* says, "Through fully knowing that eternal things are shown by one's own mind, there occurs the revolution at the personality-base of discrimination, which is liberation and not destruction."

The Yogācārin Sūtras *(Laṅkāvatāra, Śrīmālā-devīsiṃhanāda,* and do on) equate the store-consciousness with the womb of Tathāgatahood (tathāgata-garbha), a concept of great soteriological importance. *Garbha* has a twofold general meaning: first, the womb, and by extension, an inner room, the calyx of a lotus; and second, the womb's contents, that is, an embryo, fetus, child. In the first sense, the purified store-consciousness is the womb where the tathāgata (the Enlightened Being) is conceived and nourished and matured.

The *Prajñā-pāramitā Sūtras* had already introduced the uteral metaphor when they declared that the Prajñā-pāramitā (Perfection of Wisdom) is the mother of all the Buddhas (see p. 99). The new term just makes it more physiological. In the second sense, the womb of Tathāgatahood is the embryonic Buddha consisting of the pure dharmas in a person's store-consciousness. The *Lotus Sūtra* proclaims that the Buddha will enable all beings to attain final nirvāṇa but does not examine the implicit idea that every living being harbors the capability or potentiality of Buddhahood.

The later Sūtras originating in India specify that the womb of Tathāgatahood is innate to all living beings, since they are irradiated by the pervading power of the Buddha, and since through time without beginning they have grown a stock of good dharmas under the influence of this radiating grace. If this womb did not exist, a person could not take religious initiative, could not turn from saṃsāra and aspire to nirvāṇa. This womb is always intrinsically pure, and is synonymous with suchness, which is identical in everyone. In ordinary beings, it is covered with adventitious defilements; in the bodhisattvas, it is partly pure and partly impure; and in the Buddhas, it is perfectly pure.

The womb of Tathāgatahood is described in a series of similes. It is like the Buddha in a faded lotus, honey covered by bees, a kernel of grain in the husk, gold in the ore, a treasure hidden in the earth, the fruit in a small seed, a Buddha-image wrapped in rags, a great king in the womb of a low-caste woman, and a precious statue covered with dirt. These similes fall roughly into two classes, the organic and the mineral. Of the former, two imply growth: The small seed grows into a fruit tree, and the fetus grows into a great king. Most of the similes connote an immutable thing that will emerge unstained when it is unwrapped or washed. It is no wonder that the *Laṅkāvatāra* has to protest that the womb of Tathāgatahood is not the same as the Hindu ātman. To the ordinary person, gems and gold and statues are enduring things, as close to eternal immutables as a commonsense example can come.

The womb of Tathāgatahood contains the causes from which pure as well as impure dharmas arise. It is the source of the phenomenal world, of good things and bad alike. This follows from its office as a storeroom for the seeds of past karman. But since the womb of Tathāgatahood is synonymous with the Dharma-body (see below) of the Buddha, this leads in a tortuous way to the conclusion that the Buddha creates the world. For centuries, the Buddhists had been striving to avoid conceding the role of an agent to their ultimate entity (nirvāṇa, suchness, Dharma-realm, tathāgata). Embarassed Yogācārins insisting that their theory of individual and cosmic genesis is different from the Brahmanical creation theories sound rather like East European Communists in the late 1960s protesting that adoption of the profit principle and market-responsive pricing did not mean they were turning to capitalism. In both instances, the advantageous features borrowed from rival systems are subordinated and integrated into the established structure without sacrificing its essential characteristics. But this fact is easy for the unsympathetic critic to overlook.

Earlier Buddhist schools had dealt awkwardly and unsatisfactorily with the facts of psychic continuity. They had restricted the six sense-consciousnesses to witnessing present objects, and so had disqualified them as regents of memory. Yogācāra introduced two extra consciousnesses, store consciousness and mind, which between them have charge of storing the impressions deposited by experiences and projecting them into new events when they ripen. This explanation was applied to memory, the continuity of personality through sleep and deep trance, and the transmission of identity between successive lives.

The store-consciousness is both individual and collective. It receives the impressions of individual deeds, harbors them, and projects the phenomenal world, which consists of: (1) the "receptacle world" of space-time, and (2) the psychophysical individual. The purified mind of the saint no longer projects a phenomenal world of its own, but it sees the world projected by the minds of ignorant people.

Whereas Mādhyamika posits two "truths," the relative and the absolute, Yogācāra sets up three "natures" *(svabhāva)*, the absolute, the relative, and the imaginary. Practice of the Path purges the imaginary out of the relative and so refines it into the absolute. Mādhyamika ridicules the idea of a coupling of the real and the unreal, but this is just what the Yogācārin relative nature is. Furthermore, the imaginary has its basis in the absolute. After all, where else could illusion have its source except in reality?

The Yogācāra introduced the doctrine of the three bodies of the Buddha. The first is the apparition-body *(nirmāṇa-kāya)*, which corresponds to the apparition or form-body *(rūpa-kāya)* of Siddhārtha Gautama of the earlier teachings. The third is the Dharma-body, the unconstructed, infinite, and perfectly pure reality, a Mahāyāna formulation of nirvāṇa. The second is a Yogācārin innovation, the recompense or enjoyment-body *(sambhoga-kāya)*. It is the glorified body that the Buddha attains as a reward for his bodhisattva practices, and it is the transfigured body which the great bodhisattvas apprehend when they see the Buddha. For example, the Buddha Amitābha in his Pure Land is apprehended in his enjoyment-body by the bodhisattvas there, while he appears in his apparition-body to favored persons in this world.

Vasubandhu, coarchitect of the Yogācāra system, was also the greatest of the Abhidharmists. He wrote the *Abhidharmakośa (Compendium of Abhidharma)*, a brilliant polemical work that became the standard Mahāyāna Abhidharma text. For better or worse, the new school took over the Abhidharma enterprise, pulled together all the classifications, subclassifications, lists, and numbers that appeared in the Sūtras and treatises and proceeded to invent more and more. The system became very unwieldy, providing an occupation for monks with plenty of time who would rather study than practice. There is, nonetheless, a sort of religious exaltation to be derived from contemplating this architectonic scholastic edifice; and, since Vasubandhu and Asaṅga wrote short and fairly clear summaries of their system, those who wanted to bypass the luxuriant detail could do so.

6.
Soteriology and Pantheon of the Mahāyāna

THE BODHISATTVA PATH

Mahāyāna is synonymous with the course *(yāna)* or career *(caryā)* of the bodhisattva. In the early Mahāyāna Sūtras (composed before the second century A.D.), this is a simple path beginning with arousing the thought (that is, aspiration) for supreme, perfect enlightenment, and practicing the six pāramitās (perfections) until the goal is reached. Between 100 and 300 A.D., the doctrine of the ten bodhisattva stages *(bhūmi)* was introduced, and an elaborate schema of paths and stages was devised.

The Buddha Amida. (From a twelfth century Japanese silk painting.)

The Mahāyāna Sūtras address their teaching equally to the monastics and laity, exhorting both to recite, copy, and explain the Sūtras, an enterprise which monasticizing Hīnayāna sects reserved for the monks and nuns. But though the laity and monastics were regarded as equal in some respects, both sects still maintained that the monastic orders were superior, and the layman still had to pay formal honor to the monk. Only some Sūtras, the libertarian ones, authorize the laity to preach Dharma to monks. The most famous of such Sūtras, the *Vimalakīrti*, shows the householder bodhisattva[1] encouraging a crowd of young patricians to leave the household life. When they protest that they cannot do so without their parents' permission, Vimalakīrti tells them to arouse the thought of enlightenment and practice diligently, since that is equivalent to "going forth." Far from diminishing the monastic vocation, this concession is a second-best for those unable to take the yellow robe.

Nothing like European anticlericalism is found in the Sūtras of the Great Vehicle. There is one lurid description of corruption in the monasteries, of wicked monks who, "destitute of shame and morality, impudent as crows, arrogant, ill-tempered, consumed by jealousy, conceit, and presumption," engaged in commerce and litigation and cohabited with women. Evidently some monasteries fell into the hands of opportunists who disregarded the Vinaya while enjoying use of the Saṅgha's property and privileges.

Though the literature reveals a number of lay preachers, it mentions no legitimate noncelibate communal life and no householder clergy. The householder bodhisattva was welcome to study meditation and philosophy and probably was allowed to spend protracted periods of retreat in the monasteries. He could teach the doctrine, and was encouraged to propagate it. But, so far as we know, the Mahāyāna Sūtras were composed by monks, and there is not a single important treatise attributed to any Indian Buddhist layperson.

The bodhisattva saṅgha was evidently a fraternity within the general Buddhist Community. It had no special monastic rule, and its householder sections were probably loose-knit associations like those that gather around modern Hindu holy men and temples. There was also an ordination rite for the lay bodhisattva, modeled on the bhikṣu's ceremony rather than on the less solemn Hīnayāna lay initiation.

The bodhisattva's path begins with instruction from a Buddha, a bodhisattva, or some other spiritual friend. Seeds of virture are planted in the mind of the hearer, and from much hearing he comes to perform good deeds, through which he acquires more and more roots of goodness. After many lives, thanks to the infused grace of the various teacher-saviors and the merit earned by responding to them, a person becomes able to put forth the bodhicitta (thought of enlightenment). The two motives for this aspiration are one's own desire for bodhi, and compassion for all living beings who suffer in saṃsāra. Initially the motivation is both egotistic and altruistic, but along the path one realizes the sameness of self and others and transcends the duality of purpose. Arousing the bodhicitta is an extremely meritorious deed. It cancels past bad karman, increases merit, wards off bad rebirths, and ensures good ones. In these respects, it corresponds to "winning the stream" in early Buddhism, since the srotāpanna, too, will never be reborn in the woeful destinies and is confirmed in the course of enlightenment (see p. 44). "Arousing the thought of enlightenment"[2] is a decisive conversion experience with profound psychological effects. It is compared to a pearl, the ocean, sweet music, a shade-giving tree, a convenient bridge, soothing moonbeams, the sun's rays, a universal panacea, and an infallible elixir.

The new bodhisattva proceeds to consolidate his bodhicitta and advance on the Path by cultivating good qualities and working for the welfare of living beings. He makes a set of vows or earnest resolutions *(praṇidhāna)*. Some vows are quite general; for instance: "When we have crossed the stream, may we ferry others across. When we are liberated, may we liberate others." Some bodhisattvas' vows are very specific and pragmatic, for example, those of Dharmākara, who later became the Buddha Amitābha. He made three or four dozen vows in the form "May I not attain supreme, perfect enlightenment until such-and-such a benefit is assured beings who are born in my Buddha-land" (where he [Amitābha] lives and teaches the Dharma). Taking the precepts is an early Buddhist forerunner of Mahāyāna vow-making in that it is a formal act of commitment and involves a greater forfeiture of merit if one transgresses than if one had not made a vow. Bodhisattva vows are usually binding until the end of the bodhisattva career, a matter of eons. Even when the great bodhisattva has passed beyond dualistic cognitions and intentions, he is motivated, as if on automatic pilot, by the force of his original vows.

The bodhisattva is supposed to declare his vows in the presence of a Buddha, which means that he must wait until a Buddha appears in the world. The Tathāgata then gives the bodhisattva a prediction (see p. 44) that after x number of ages he will become a Buddha of such-and-such a name, reigning in such-and-such a Buddha-land, (a world created by a particular Buddha for the salvation of his devotees), which will have such-and-such excellences. Ordinary bodhisattvas who have not yet had the good fortune to be born in the same generation as a Buddha make their vows in the presence of other human bodhisattvas, or even with the Buddhas and bodhisattvas of the ten directions as their witnesses.

The six pāramitās are the main course of the bodhisattva career. As we have noted (p. 70), these virtues are all advocated in the early Buddhist Canon, and extreme instances of them are extolled in the *Lives Tales (Jātakas)*. Mahāyāna differs from Hīnayāna in making the extremes the model for ordinary devotees.

A virtue is practiced to perfection when the most difficult acts are executed with a mind free from discriminatory ideas, without self-consciousness, ulterior motives, or self-congratulation. The perfect giver, for example, does not think "I give," and has no fictive concepts about the gift, the recipient, or the reward that ensures from the act. Thus prajñā-pāramitā (perfection of wisdom) is necessary in order to attain the other five perfections.

The perfection of giving *(dāna)* consists of giving material things, Dharma-instructions, and one's own body and life to all beings, then in turn transferring or reassigning the ensuing merit to supreme enlightenment and the welfare of other beings,[3] rather than allowing it to earn one future bliss in the world. The bodhisattva practices giving donation, and stimulates others to do likewise.

The perfection of morality *(śīla)* consists of following the ten good paths of action, transferring the merit, and prompting others to do likewise. The ten are: not killing, stealing, or fornicating; not lying, slandering, speaking harshly, or chattering frivolously; and not having covetous thoughts, hostile thoughts, or false views.

The perfection of patience *(kṣānti)* is founded in nonanger and nonagitation. It means patient endurance of hardship and pain, forbearance and forgiveness toward those who injure and abuse the bodhisattva, and patient assent to difficult and uncongenial doctrines.

(4) The perfection of vigor *(vīrya)* means unremitting energy and zeal in overcoming one's faults and cultivating virtues, in studying Dharma and the arts and sciences, and in doing good works for the welfare of others. *Vīrya* is derived from *vīra* (a martial man, a hero). It corresponds to right effort, the sixth member of the Holy Eightfold Path of early Buddhism, but more explicitly signifies heroic endeavor to benefit other living beings. ?

(5) The perfection of meditation *(dhyāna)* consists of entering all the meditative trances, concentrations, and attainments, yet not accepting rebirth in the paradises to which such states normally destine one in the next life.

(6) The perfection of wisdom *(prajñā-pāramitā)* is personified as a goddess, because *prajñā* is grammatically feminine. She is the mother of all the Buddhas since through her they become Enlightened Ones. A famous hymn endows her with feminine traits and maternal loving-kindness.

The Goddess Prajñāpāramitā. On the lotus is wisdom in the form of a Prajñā-pāramitā Sūtra. (From thirteenth century Java.)

The *Prajñā-pāramitā Sūtras* say over and over again that the doctrine that things neither arise nor cease is supremely difficult, that it causes fear and aversion in the tender-minded, and that the bodhisattva who can accept it is a great hero *(mahāsattva)*. Three degrees of assent are distinguished. The first is acceptance of the words of the teaching. The second is conforming assent, attained in the sixth bodhisattva-stage, and consisting of an intense but not definitive conviction. The third is patient acceptance that the dharmas are nonarising. It is said by later texts to be attained in the eighth stage and it is concomitant with reaching the nonrelapsing state. We have seen that the nonreturner is the second highest level of holy person in early Buddhism, and that the stream-winner is assured of not falling back into the states of woe (see p. 44). The Mahāyāna concept of nonrelapsing is a reworking of the old ideas.

The early theory of stages seems to have recognized just seven bodhisattva-stages, with acceptance that the dharmas are nonarising and that the nonrelapsing states occur in the seventh stage. The number of stages was increased from seven to ten about 200 A.D. Variant lists of stations and stages circulated for a while, but eventually the following became standard:[4]

(a) The stage of the "lineage," where the beginner strives to acquire a stock of merit and knowledge. It extends from the first thought of enlightenment until the "experience of heat," the first signpost of success in meditation.

(b) The stage of "practicing with conviction." Here the bodhisattva cultivates four "factors of penetration," namely "meditative heat," "climax," "patience," and "highest mundane Dharma." These meditative experiences overcome and expel the antithesis between subject and object, and lead to nondiscriminative knowledge. Stages *a* and *b* can be considered preparatory stages.

(c) The ten bodhisattva-stages, namely: (1) the joyful, (2) the stainless, (3) the illuminating, (4) the flaming, (5) the very-hard-to-conquer (6) the face-to-face, (7) the far-going, (8) the immovable, (9) good-insight, and (10) Dharmacloud.[5] Each successive stage is supposed to be practiced in concert with a pāramitā. Four pāramitās were added to the early list of six for the sake of symmetry: (7) skill in means, (8) vows, (9) power, and (10) knowledge. The first bodhisattva-stage corresponds to the path of vision, which follows immediately after "highest mundane Dharma," and is characterized by nondual awareness. Stages two to ten correspond to the path of meditative cultivation, in which the bodhisattva continues to enjoy nondiscriminatory supramundane knowledge.

(d) The Buddha-stage follows the diamond-like samādhi (concentration), which is the last event on the path of cultivation. This samādhi plays an important role in Abhidharma, too, where it is realized by the bodhisattva as he sits on the Diamond Throne of Enlightenment, and in it he fulfils the perfections of dhyāna and prajñā in the moment just before he attains bodhi. It is this samādhi which destroys all the residues of defilement. Mahāyāna doctrine maintains that the terminal path consists in awareness that the causes of suffering have been destroyed and will never arise again. In other words, the bodhisattva's final realization is identical with the arhant's (see p. 00).

There were some differences of opinion about the duration of the bodhisattva career, but the prevalent view was that it takes three immeasurable aeons: one to or through the first bodhisattva-stage, one from there through the seventh stage, and one for stages eight to ten.

How seriously should we take this intricate and pedantic-looking schematization of the Path? The correspondence between the stages and pāramitās is contrived, and it conflicts with the earlier teaching that the first five pāramitās cannot be attained until the sixth, prajñā, is achieved. The spiritual states described are very similar to those in Hīnayāna descriptions of the arhants' path, for which no such long ages are deemed necessary. The overall progression, from good works and faith through aspiration and training to realization, from deliberate practice to spontaneous exercise, and from mundane knowledge to transcendental wisdom, rings true to experience. It is an unusually detailed account of the universal path by which men learn and mature, and of the way of holiness in many diverse religions. The seven or ten bodhisattva-stages, with their vivid metaphorical names, may have begun with the actual experience of a meditator or a small school of contemplatives for whom the series was a firsthand description. The list may then have passed into the hands of outsiders to whom the experiential references were unknown, and who consequently elaborated scholastic fantasies about them. The doctrine of three immeasurable aeons was taken literally by Indian schoolmen, but rejected by some Chinese schools and bypassed in later Indian sects. It is patently hyperbolic, and serves merely to make graphic how long and arduous the course is, and how great a distance stands between the beginning bodhisattva and the great savior bodhisattvas on the highest stage.

THE CELESTIAL BODHISATTVAS

Many Mahāyāna Sūtras begin with a catalog of the assembly present on the occasion when the Sūtra was uttered by the Buddha. The *Lotus Sūtra,* for example, opens with Śākyamuni sitting on Mount Gṛdhrakūṭa (Vulture Peak) surrounded by twelve hundred arhant bhikṣus, eighty thousand nonrelapsing bodhisattvas, Śakra, the Four Great Kings, Śiva, Brahmā, and contingents of spirit beings. This is a laborious though dramatic device for expressing the early Buddhist claim that Śākyamuni is the teacher of gods and men. It also catalogs the pantheon, the personages to whom the Mahāyānist should offer worship, veneration, and propitiation.

The chief innovation in this Mahāyāna pantheon is the class of great bodhisattvas, also called great beings *(mahāsattvas).* The *Lotus Sūtra* mentions by name twenty-three; the *Vimalakīrti* names some fifty. Of these, the most important are Mañjuśrī, Avalokiteśvara, Mahāsthāmaprāpta, and Maitreya. All four figure as interlocutors in Mahāyāna Sūtras, where they appear as men and converse with the great disciples and Śākyamuni. These great beings are nonhistorical; there is no evidence that any one of them is an apotheosis of a human hero, as Rāma certainly was and Krishna probably was. Strangely, no Sūtra preaches devotion to a celestial bodhisattva until the third century A.D., a full three centuries after these beings entered the literature. The strategic function of these bodhisattvas is to serve as Mahāyāna counterparts to the great arhants in the Pali Sūtras. The nonrelapsing bodhisattva stage is so exalted that no actual persons could be found to represent it.

Maitreya

Maitreya is the earliest cult bodhisattva. A Pali Sūtra predicts that in the distant future there will arise in the world a Blessed One named Metteya (Pali for Maitreya), who will have thousands of disciples just as Śākyamuni has hundreds. Another Pali Sūtra lists, with particulars, six Buddhas of the past

Maitreya, in a twelfth century representation from Bengal.

whom Gautama remembers through his own paranormal powers, as well as through revelation from the gods. Stūpas of the former Buddhas were built as early as the third century B.C.; but if the extinct Buddhas were worthy of reverence, how much more so the coming one, now a bodhisattva residing in the Tuṣita heaven (where traditionally future Buddhas spend their last life) and awaiting his last birth? The pious might look forward to the utopia, and to pass the interlude happily and be sure of rebirth along with Maitreya when he comes, they could seek rebirth in the Tuṣita paradise. An efficacious means to secure a desired rebirth is to concentrate one's thoughts on it at the moment of death. Thus, King Duṭṭhagāmaṇi of Ceylon, dying in 80 B.C., fixed his last thoughts on Maitreya's paradise where, the chronicles assure us, he was reborn.

While Mahāyāna affirmed that saṃsāra is suffering and that one should try to get out of it, and while it promised eventual nirvāṇa to all or most adherents, its willingness to postpone attainment for vast ages betrays an accommodation to saṃsāra that was foreign to the early teaching. Like the youthful Augustine, who prayed "Lord, give me chastity, but not yet," the bodhisattvas were quite content to wait. This attitude also appears in the Theravāda tradition. On his deathbed the Elder Saṅgharakkhita disclosed that, contrary to popular belief, he was not an arhant: "Thinking to see the Blessed One Metteya, I did not try for insight." But so as not to disappoint the crowds who had gathered, he made an effort and immediately became an arhant.

All Hīnayāna sects acknowledged Maitreya, and the Theravāda tradition recognizes no other bodhisattva in the present age. He was conceived of as a historical bodhisattva, and where the Canon had nothing to say, extracanonical tradition invented history.

Maitreya, unlike the Buddhas before him, is alive, so he can respond to the prayers of worshippers. Being compassionate, as his name indicates (its Sanskrit root means benevolent), he willingly grants help; and being a high god in his present birth, he has the power to do so. His cult thus offers its devotees the advantages of theism and Buddhism combined.

India was caught up in the surge of messianic expectations which, originating probably in present-day Iran, coursed through the Mediterranean world after 200 B.C. Buddhism was more hospitable than Hinduism to the messianic idea because it was more open to Western influences, and because from the first it took history and pseudohistory more seriously. Accustomed to thinking of the past in terms of teacher-pupil lineages, Buddhists came in due course to anticipate the future sage, just as the Hebrews came to dream of a future anointed prophet-king after musing long on the series of prophets and kings in their ancient history. Each Messiah, though, accrued collateral attributes and functions. Christ assimilated the figures of the suffering servant, the Son of God, and the dying God into the nuclear concept of the coming king and judge. Maitreya proved no less accommodating. He became a god of light, like Ahura Mazda, Jehovah, Christ, Krishna, and all the Buddhas and other bodhisattvas. This was probably not due to Persian influences (Iran is not the only place where the sun shines), but it undoubtedly made the cult more congenial to worshippers of the sacred fire, of Ahura Mazda and Mithra. As a figure of light and of the future, Maitreya came to be the inspirer, a role he shares with Mañjuśrī and with Brahmā.

Just as the Buddha had received revelations and inspirations from the gods *(devas)*, Mahāyāna masters went into trance and journeyed to the Tuṣita heaven, where Maitreya revealed Dharma-themes to them. On occasion, too, he descended to earth to divulge texts, which makes it exceedingly difficult to decide whether the Yogācārin texts attributed to "Lord Maitreya" are or are not the works of some human author who took that name. As the "Friendly One," Maitreya became the consoler of Dharma-masters and seekers when they were afflicted with doubt and discouragement. In his capacity as the Friend, he also receives confessions of sins, and guides the departed after death, an office the Bodhisattva Avalokiteśvara and the Buddha Amitābha also perform. If the devout are bound for Maitreya's paradise when they die, what more natural than that he should come and welcome them?

Mañjuśrī

Mañjuśrī shares with Maitreya preeminence among the bodhisattvas in Mahāyāna Sūtras up to 300 A.D. In the *Lotus Sūtra* he remembers deeds of former Buddhas which were unknown even to Maitreya. In the *Vimalakīrti*, he alone of all Śākyamuni's disciples has wisdom and eloquence enough to stand up to that formidable householder, Vimalakīrti. In the *Gaṇḍavyūha*, he counsels the youth Sudhana in his search for enlightenment. Many smaller Sūtras are devoted to his legend, his attributes, and his teachings. Curiously, he is scarcely mentioned in the *Prajñā-pāramitā Sūtras*. And he is absent from the Buddhist art of all schools—Gandhāra, Mathurā, Amarāvatī, Nāgārajuna-koṇḍa—prior to 400 A.D. When he does appear in art, he is shown as a bodhisattva bhikṣu, with a five-pointed coiffure or tiara, a sword (to cut ignorance) in his right hand, a book (the *Prajñā-pāramitā)* in his left, and a lion for his mount.

The name Mañjuśrī means "gentle or sweet glory." He is also called *Mañjughoṣa* ("Sweet Voice") and *Vāgīśvara* ("Lord of Speech"). This last epithet also belongs to Brahmā, whose roles as patron of science, custodian of memory, lord of inspiration, and most ancient of beings Mañjuśrī takes over in the Mahāyāna pantheon. The nucleus around which this bodhisattva-figure grew is a celestial being *(Gandharva)* named *Pañcaśikha* ("Five-Crest"), who appears in wonder-tales in the Pali Sūtras. In one tale, Śakra and the Gods of the Thirty-Three are assembled in their annual convention. A radiant splendor announces the imminent manifestation of Brahmā Sanatkumāra ("Forever-a-youth"). This great god's proper form is too subtle to be visible to the Gods of the Thirty-Three, so he creates an apparition-body "in appearance like the youth Five-Crest." Just as a golden image outshines humans, so Brahmā's apparition outshines the other gods in color and in glory. His voice is fluent, intelligible, sweet, audible, continuous, distinct, deep, and resonant. In this guise, Brahmā proceeds to preach the Dharma to Indra and his hosts.

Mañjuśrī's standard epithet is *kumāra-bhūta*, "in the form of a youth," or "having become the crown prince." The former meaning is the earlier, and applies equally to a celestial being (Gandharva), who like all angels never grows old, and to Brahmā, whose epithet is "Forever-a-youth." Mañjuśrī is the crown prince of Dharma because, like other tenth-stage bodhisattvas, he will next become a King of Dharma, a Buddha.

In due course, devotees endowed Mañjuśrī with a history invented out of whole cloth. Seventy myriads of aeons ago and seventy-two hundred billion Buddha-fields to the east of this world, Mañjuśrī was a pious king who offered worship to a Tathāgata and aroused the bodhicitta. He resolved to pursue an endless career to the end of saṃsāra, and not to hurry to enlightenment but to stay in saṃsāra as long as there remained even one being to be saved. Though he has now fulfilled all the virtues of a Buddha, he has never considered becoming one. But eventually he will become a Tathāgata. This implies that there will come a time when the last living being has been saved, a rare eschatological statement in the Buddhist tradition.

The doctrinaire thesis that all bodhisattvas take three immeasurable aeons to reach their final goal is contradicted by the *Larger Prajñā-pāramitā Sūtra*. It says that some bodhisattvas obtain supreme perfect enlightenment as soon as they arouse bodhicitta, while others, animated by great love and compassion, devote the longest possible time to the welfare of all living beings. Mañjuśrī took as long as possible to reach the tenth stage and will stay there until universal salvation is reached.

Tenth-stage bodhisattvas have the ability to manifest themselves anywhere in any condition. They enter the Hero's-journey Concentration *(śūraṃgama-samādhi)*, manifesting themselves in all parts of the universe as bodhisattvas at various stages, as residents of the paradises, and as Buddhas. They go through the standard episodes of a Buddha's career and enter parinirvāṇa, but do not in fact become extinct. The Sūtras mention Mañjuśrī as residing in diverse Buddha-fields in the present and in the past, and as being in other world-realms now, as well as ages ago.

Mañjuśrī usually appears to human beings in dreams. The chronicles record that a dozen or more great masters "saw the face of Mañjuśrī." Merely hearing Mañjuśrī's name uttered subtracts many aeons from one's time in saṃsāra. Whoever worships him is born time and again in the Buddha-family and is protected by Mañjuśrī's power. Those who meditate on Mañjuśrī's statue and his teaching will be similarly fortunate and will reach enlightenment. If a devotee recites the *Śūraṃgama-samādhi Sūtra* and chants Mañjuśrī's name, then within seven days Mañjuśrī will come to the worshipper, appearing in a dream if bad karman hinders the supplicant from receiving direct vision. Mañjuśrī also takes on the form of a poor man or an orphan and appears to those who are devoted to him. The wise man should contemplate Mañjuśrī's superhuman physical marks. If he does so, he will soon see the Bodhisattva.

Avalokiteśvara

Avalokiteśvara (Chinese Kuan-yin) first appears as a mere name in the lists at the beginning of the *Vimalakīrti* and, later, the *Lotus Sūtra*. His first significant role is in the *Sukhāvatī-vyūha Sūtra*, where he and Mahāsthāmaprāpta are Amitābha Buddha's chief attendants. They are the only Bodhisattvas in Sukhāvatī (see pp. 112–115) whose light is boundless, and, owing to them, that world-realm is luminous always and everywhere. The two of them used to be men in this world, and upon dying went to Sukhāvatī.

The *Avalokiteśvara Sūtra* was incorporated into the *Lotus Sūtra* as late as the third century A.D. To this day, though, it circulates as an independent work in China and Japan, where it is the main item in the liturgy of the Kuan-yin cult. A few verses at the end describe Sukhāvatī, and say that Avalokiteśvara stands now to the left of Amitābha and fans him. The rest of the text says nothing about Amitābha, but shows Avalokiteśvara as an omnipresent, omnipotent savior-deity subordinate to no one. He has purified his vows for countless aeons under millions of Buddhas. He possesses all virtues, and is especially rich in love and compassion. His skill in means is infinite, and through it he takes whatever form will help living beings. He adopts the guise of a Buddha, a bodhisattva, a disciple, Brahmā, Indra, and other gods. Like Mañjuśrī, he has played the role of a Buddha and will play it again, without getting trapped in extinction. In this respect the celestial bodhisattvas are superior to the Buddhas.

Avalokiteśvara grants multifarious boons to those who remember him and recite his name. The merit from adoring him is equal to that from worshipping and serving an incredible number of Buddhas. Those who adore him are saved from lust, hostility, and folly. A woman who worships him will get a son or daughter, whichever she wishes. Anyone in distress will be freed from danger and anxiety. For example, if you fall into a fire, think of Avalokiteśvara and it will be quenched. Similarly, he rescues those who invoke him from shipwreck, falling off a precipice, missiles, armed robbers and enemies, execution, chains and shackles, witchcraft, demons, wild beasts, snakes, and thunderbolts.

This Bodhisattva is usually represented in art as a bejewelled layman wearing a high crown with a cross-legged image of Amitābha in the front of it. He often holds a lotus in his hand. In the Tantric period (600-1200 A.D.), he came to be represented with eleven heads, or with four, ten, twelve, twenty-four, or a thousand arms. In China he was even metamorphosed into a female.

The Bodhisattva Avalokiteśvara, who holds a lotus in his hand (Padma-pāṇi), his eyes looking down out of compassion for beings. (From a wall painting in Cave 1 at Ajantā. Sixth century A.D.)

Mahāsthāmaprāpta

Mahāsthāmaprāpta is mentioned in the lists at the beginning of the *Lotus Sūtra* and the *Vimalakīrti*. Śākyamuni addresses a discourse to him in Chapter 19 of the *Lotus*, and as already noted, the *Sukhāvatī-vyūha Sūtra* places him on a par with Avalokiteśvara as an attendant of Amitābha's. In Far Eastern art he is frequently represented standing on the right of Amitābha while Avalokiteśvara stands on the left.

Samantabhadra

Samantabhadra (Universal Sage) became popular rather late. He is not mentioned at the beginning of the *Lotus Sūtra,* but in Chapter 26, a late addition, he comes to the world with a fabulous retinue to ask Śākyamuni to expound the *Lotus Sūtra*. He promises to protect the monks who keep this Sūtra, to avert the menaces of human enemies and demons. Mounted on a white elephant with six tusks, he will accompany the preacher and will appear and remind him when he forgets part of the text. If the devotee circumambulates for twenty-one days, then Samantabhadra will show his body on the twenty-first, will inspire the devotee, and will give him talismanic spells.

THE CELESTIAL BUDDHAS

Śākyamuni was reportedly the object of adoration even during his lifetime. He reproved Vakkali, "the highest of those who have faith," for being so attached to the Tathāgata's person and told him to concentrate instead of the Dharma. The idea was, "Whoever sees the Dharma sees me (the Buddha)." He also said, "Those people, enthralled by ardent desire, who saw me by (my) form and followed me by (my) voice, do not know me." He regularly referred to himself not by his name but as the Tathāgata. An occasional synonym of Tathāgata is *sattva*, "living being, true essence." These words signify the purified inner quality of the saint who has "become Dharma," who is "born of Dharma, formed by Dharma, heir of Dharma," who "had Dharma as his body."

Multiple Bodies of the Buddha

From the first the Buddha was held to have two bodies *(kāya),* the form-body (rūpa-kāya) and the Dharma-body (Dharma-kāya). In addition, he could conjure up apparition-bodies (nirmāṇa-kāya) through his magic powers, and in mind-made bodies (manomaya-kāya) he could travel to the heavens. Devotion to Dharma was encouraged, but adoration of form (rūpa) was disparaged as a sensual fetter. Nonetheless, over the centuries piety glorified Śākyamuni's body, ascribed to it the thirty-two major and eighty minor marks of a superman, extolled its radiant complexion, stated that rays of six colors constantly shone from it, and that it exuded sweet perfume.

   Dharma was from the first a transcendental principle immanent and operative in the world. It is the constant, the real, the true, the good, the valuable, the harmonious, and the normative. Perception of Dharma in the moral sphere is the Buddhist version of conscience. Intellectual penetration of the Dharma-realm is bodhi, the goal, enlightenment. The nature of things, Dharma-ness *(Dharmatā)* is like the medieval idea of natural law. It is the fixity, regularity, and necessity in phenomenal occurrences. The Buddha taught Dharma—it is in some sense expressible—but Dharma is not just doctrine. It is a real and holy force that governs the destiny of individuals and peoples. It should be not merely respected but worshipped and sought as a refuge. The Buddha and the Saṅgha are to be revered because they "have become Dharma." When the early sects agreed that the real Buddha is the Dharmabody, it was not that they were personifying the Teaching, but that in their view the Buddha actualized the Dharma which his Teaching then revealed.

   Among the early schools, it was the Mahāsaṅghikas (see p. 68) who maintained that the Buddha is supermundane and yet forever active in the world, infinite and eternal, transcendental and immanent. Since Dharma is all these things, it stands to reason that his Dharma-body should be likewise. The early sects all wrestled with the apparent anomaly that the Buddha, though extremely wise, powerful, and good, lived a mere eighty years and then ceased to function in saṃsāra. If he could have lived for an aeon, why did he not do so? (p. 60). Over the centuries, the steady pressure of wishful thinking produced an answer: Gautama didn't really enter extinction; he only seemed to do so. His form-body was just an apparition (nirmāṇa), a māyā (conjurer's illusion). Though Buddhism denied that there is a personal Creator, it assigned the same functions to Dharma (= pratītya-samutpāda), and by emphasizing the fictive, insubstantial, and transient character of phenomena, came to view the conditioned world as a figment of cosmic imagination. So when the historical Buddha was considered an apparition, he was not held to be less real than anything else in the world. (See Yogācāra classification of the three bodies, p. 95).

Once granted that the historic Gautama was an apparition of the everlasting Dharma-body, it seemed reasonable that there should be apparition-bodies in all times and places, that benevolent omnipotence should respond to the needs of all suffering beings. There must be Buddhas elsewhere in the universe, as well as in the past and future of this world-realm.

Early Buddhist cosmology had posited just one world system *(loka-dhātu)*, consisting of four continents on earth and assorted hells below and heavens above. Later it came to be held that the immediate universe, "the three-thousand great-thousand world-realm" consist of 1000^3 such worlds. In the ten directions (East, Southeast, South, Southwest, West, Northwest, North, Northeast, Nadir, and Zenith), there are universes "as numerous as the sands of the Ganges." Some but not all of these universes are Buddha-lands, in each of which a Tathāgata lives and teaches the Dharma.

The Mahāsāṅghikas very early asserted that there are Buddhas in all directions and in all the universes. What the Mahāyāna did was to produce names for such Buddhas and their countries, legends about their origins, and vivid circumstantial descriptions of the scenery and spiritual amenities of certain Buddha-lands. Guatama's career is the paradigm for all these other Buddha's legends, and the celestial Buddha-lands are Never-Never Lands fashioned after terrestial models. These tales undoubtedly have an experiential basis in the visions of Buddhas, bodhisattvas, and paradises that resulted from the meditation on the Buddha and the gods that is recommended even in Theravāda works. We have seen already that much of Mahāyāna meditation seeks to obtain the appearance of bodhisattvas in dreams or in trance-visions. Manifestations of Buddhas and Buddha-lands were sought and obtained by the same means. In addition, it was believed that Gautama and his great bodhisattvas could reveal other Buddha-lands through their superknowledges and supervening powers so that ordinary people could see them directly.

This Mahāyāna space fiction expresses a radical expansion of world view and a corresponding change in values. The drama of salvation was no longer confined to this world-realm, and help from outside might be expected. Śākyamuni's followers were not spiritual orphans, because extraterrestrial friends stood always ready to protect them—not only gods like Śakra, Brahmā, and the Four Great Kings, but great bodhisattvas and Buddhas also. This feeling of endless space populated by spiritual beings is perhaps the nuclear world view of classical Indian civilization.

Śākyamuni According to the Lotus Sūtra

Śākyamuni remained the foremost of the celestial Buddhas until Tantrism transformed the Indian Buddhist pantheon. The *Lotus* ranks among the greatest of the Mahāyāna Sūtras not because of profound technical philosophy, of which it contains only a few fragments, but because it teaches artfully, in graphic parables and concrete religious language, that the historical Gautama is in reality an everlasting, ever present cosmic father. As the Sūtra opens, Śākyamuni enters samādhi, the earth quakes, and a ray shoots forth from the tuft of hair between the Buddha's brows, illuminating myriads of Buddha-fields in the eastern direction and revealing their inhabitants from denizens of the hells up to the Buddhas and their assemblies. Maitreya asks Mañjuśrī what event this prodigy portends; Mañjuśrī replies that the Buddha intends to deliver a grand discourse on Dharma. In the past, Mañjuśrī remembers, a similar marvel had presaged another Buddha's preaching the *Lotus Sūtra.*

In Mahāyāna as in Hīnayāna, the Buddhas are preeminently teachers and revealers. They do not grant mundane favors such as children for the childless, wealth for the poor, and rescue from danger. The extraordinary appearance of many worlds is a concrete harbinger of more abstruse revelations to follow. It serves to establish the Buddha's stupendous power and knowledge and to set the scale for his saving activities.

The Buddha then tells Śāriputra, one of his two chief disciples, that only a Tathāgata knows all the dharmas (factors of existence) as they really are. As the Dharma (Teaching) is exceedingly difficult, the Buddhas employ their supreme skill in good means to accommodate the doctrine to living beings' varying capacities. Śāriputra pleads with the Buddha to reveal the True Dharma. The Buddha consents, and declares: "It is for a sole aim that the Tathāgata appears in the world, namely to impart to living beings the knowledge and vision of a Tathāgata." The Buddhas, furthermore, preach the Dharma by means of just One Vehicle, the Buddha-vehicle (Buddha-yāna). But when a Buddha appears in a degenerate epoch, among beings who are corrupt and lacking in merit, he uses the expedient device of the Three Vehicles (arhant, private-buddha (pratyeka-buddha), and bodhisattva). Śāriputra rejoices to hear the Buddha say that the arhants are not condemned to an inferior nirvāṇa, that they too will reach supreme, perfect enlightenment. Śākyamuni then predicts that Śāriputra will become a Buddha in the distant future.

Śāriputra asks the Buddha to dispel the perplexity that the idea of the One Vehicle has occasioned among sincere Hīnayānists in the assembly. Gautama then tells the parable of the burning house. A rich householder had a vast and decrepit mansion inhabited by hundreds of living beings. A fire broke out, and the man devised a stratagem to get his twenty young sons out of the house. They did not come when he called them, because they were too busy playing to notice the flames. So he told them that toy carts—bullock carts, goat carts, and deer carts—awaited them outside. The boys came out, and found that there was only one kind of cart, a magnificent bullock cart.

Śāriputra agrees that the father was not guilty of falsehood as his story of the three carts was an expedient to save his children. Śākyamuni says that the Buddha, being the father of the world, is not guilty of falsehood, either, when as employing skillful means *(upāya)* he announces that there are three vehicles. Just as the rich man gave each of his sons the best of carts, even so the Buddha leads all beings to the same supreme enlightenment.

The Buddha tells another parable. A rain cloud comes up and pours water equally upon all kinds of grass, shrubs, and trees. Rooted in the same soil and vivified by the same water, they nonetheless grow to different heights according to their natures. Likewise, the Dharma of the Tathāgata is of one essence, yet one responds according to one's capacity. The bodhisattvas are the trees, while the Hīnayānists (men of the first Two Vehicles) are the lesser plants.

A giant stūpa arises in the sky and hovers there, resplendent with jewels and ornaments. A voice from it praises Śākyamuni for proclaiming well the *Lotus Sūtra.* When the multitude is gathered, Śākyamuni opens the stūpa, and there is revealed the body of the "extinct" Buddha Prabhūtaratna, sitting cross-legged as if in samādhi. He repeats his praise of Śākyamuni, to the astonishment of the assembly, who think Prabhūtaratna has been extinct for many aeons. Prabhūtaratna moves over, and Śākyamuni sits beside him.

The point of this episode is that a Tathāgata who enters parinirvāṇa may not actually be extinct; he may only seem so. Likewise, what seems like a live Buddha may be an apparition magically created by Śākyamuni.

Śākyamuni states, "Many trillions of aeons ago, I realized supreme perfect enlightenment." When the Tathāgata who so long ago reached perfect enlightenment goes through a semblance of attainment, he does so in order to lead beings to maturity. Without becoming extinct, he makes a show of extinction so that weak beings will not take his continuing presence for granted. When these people are convinced that the apparition of Tathāgatas is rare, they become more zealous.

Śākyamuni declares that he resides forever on Mount Gṛdhrakūṭa, preaching the Dharma. When the unenlightened imagine that this world is engulfed in flames at the end of an aeon, it is really a paradise with gardens, palaces and aerial cars, teeming with gods and men.

The notion that this wretched world is really a splendid, pure Buddha-field occurs also in the *Vimalakīrti.* This idea has also enjoyed considerable currency in Chinese and Japanese Zen. As the Japanese Zen master Hakuin said, "This very place is the Lotus Land, and this very body is the Buddha."

The *Lotus* gospel is no more one of salvation by faith than is the early Buddhist teaching. Acts of faith, making vows, and affirmations of commitment lead to hearing the Dharma. The works of the devotee and the gifts of the teacher-savior are equally indispensable parts of an interaction cycle.

Akṣobhya is the earliest attested of the nonhistorical celestial Buddhas. In the *Vimalakīrti-Nirdeśa* Gautama says: "There is a country named Abhirati and a Buddha named Akṣobhya. This Vimalakīrti died in that country and came to birth here." To satisfy the Assembly's longing, Vimalakīrti entered samādhi, and grasped Abhirati and set it down in this world to be seen. Afterward it returned to its proper place, in the East. In the *Small Prajñā-pāramitā*, Śākyamuni exerts his wonder-working power and enables his Assembly to see Akṣobhya and his retinue. Neither Sūtra advocates devotion to Akṣobhya. Apparently, though, rebirth in Abhirati was sought by some people. It could be attained through moral acts, or even through hearing the name of Akṣobhya. This Buddha became moderately popular in Tantrism. In art he is represented as blue, holding a thunderbolt *(vajra)* in his right hand, his left hand in the earth-witness gesture *(bhūmi-sparśa-mudrā)*, with a blue elephant for his mount. The name Akṣobhya means "immovable" or "imperturbable." Legend says that while he was just a bodhisattva he made a vow to practice deeds without anger. The bodhisattva who does likewise will go to birth in Abhirati.

Amitābha (Amida)

Amitābha ("Unlimited Light") and *Amitāyus* ("Unlimited Lifespan") are alternate names for the same Buddha. Chinese A-mi-t'o and Japanese Amida transliterate a short form, Amita. The cult of this Buddha goes back at least to 100 A.D.[6]

Countless aeons ago a bhikṣu named Dharmākara ("Mine or Treasury of Dharma") heard the Buddha Lokeśvararāja preach and expressed a fervent desire to become a Buddha like him. He implored the Buddha to teach him the way to supreme perfect enlightenment and the qualities of a pure Buddha-field. The Tathāgata then taught him for ten million years the excellences and amenities of innumerable Buddha-lands. Dharmākara took all these good qualities, concentrated them all on one Buddha-land, and meditated on them for five aeons. Then he went to his future Buddha-land.

In his Buddha-land, said Dharmākara, there will be no evil destinies (hell, animals, ghosts). In other words, everyone born there will be at least a stream-winner (see p. 44). There will only be a nominal difference between men and gods in that Buddha-land. All beings born there will be almost, but not quite, arhants. They will all be destined for consummation in nirvāṇa, and, unless their bodhisattva vows bind them to more rebirths, they will only be reborn once. But their life span in Sukhāvatī ("Happiness-having") will be unlimited. Evil will not be known there even by name. All beings there will be able to hear automatically whatever Dharma-theme they wish; but there will be neither teaching nor learning, because all will possess direct cognition and will be able to recite the Dharma informed by all-knowledge.

The Buddha Amida will have unlimited light and unlimited life. His congregation of disciples will be countless, and innumerable Tathāgatas in other Buddha-lands will proclaim his fame and praise. In return, bodhisattvas from Sukhāvatī will travel everywhere to visit and worship the other Buddhas, while beings who stay in Sukhāvatī have merely to think of making offerings to Buddhas elsewhere and the gifts will automatically spring into being and be accepted. Bodhisattvas in that country will be able at will to convert their merit into precious substances, incense, robes, umbrellas, flags, lamps, dancing, and music. Just by wishing, the bodhisattvas will produce masses of superb ornaments from the jewel trees of the land. There will be a myriad of incense burners always emitting fragrance.

Dharmākara, when he becomes a Buddha, will exercise tremendous outreach. Other Buddhas everywhere will declare his name and fame, and from hearing his name living beings will derive manifold benefit. Women who hear the name of Amida will never again be reborn as women. (This is not just masculine arrogance, but a judgment on women's life in ancient Asia with which women generally concurred.) Living beings in other Buddha-lands who hear Amida's name will be released from birth and gain knowledge of the spells (dhāranīs). Through hearing his name they will attain birth in a noble family. Bodhisattvas who hear Amida's name will be honored by gods and men if they worship him. They will attain a samādhi in which they will dwell continually, seeing countless Buddhas, until they reach bodhi. They will earn merit by rejoicing in the bodhisattva course. No bodhisattva who hears Amida's name will ever relapse or forsake the Three Jewels, Buddha, Dharma, and Sangha.

The most crucial question concerning a Buddha-land is how to attain rebirth there. Dharmākara's vows give a specific answer to this, though different versions of the Sūtra vary significantly. The second-century Chinese translation says that if those who have aroused the thought of bodhi always meditate on Amida with a faith-filled mind, then at their death, Amida and his retinue will come to escort them to Sukhāvatī. On the other hand, if those who have done evil in former lives hear Amida's name and sincerely aspire to birth in his land, they will not endure bad destinies when they die but be reborn in Sukhāvatī.

The third-century translation distinguishes three classes of candidates for rebirth: evildoers, good Buddhists, and practicing bodhisattvas. The general prerequisites for rebirth are a desire to be reborn in Sukhāvatī and good conduct (with dedication of the resultant merit to rebirth and bodhi). The sinner must hear Amida's name, and repent and reform. The ordinary devotee has to perform worship and donation. The bodhisattva must meditate, presumably upon Amitābha and his paradise. Note that faith is not mentioned at all.

In the Chinese version adopted as orthodox by the Chinese and Japanese Pure Land sects, Amida's eighteenth vow says that all living beings in the ten directions who with sincere faith desire rebirth in Amida's country, by calling this desire to mind even ten times, will attain it. Only those who have committed atrocities or slandered the True Dharma are excluded. The nineteenth vow says that all living beings in the ten directions who arouse the thought of bodhi, cultivate all the virtues, and wholeheartedly vow to be reborn in Amida's country will, when they die, see Amida and a large retinue before them. The twentieth vow says that if living beings in the ten directions hear Amida's name, fix their thoughts on his country (that is, meditate on it), plant all the roots of virtue, and wholeheartedly dedicate (the resulting merit) desiring rebirth in his country, then it will happen that way. Here the general prerequisites are a desire for rebirth and good conduct. (Presumably dedication of merit is required by all three vows.) No distinction is made between classes of devotees. One may meditate with sincere faith as little as ten times. Or one may arouse the thought of bodhi. Or one may hear Amida's name and meditate on his country. But faith alone is not stated to suffice for rebirth.

The foregoing excursion into textual criticism has been necessary because the whole edifice of Far Eastern Pure Land dogmatics rests on the interpretation of these three vows. The issue is whether salvation requires both faith and works, or faith alone. On the evidence of the Sūtra in all surviving versions, faith is just an adjunct to meditation. The concentrated, aspiring mind is faith-filled. Salvation, furthermore, is not effected by Amida's power alone. The candidate, too, must make an effort. The Buddha's name is a talisman for those who lack merit, but in the early and detailed third-century translation, the sacred name alone does not cancel one's sins; repentance and reform are needed, too. In India the Amitābha cult was a religion of devout contemplation rather than of pure faith. It was a road to salvation not through "Other-power," but through interaction of Amitābha's supervening power and the devotee's own exertions.

Having proclaimed his vows, Dharmākara practiced the bodhisattva course as affirmed by the Chinese Pure Land Master T'an-luan in the sixth century and by Shinran in thirteenth century Japan (see below, pp. 115 and 177–178), for a trillion years. He established innumerable living beings in supreme perfect enlightenment. He worshipped countless Buddhas. Gradually his body became transformed, a sweet scent issued from his mouth and pores, and he acquired the signs and marks of a Great Person. Finally, ten aeons ago, he became the Tathāgata Amitābha presiding over the world-realm Sukhāvatī, a trillion Buddha-fields away to the West, a realm endowed with all the virtues he had vowed that it would have.

Certain features of the Mahāyāna paradises[7] deserve comment. Their penchant for jewels, jewel-trees, and diamond bodies indicates a low opinion of organic matter, because it is so perishable and "impure." Minerals, on the other hand, are durable and pure. Jewels, moreover, possess occult properties and radiate spiritual forces. They are visionary substances. Concentrating on them induces trances, and paradise visions tend to be bright, with gem-like colors and shapes.

The Buddha-lands differ from the heavens of the gods in that they are presided over by a Buddha so that the inhabitants can practice the Way, earn merit, and gain wisdom. In the heavens of the gods, a nonreturner can attain arhant-ship only through the maturing of merit previously earned as a human being. But the characteristics of the celestial Buddha-lands are very much like those of the heavens of the gods. The inhabitants of both are freed from labor, and the necessities of life come to them for the mere wishing. Sex is attenuated or entirely eliminated, and birth takes place without coitus or gestation.

The pure Buddha-lands differ from the Iranian, Christian, and Muslim paradises in that their delights are a means to a goal of bodhi rather than an end in themselves. All who go to Sukhāvatī are assured that they will attain enlightenment there, but residence there is neither an equivalent nor a substitute for nirvāṇa. Some inhabitants of Amida's land are disciples *(śrāvakas)*, and they become arhants and enter parinirvāṇa, which of course is not localized in any world-realm. Others are bodhisattvas; being bound by their vows, they do not enter cessation when they attain the highest stage, but appear at will throughout all the worlds in order to benefit living beings.

Vairocana

Vairocana ("Shining Out") is an epithet of the sun. Originally it was just an epithet of Śākhamuni, but in due course the name acquired separate identity as a celestial Buddha. In the Tantric set of the Five Tathāgatas, he occupies the center, which is Śākyamuni's position in the exoteric Mahāyāna maṇḍala. The Chinese scholastic view that Vairocana is the Dharma-body of Śākyamuni thus reaffirms the identity from which Vairocana had historically been derived.

We have seen that solar traits characterize the early accounts of Śākyamuni's Enlightenment (pp. 29–30). Ignorance was paired with darkness, and knowledge with light. Daybreak and the Enlightenment were synchronized. The *Lotus Sūtra* represents the Buddha's revealing act as a beam of light shooting from the wisdom-eye between his brows. Amitābha's very name signifies that he is a luminary deity, and his Buddha-land is suffused with radiance in all the hues of the rainbow. It is a land of eternal daylight, devoid of shadows.

The *Mahāvairocana Sūtra,* a Tantric work composed in about the seventh century, consists of Vairocana's revelations to the Tantric equivalents of Bodhisattvas. The venue of the Sūtra is frankly nonterrestrial: the residence of Śiva at the top of the form-realm.

Vairocana did not become popular either in art or in cult until the seventh century, when his role as Śākyamuni's transcendental counterpart gave him preeminence in the Tantric cosmoplans (maṇḍalas) and the associated rites.

7.
Buddhist Tantra and the Demise of Buddhism in India

BUDDHIST TANTRA

Buddhist Tantra is a mysticism mixed with magic, amalgamating elements some distinctly Buddhist, others traditionally quite non-Buddhist. Tantra, like yoga and *bhakti* (devotionalism), is a pan-Indian religious form, not limited to any one Indian religion. There were Hindu and Jain Tantrisms, just as yoga and devotionalism were a part of all three.

Buddhist Tantra originated primarily in the frontierlands of classical India, somewhere around the sixth century A.D. It flourished both in the far northwest, where it was influenced by Brahmanical and perhaps Chinese and Central Asian elements, and in the northeast of India—in Bengal, Orissa, and Assam. There Tantra drew inspiration from local magic and occult arts. Buddhist Tantra especially prospered from the eighth century on, under the Pāla dynasty of Bengal (circa 750–1150 A.D.). At Nālandā, the great center of Buddhism at that time, Prajñā-pāramitā ideas combined with Tantra, uniting metaphysics with ritual, magical practices. Tantra was exported throughout Southeast Asia, from Ceylon and Burma to the Indonesian isles, where it found its greatest success; but eventually it failed, defeated by Theravāda, or syncretized with Śaivism and then disappearing, or repressed by Islam. Since the Buddhism of the Tibetan culture area was exported from India during this period, it is predominantly Tantric. In the eighth century, three Indian monks took a school of ritualized Tantra *(Chen-yen)* to China, where it won favor at the court of the T'ang emperors but did not last more than a century. At the beginning of the ninth century, Kūkai introduced it into Japan as the Shingon school. It became popular among the nobility and continues so until the present day.

Part of the amalgam of Buddhist Tantra is the culmination of trends long present in Buddhism. Magic was explicitly allowed by the Buddha and the early Canon in the spells (Pali: *paritta)* which, when repeated, offered protection from such dangers as snakebite. Magic spells *(dhāraṇī)*[1] also occur in the Mahāyāna Sūtras as early as 200 A.D. These were supposed to epitomize the doctrine of the Sūtras and thus make available a short-cut to enlightenment to those who repeated them. By the seventh century, Buddhism had also incorporated the Hindu notion of inherently efficacious sounds such as *Oṃ* (Aum) and had elaborated a set of magical syllables, associating one with each major figure in the Tantric pantheon and with each "center" *(cakra)* in the mystic physiology of the meditator's body.

Another specifically Buddhist feature was the maṇḍala, or magic circle. It derived many of its features from the early religious architecture of the stūpa. The first of these shrines, with their railings separating sacred from profane ground, were intended as replicas of the cosmos. When the Buddha-image came into use, about 100 A.D., images were placed on the stūpa, or at its cardinal points or those of the courtyard surrounding it. The shrine thus became a three-dimensional maṇḍala.

The Tantric innovation was to turn the creation of maṇḍalas into an "actualization,"[2] a rite in which the agent becomes the deity conjured up. Probably Yogācāra meditation, which specialized in elaborate investigation of meditative states, greatly facilitated this development. Even in the beginning, the Canon indicates that monks meditated on external figures *(kasiṇa)* such as colored circles as supports for their practice of meditative visualization. All this fed the growth of Buddhist Tantra. Maṇḍalas can be depicted in painting; in three-dimensional models; by a troupe dramatically acting one out; or by a yogin visualizing the setting and the figures, basing the imaginative recreation of the mystic diagram on an external text or painting (such as a hanging scroll) for meditative support.

The maṇḍala is a divine cosmoplan and a theophany, able to manifest divinity itself when used by the meditator as a meditative object. Like the Vedic altar, it received the gods into its sacred space, making the divine immediately accessible to human beings. It was the site of communication with other worlds and the invisible gods. In its center, and in its complex design consisting of variously colored circles, squares, and triangles, were placed the gods, as if residing in their labyrinthine, divine palace complete with rooms, towers, and gardens. On its periphery were four entrances or doors through which the meditator could enter, symbolically receiving thereby initiation into the exclusive world of divine reality. The complex symbolism of the maṇḍala was fully used in Tantric meditations.

Tantric practices had a venerable Brahmanical ancestry as well. Buddhist Tantra was a radical departure from the classical Buddhist tradition, allowed primarily by Mādhyamika metaphysics which had declared the world empty, hence in principle essentially pure. This permitted, for one, incorporating unorthodox components into Buddhist ritual, including erotic elements. A considerable amount of esoteric yoga practice was taken over from independent circles of yoga practitioners, including Haṭha yoga, along with elements of popular and magical ritualism. Perhaps mostly from the northwest, traditionally a stronghold of Brahmanism, came such forms of Hindu ritualism as magical rites, instructions for ceremonies, and their formulas *(mantras)*. Another influence was the Hindu emphasis on the necessity for having a *guru* or preceptor to direct one's difficult learnings and transformations. These were prefigured in the Bhagavad Gītā's emphasis on Krishna as the divine teacher from whom mystic vision comes, and on the earlier Vedic preceptor. Even the rationale of the Vedic sacrifice was adopted, since we read of a fire sacrifice that would impart immortality in an early text from the northwest, the *Śatapaṭhabrāhmaṇa*. The highest purpose of Tantric ritual actualizations, though, is attainment of enlightenment, the conventional Buddhist goal. If magic power also resulted, this was nothing new since Buddhist meditators from the beginning had experienced extraordinary powers *(siddhi)* born of their contemplative disciplines.

Mantras were so much a part of Tantric meditation that Tantra (Buddhist as well as Śaivite) received the alternate name *Mantrayāṇa*, the Mantra Vehicle or Course. To call the use of mantra a *yāna*, or vehicle, accorded it the dignity of being a legitimate, distinct path to salvation. The term mantra was first used in Vedic Sanskrit to designate a verse, particularly one used to invoke or call up a deity, or to bring the gods from afar to the sacrifice for whose success their presence was required. From the beginning, mantra was not prayer but an "instrument of mind" (its etymological meaning), which, via speech, influenced cosmic forces. In the *Ṛg Veda*, mantra is also associated with the safety or protection that comes from the god's response to the recited "mantra of the praising poet." These meanings are remarkably continuous with Tantra. The scholar Jan Gonda's definition of mantra according to its etymology and earliest textual meanings applies almost as well to the much later Buddhist use: "word(s) believed to be of 'superhuman origin,' received, fashioned, and spoken by the 'inspired' seers, poets, and reciters in order to evoke divine power(s) and especially conceived as means of creating, conveying, concentrating, and realizing intentional and efficient thought, and of coming into touch or identifying oneself with the essence of the divinity which is present in the mantra." The continuity of the Vedic use with that of Buddhist Tantra recalls the remarkable resistance Indian traditions have had against extinction.

In Buddhist Tantra mantras were used as a means of evoking the deity so that the meditator might become one with him or her. In this sense their full soteriological import becomes apparent. They were also a means of protection against evil forces and adverse events. A mantra could be used as a meditative object from which to gain insight or to induce mental calm through repeated repetition, silent or vocal. One of the most famous Buddhist mantras, recited literally uncountable times, is "Oṃ maṇi-padme hūṃ." Often a mantra's form is so compressed that it even fails to conform to ordinary Sanskrit grammar, but this one means, roughly, "Oṃ in the lotus a jewel, hail!" Its symbols are thoroughly Buddhist: the lotus (padma) is the material world, the Wheel of Life, saṃsāra. But in it is the jewel *(maṇi)*, which may be colored by an adjacent object (as a diamond would reflect a nearby rose) but which is not in its essence of that color. Uncut by any other substance but itself, the jewel is a symbol of the unconditioned, nirvāṇa, or of the natural, essential purity of mind (citta).

Another famous Buddhist mantra, "Gate, gate, pāragate, pārasaṃgate, bodhi svāhā," is recited by the Goddess of Perfect Wisdom at the end of the

Heart Sūtra, by far Buddhism's best-known and most concise statement of its wisdom, to summarize and evoke Prajñā-pāramitā, the perfection of wisdom. It means: "Gone (gaté), gone, gone beyond, completely gone beyond, enlightenment hail!" This mantra, even though it begins with the Vedic invocatory initial *oṃ* and ends with the Vedic final *svāhā,* can open the mind to Buddhist enlightenment. The "beyond" it refers to is nirvāṇa, the other side of saṃsāra, the ocean of existence. Hsüan-tsang recited this mantra while traversing the Gobi desert to fend off demons and goblins. Tārā's mantra, "Oṃ, tāre tuttāre ture svāha" (untranslatable but verbally playing on her name), evokes protection of the goddess Tārā from dangers, both physical and spiritual. A mantra which avows the truth of the teaching of emptiness goes: Oṃ śūnyatā-jñāna-vajra-svabhāvātmako 'haṃ"—"Oṃ, I am a self whose essence is the diamond knowledge of emptiness." A similar mantra states: "Oṃ svabhāvaśuddhaḥ sarva-dharmāḥ svabhāvaśuddho 'haṃ." This mantra, encapsulating the teaching of the emptiness of self and dharmas, means, "Oṃ by essential nature all the dharmas are pure, by essential nature I am pure!"

Many have observed that some Tantric ritual procedures including the erotic and magical practices that its emptiness metaphysic allows, are incongruous in the Buddhist context. But this view runs counter to the way religions actually develop and evolve. The result of both Buddhist and non-Buddhist influences was Tantra, some of whose rites, while violating traditional Buddhist precepts, still sought the traditional Buddhist goal, although they imbued it with new doctrinal significance and converted it into a sacramental means of realization. Tantric masters systematized these rites and eventually wrote them down in the form of *Tantras* (ritual manuals). The *Tantras* were intended as aids for initiants training under a master. They were not for public perusal, and their secrets were safeguarded by an argot called twilight speech[3] in which, for example, semen was called "camphor," *"Bodhicitta"* (thought of enlightenment), and "elixir"; the male and female genitals were called "thunderbolt" and "lotus"; and the corpse of an executed criminal was called a "banner."

It is not surprising that Tantra has been excoriated by many modern writers. It has been said that Tantrism was a degeneration, that it grafted the Hindu cult of female energies onto Buddhism, and that the graft became a parasite which in due course crushed the life out of its host.

What happened was in fact the reverse. The main Buddhist tradition assimilated diverse non-Budddhist elements, restructuring and reinterpreting them, until it would be more correct to say that pure Buddhism crushed the life out of the *Tantras.* By 800 A.D., Tantric studies had achieved the dignity of an academic discipline. Learned scholars in Bengal and Bihar were writing commentaries; giving glosses for the "twilight speech"; explaining the symbolic meanings of the ritual objects, persons, and acts; and suffusing the subject with a refined and ethical tone. The practitioners who wrote the *Tantras* considered that the accompanying mental exercises were more important than the physical acts of the rites. It was a commonplace that everything is mind-only, so it was not always necessary to perform the rites in imagination. After a time, most Tantric schools ceased to perform those rites which infringed the precepts. Tantra became respectable exercises in pure contemplation.[4]

A typical contemplative visualization uses the characteristic devices of Tantric meditation. An alternate reality, a "maṇḍala-world" peopled by divinities, is generated by chanting and thinking of mantras and by meditative visualization. The process is not so different from the early Buddhist contemplative practice of visualizing various kinds of circles, only the meditative object is more complex. The meditator envisions himself as the central Buddha of the maṇḍala, as if to abide in an "interior castle" or divine mansion strikingly similar to the one experienced in meditation by the medieval Spanish mystic, St. Theresa of Avila. The meditator's purpose is to gain access to the knowledge and divine power of Buddhahood by a direct, ritual assault on Buddhahood itself.

He begins with traditional preliminary meditations, going for refuge, cleansing himself of sins, praying to the masters and worshipping them, practicing the four immeasurable meditations, and erecting around himself a protective, magic circle which defined the sacred space of the alternate reality he was creating. To take on the being of the deity, he disperses all appearances of the world into emptiness. Then he generates himself as the god, many-armed and in sexual union with his consort, seated on the central throne of his maṇḍala. All the Buddhas enter the interior castle of the maṇḍala and the meditator assimilates them in his body and senses, thereby attaining immanent divinity. He receives Buddha-knowledge from the god and is initiated into his new divinity by goddesses who serve him. Then, as a god, he receives offerings, his speech becomes divine speech, and he can perform any of the deity's powerful functions. Finally possessed of the mind of the god, he has Buddha-like divine understanding and returns to the world in this state of ineffable, realized power.

Tantric practice is based in part on the Mādhyamika principle that saṃsāra and nirvāṇa are not different. As Nāgārjuna said, "The limit of saṃsāra is the limit of nirvāṇa. Between these two there is not even the subtlest something." Also, "Unrelated to the pure there is nothing impure with reference to which we can designate the pure. Therefore even the pure is not a matter of fact." An early Buddhist maxim says: "Living beings are defiled through defilement of the mind, and purified through purification of the mind."[5]

Referring back to a popular Mahāyāna Sūtra, clearly not Tantric, shows how Mahāyāna metaphysics could provide a basis for Tantric practice. The *Vimalakīrti-Nirdeśa* Sūtra shows the great bodhisattva accepting gifts of maidens and garlands which the monks refused, fearing they would be contaminated by them. The blossoms stuck to the arhants, because they discriminated lawful and unlawful, but did not stick to the bodhisattvas, who discriminated nothing. Many sayings in this Sūtra have a very Tantric ring: "Only for conceited men does the Buddha preach that separation from lewdness, anger, and folly is liberation. For men without conceit, the Buddha preaches that lewdness, anger, and folly are indeed liberation." "The bodhi-sattva seems to proceed in precept-breaking, yet persists in pure morality and feels great fear even at the smallest sin. He seems to proceed in the passions, yet is always pure in mind. He seems to have wives and concubines, yet always keeps far away from the mud of the five lusts." "Just as lotus flowers do not grow on a high plain of dry land but only where there is low, moist mire, even so, only in the mire of passions are there living beings to produce the Buddha-qualities." "He appears to indulge the five lusts, but also seems to practice meditation. A lotus blossom that grows in a fire has to be described as a rarity. One who lives in lust yet meditates constitutes as great a miracle."

The Tantric poet Saraha says, "Here there's no beginning, no middle, no end, no saṃsāra, no nirvāṇa. In this state of supreme bliss, there's no self and no other." "Just as water entering water becomes of the same taste, so when the sage thinks vices and virtues the same, there's no polarity." In other words, the enlightened man is beyond good and evil.

The crux of the matter is skill in means. The *Hevajra Tantra* says, "The unknowing worldling who drinks strong poison is overpowered; he who has expelled delusion, with his mind on the truth, destroys it utterly." What is licit under the direction of a preceptor *(guru)* and within the consecrated maṇḍala is still illicit for ordinary people. When the tabus are broken, they must be broken with a pure mind and not for worldly pleasure.

The aim of the Tantric devotee is to destroy the passions by means of the passions. As the *Hevajra* says, "The expert in poison repels poison by that very poison, a little bit of which kills most people. . . . Those who have 'means' are liberated from the bondage of 'becoming' through the very thing by which wicked people are bound. The world is bound by lust, and released by the same lust."

Who should ritually break the tabus, and who should not? Tantric doctrine classifies people into five "tribes" or "families" according to person-ality type and prescribes a different method of meditation for each tribe. Earlier meditation manuals recommended different meditations depending on the student's dominant passion. The lustful type should meditate on impurity, the hostile type on compassion, and the foolish type on causal relations. The classical prescription for the hostile type is cultivation of compassion and friendly love. Tantrism prescribes for such a one the performance of erotic rites. "Compassion" is twilight speech for "sexual love." Tantra fuses spiritual and physical love, in idea and in practice.

Already, in the *Prajñā-pāramitā Sūtras,* Mahāyāna thinkers had held that enlightenment requires perfection of wisdom (prajñā) and development of skill in means *(upāya).* Wisdom soon became a goddess (see p. 99). The Tantras made Means a male divinity. The union of Wisdom and Means produces the Bodhicitta (thought of enlightenment). In the maṇḍala of Hevajra, the goddess Nairātmyā ("No-self") stands for Wisdom, and Hevajra stands for Means. When the maṇḍala is acted out, the yogin impersonates Hevajra, and his consort takes the part of Nairātmyā.

The rites are practiced long and thoroughly in contemplation before they are actually performed. The yogin imagines the maṇḍala and the goddess around the circle and mentally envisages the rites with himself as the deity. Having conjured up this vivid drama, he contemplates that these phenomena, like all others, are empty—that there is neither subject nor object, thought nor thinker.

Such visualizations are a considerable psychological feat. Images and paintings are used to support the imagination, and in turn the artist pictures the themes mentally before executing the painting or the statue.

The body, which earlier Buddhism tended to devalue in one way or another, received its due in Tantra. Saraha says: "Here's the Jumna, river of gods, and here's the Ganges' flood; here are Prayāga and Benares, here are the Moon and Sun. In wandering, I've visited all kinds of Tantric meeting-places, but never have I seen another holy place as blissful as my body." Tantric physiology is mystical rather than anatomical. It confounds the circulation and nervous systems, for example. It posits four psychic centers (navel, heart, throat, and brain) and three main channels, one corresponding to the spinal column and the other two to the jugular veins. It says that the bodhicitta ascends at the moment of Great Bliss (orgasm) until it reaches the highest center.

The *Tantras* do not advocate murder, even ritually, and they observe the general Buddhist prohibition against animal sacrifice, which Hinduism allowed as an exception to its precept against injuring sentient things. But the *Tantras* do enjoin illicit and even incestuous sexual relations, and they do prescribe drinking wine and eating the flesh of men, cows, elephants, horses, and dogs. Early Buddhism was not vegetarian, but during the fourth century A.D. Mahāyāna adopted vegetarianism from the Hindus. Cow slaughter had become a heinous crime by Tantric times, so for an upper-caste Indian, whether brahmin or Buddhist, eating beef was virtually as repugnant as cannibalism.

Much Western horror at Tantric practices stems from cultural astigmatism. The imagery of human sacrifices and the eating of human flesh underlie the greatest of all Christian sacraments. If a Tantric deity holding a skull filled with blood seems morbid, consider the phrase "washed in the blood of the Lamb" and its origins in the animal sacrifices and belief in the purifying power of blood of the ancient Hebrews.

The religious character of sexual acts goes back a long way in India. The *Bṛhad-āraṇyaka Upaniṣad* likens sexual union to a sacrifice. The woman is the fire into which the oblation is offered. In the Vedic royal horse-sacrifice the queen ritually copulates with the horse immediately after it is strangled so as to acquire its power and transmit it to the king. Orgiastic fertility cults have survived among the tribal peoples of northeast India to the present day, and it was in this region that Tantra perhaps first developed.

That mystical realization is, or is like, erotic consummation is not just an Indian idea, though it is fundamental to Hindu devotional cults. Traditional Christian interpretation made the Song of Solomon an allegory for the spiritual marriage, a concept that was popular among medieval European mystics. In China the shaman's songs of the *Songs of the South* (Ch'u-tz'u) treat the meeting between shaman and spirit also as an erotic encounter.

The Tantric spirit brought a needed revival to Buddhism in its later Indian stages, in the same way that Zen masters cut through the oversystematized Mahāyāna Buddhism of China to its essentials. The effectiveness of the Tantric path is witnessed by the great saints it produced. Each major Buddhist movement has created its own type of holy individual and incited the zeal of its followers by pointing to living exemplars. In the Buddha's day, many attained arhant-ship. As the generations went by, the ideal faded and fewer attained it. Then in early Mahāyāna the bodhisattva path offered human saints of modest attainment fellowship with the celestial bodhisattvas. But the latter were so extolled that they eventually robbed earthly bodhisattva-hood of all glamor. Seventh-century China circumvented the scholastic claptrap concerning the bodhisattva course and created a new type of holy man in the Zen master. The Tantric accomplished ones *(siddhas)* combined features from most of the preceding Indian types of wizard and saint and added some new traits, both bizarre and admirable. They usually lived and operated outside the regular monastic communities, which continued their old style of life throughout the Tantric period. Some Tantric adepts were bhikṣus, but some, too, were householders. They were recruited from all castes and classes, and they wandered around the country, mixing freely with out-castes and tribal people, begging from door to door, frequenting cremation grounds and haunted places. They trafficked with demons and took outcaste girls for their ritual consorts. Some achieved success with very little instruction, and some went through many years of ordeals under stern and capricious masters.[6] The one great rule for the Tantric student was absolute obedience and devotion to his preceptor *(guru),* whom he must revere as a very Buddha. Success depended on the preceptor's ability to identify the student's problems and understand his karmic states of mind, manipulate him through personal interaction, and use charisma to overcome blocks that the student could not surmount by himself. The Tantric preceptor is thus a variant of the pan-Buddhist teacher-savior type.

THE DEMISE OF INDIAN BUDDHISM

In the seventh century, Buddhism was fairly strong in most parts of India. Hsüan-tsang, the seventh-century Chinese pilgrim who studied in India, reported quite a few deserted monasteries here and there, but prospering centers were numerous and widely distributed. However, archaeology tells the tale of a steady decline over the next several centuries in most regions. After 600, Buddhism in the south gradually gave way to the devotional Hinduism of the Tamil minstrel saints. It left its influence on Tamil theism, however, fostering the idea of a compassionate God. Kāñcīpuram (Conjeeveram) was a renowned Buddhist center, and as late as the fifteenth century a Theravāda community existed there.

The White Hun invasions of the sixth century devastated the monasteries of Gandhāra, but Buddhism continued to prosper in nearby Kashmir, where by the ninth century, though, Buddhism and Śaivism became intermingled. Muslim rulers finally stamped out Kashmiri Buddhism during the course of the fifteenth century. In Sindh, the Ganges valley, and Orissa, Buddhism flourished until the Muslim invaders sacked the monasteries and butchered the monks. Nālandā was pillaged and burned in 1198 and, though it continued to function on a reduced scale for several decades, repeated attacks by Muslim marauders eventually exterminated the institution. Buddhism lingered for a few centuries as a folk cult in Bihar, Bengal, and Orissa, then disappeared.

It has been said that Buddhism vanished from India because it was imprudently tolerant and gradually became so Hinduized that it lost all reason for a separate existence. This is at best a partial truth. Mahāyāna was quite hostile to theistic Hinduism. The householder bodhisattva pledged himself never on pain of death to worship Vishnu and Śiva. Āryadeva reportedly entered a south Indian temple and tore the eye out of a baleful idol of Śiva. The mutual antipathy was still evident about 1000 A.D., when a Bengali brahmin family strongly opposed the marriage of their daughter to Nāropa, who came from a Buddhist family. A Kashmiri play of the same general period takes the rivalry among Buddhism, Jainism, and various Hindu sects as its theme. It evinces both a strong sense of the distinctions among sects and a genial spirit of conciliation. The element of truth in this theory is that institutional Buddhism had grown self-centered, conservative, and unresponsive to the needs of the people. The great monasteries depended not on widows' mites but on landed estates and royal grants, so they neglected to maintain popular support, became divorced from the rural populace; and when the monasteries lost royal support or were destroyed by invasions, the general population had little interest in either preserving the Dharma or restoring the Saṅgha.

It is not unnatural that Buddhism should have died out in India. Mithraism and Manichaeism, widespread and powerful in their day, perished, yet scholars are not overly amazed. The Vedic religion died about the time that Buddhism arose, Christianity vanished gradually from its Oriental homelands under Muslim occupation, and in this century Confucianism has ceased to be a religion. From very early, Indian Buddhists had expected the Dharma eventually to decline and disappear. Though Buddhism in its homeland finally went the way of all conditioned things, it had by then lighted the lamp of the

Dharma in many other parts of Asia, and had endured several times as long as any empire that has ever held sway in India.

HINDUISM AND BUDDHISM

As we saw in Chapter 1, both Hinduism and Buddhism grew from religious traditions that preceded them, including that of the Indus Valley civilization, and Brahmanism. It is probably best not to speak of "Hinduism" until the time of the *Bhagavad Gītā,* whose composition began around 200 B.C. This text systematized the various strands of orthodoxy extending from the older Brahmanism and the Upaniṣads into the comprehensive vision we identify by the term Hinduism. It consciously addressed the Buddhist challenge without, however, ever directly mentioning it. The epic warrior Arjuna, who discourses with Krishna, the incarnation of Vishnu in the Bhagavad Gītā, begins the Gītā dialog by taking a Buddhist position on war, symbolic of all action and the values that direct action, and Krishna then states through the rest of the work the Hindu position on doctrine crucial to Hinduism. His instruction includes such topics as the eternal ātman, the creation of the world, and the righteousness of the Hindu social system based on class *(varṇa)* distinctions, with its attendant sense of morally correct action, about which Buddhism held significantly different views.

It is perhaps misleading to consider Hinduism and Buddhism two separate creeds within the history of religions in India. They may equally well be seen as two sides of Indian religion. The Buddhists sided with reforming ascetics and wandering mendicants in the sixth century B.C. and were considered in later classifications to be unorthodox. This meant that they opposed religious elements and traditions that came from the prior Brahmanical orthodoxy accepted by the householder tradition and the Gītā. These included the authority of the Vedic scriptures, belief in creation by a divine entity, trust in the efficacy of orthodox sacrifices and rites as practiced by the brahmins, and the validity of the Brahmanical social system.

Hinduism and Buddhism were polarized tendencies within the same religious tradition, something like Catholicism and Protestantism within Christianity or Confucianism and Taoism in China. The Buddhists were the protestants who gathered around the central figure of the Buddha. The Hindus, under Krishna's theistic banner of the Gītā, preserved the older tradition while augmenting it, consolidating it against the growing power of the Buddhists and, when necessary, incorporating doctrine from the opposition. Both have called themselves the *sanātana dharma,* the primordial religion, use similar concepts such as saṃsāra and karman, and often share common practices like self-transformative meditative discipline *(yoga).*

Out of the immensely rich and heterogeneous religious situation of the sixth century B.C., then, Indian religion developed the major divisions. The first to consolidate their Dharma were those on the Buddhist side of the coin. Buddhism emphasized the individual in pursuit of the freedom of spiritual maturity, living outside the ordinary social system as a wandering mendicant. It espoused the values of transcendence, nonviolence, and self-transformation in this lifetime. Ordinary life rules were renounced for the special virtues conducive to the attainment of nirvāṇa. No aspirants were considered excluded by birth, but all could become Āryan (noble) by their actions alone.

In the Gītā Krishna argues strongly against these values. He affirms the legitimacy of the traditional Āryan social structure, with its assumption that social status is fixed by one's birth into a particular class. He calls Arjuna's espousal of nonviolence un-Āryan (ignoble) and notes that it will not lead to heaven, the goal of the older Brahmanical orthodoxy. Arjuna counters that it is better to live by begging (like Buddhists, unmentioned but clearly meant in the text) rather than on "blood-smeared" booty won in war. Krishna strongly condemns Arjuna's quietism and argues for the righteousness of actions undertaken out of class duty and a concern for good's victory over evil.

But this is only part of the Gītā. These arguments clearly indicate the Hindu commitment to the Brahmanical heritage, emphasizing the continuity it affirmed with the older orthopraxy which Buddhists condemned as ineffective. Krishna's arguments also show Hindus accepting much that was not originally part of the Brahmanical religion which they shared, sometimes with only superficial terminological differences, with Buddhists. The world view used by Buddhists (see pp. 16–17) was also held by Hindus. Though their respective paths differ in terminology,[7] both posit transcendence of the ordinary world as the ultimate goal of religious transformation. At the conclusion of the Gītā's second chapter, Krishna calls this goal brahmanirvāṇa (release in the absolute), wedding the favored Buddhist term, nirvāṇa, to the favored Hindu-Upaniṣadic term for the absolute, Brahman. In subsequent chapters, Krishna uses other Buddhist terms, such as duḥkha, and clearly addresses himself to the problematic of bondage to karman, recurrent death, and a transient, ever-shifting saṃsāra, a problem Buddhists also made their primary concern. The Gītā's final resolution of Arjuna's ignorance is quite different, however, from early Buddhism. Its theistic commitment becomes clear when Krishna gives Arjuna the divine eye to see the ultimate dependency of the world on Vishnu, its creator. This contrasts with the Buddha's divine eye vision during the third night watch. He obtained the vision not as a gift of grace from God, but through his own effort, and saw pratītya-samutpāda, (dependent co-arising) creation not dependent on a god but the product of impersonal responses to human choices and actions.

This theism, with its attitude of devotion (bhakti) to a personalized divine figure, was also integrated via Mahāyāna into Buddhism. So the history of the two goes, one borrowing from the other for as long as Buddhism survived in India. It is pointless to list the mutual borrowings. Eventually Hinduism, which also featured monasticism, and Buddhism were no longer polarized and the polemics that had separated them from the time of the Gītā until the beginning of the second milennium A.D. lost their point. Buddhism never developed a truly separate laity in India. When its great monastic communities and universities were destroyed in the north, it eventually was no longer an alternative religious or monastic career.

Interestingly, Hinduism never succeeded well outside of India, while Buddhism transformed the rest of Asia. Again this stems from their being two separate tendencies from within the same religious tradition. Being inseparable from the underlying Indian social structure, Hinduism, except in rare instances, never survived abroad. Buddhism, on the other hand, was Indian religion for export. Unencumbered by a burdensome orthodoxy and orthopraxy, it spread freely, adapting to local conditions as it went. Buddhism was the internationalization of the Indian vision of life, while Hinduism remained solely for home consumption and naturally prevailed in its proper homeland.

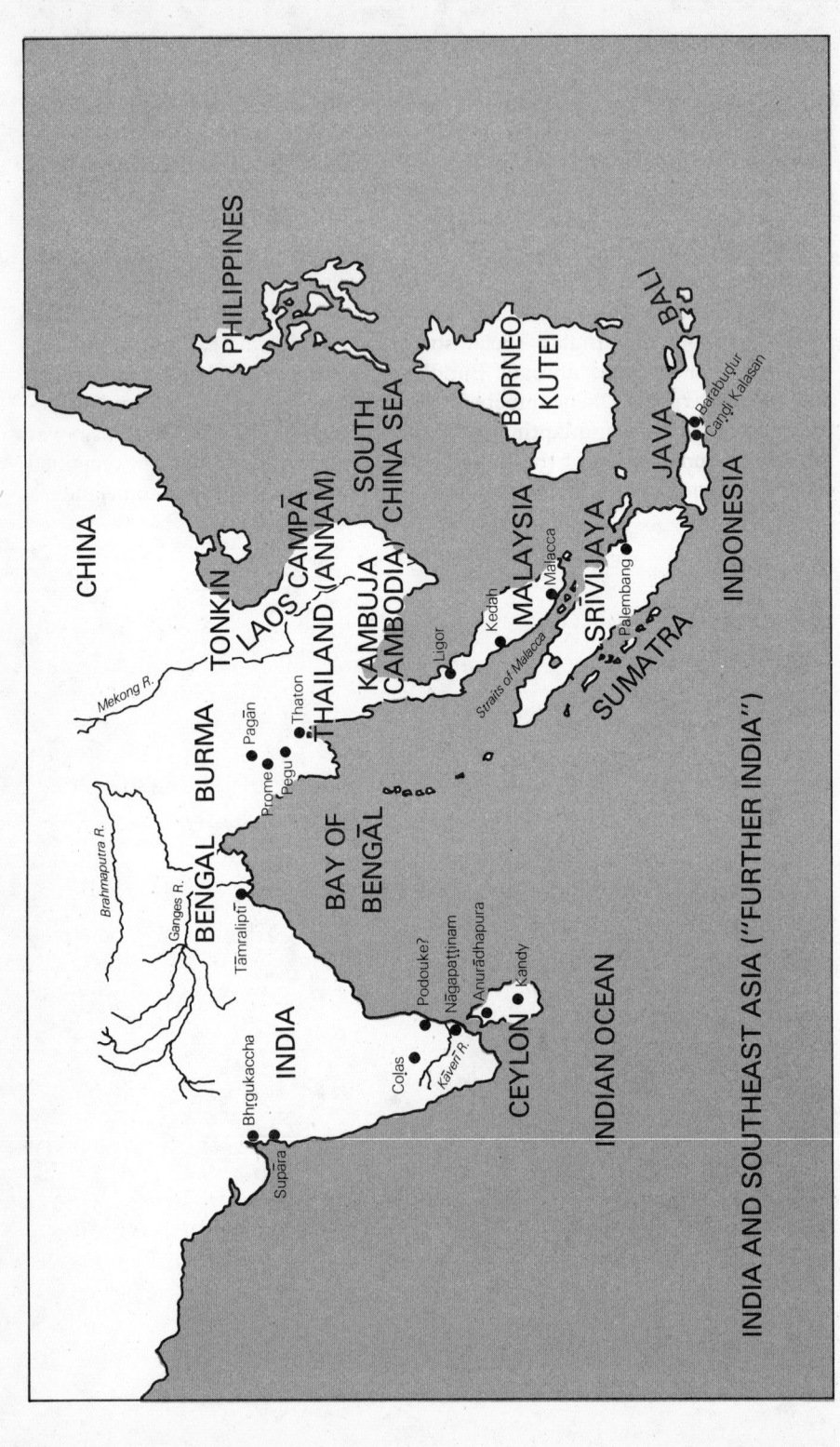

INDIA AND SOUTHEAST ASIA ("FURTHER INDIA")

Part II

THE DEVELOPMENT
OF BUDDHISM
OUTSIDE INDIA

8.
The Buddhism of Southeast Asia

BUDDHIST MISSIONARIES BEGIN

According to the Canon, the Buddha instructed all his monks to become missionaries and to spread his Word in the languages of the people they visited, far or near. In ancient India this meant using vernacular variants of the Buddha's own dialect, but it could apply to any situation, however far-flung. But it was not until Aśoka's enthusiastic royal patronage that Buddhist missionaries began taking the religion beyond the Indian subcontinent. One record indicates that in 256 and 255 B.C., Aśoka sent Dharma-envoys to various Greek rulers in the West, and later—about 247—to Ceylon, reportedly at the request of the island's ruler, Devānaṃpiyatissa. Tradition also tells that he sent a mission to Burma, where the proselytizers founded a Buddhist community. Though nothing came of the missions of the West, Aśoka's missionaries had begun the gradual spread of Buddhist and Indian culture to Southeast Asia.

After the first century A.D., Indian expansion into the area increased, until by the eighth century the entire stretch of Southeast Asia from India's eastern coast all the way to Campā (Annam in Vietnam) and Bali in the Indonesian archipelago was Indianized. There is reason to believe that the entire region was somewhat related to India before this time by a partially shared common substratum culture (perhaps Austro-Asiatic). Vigorous Indian expansion resulted in a Southeast Asian religious culture that had both a Hindu and Buddhist overlay (including Theravāda, Mahāyāna, and Tantric elements). Eventually the Theravāda Buddhists alone prevailed, midst varied survivals of older religious cultures, the ancient spirit cults, and Brahmanical customs. Only Vietnam did not retain Theravāda but adopted Mahāyāna due to its proximity to China, while Indonesia became largely Islamic after the fifteenth century A.D. The history of Buddhism in this area of "further India" is an important chapter in its development.

CEYLON (ŚRĪ LAṄKA)

Before Aśoka's missions to Ceylon in the fifth century B.C., Indo-Āryan clansmen had come to the island from the northwest or northeast Gangetic plain, bringing with them Brahmanical customs and political institutions. The Siṅhala clan dominated and founded a royal dynasty. It was their king, Tissa, who was converted by Aśoka's son and other missionaries about 247 B.C. The work of popular conversion took more time, but by the second century B.C. the Siṅhalese had thoroughly accepted the Dharma. King Tissa had well prepared the way for this victory by patronizing Buddhist missionaries and giving Buddhists a royal pavilion in a city park of his capital, Anurādhapura, from which they organized their conversions of the royal entourage and the people. A great monastery was established, a shoot of the Bodhi Tree was brought from Bodh-gayā by Aśoka's daughter (who also founded an order of nuns), and a huge stūpa was constructed for popular worship.

Thus, from the beginning the Buddhist Saṅgha in Ceylon maintained close relations with the government, becoming the state religion. Buddhists had no trouble accepting the Brahmanical political institutions of the ruling dynasty. Kings became practicing Buddhists and patrons of Buddhist works of art, learning, culture, and worship. They had shrines and monasteries built and helped regulate the affairs of the Saṅgha. Nobles and commoners supported Buddhism too; beautiful monuments were built, adorned with Buddhist art, and monasteries became centers of culture and learning. For over two millenia Theravāda has been closely linked with the fortunes of the Siṅhala monarchy. Its conservative, archaistic character has been preserved through the common efforts of kings and elders to guard a perennially threatened national heritage. Buddhism in Ceylon has had a longer continuous existence than anywhere else in the world. Throughout its history Ceylon has relied heavily on India for its literate culture. From the early centuries of the Christian era on, Hindu Tamils migrated there from nearby southern India, so that the island came to have both Buddhist and Hindu populations under a Brahmanical-style monarchy.

The history of Ceylon has been a continual struggle against foreign invaders. South Indian Coḷas were expelled as early as the first century B.C. by a king who stated his motive to be the protection of Buddhism. Buddhists on the island maintained contacts with the Buddhist homeland, particularly via Indian west coast ports. Gradually the entire Buddhist Canon was transmitted and written down. The sect of the Theravādins became dominant and is today the sole surviving Hīnayāna sect of Indian Buddhism anywhere. By the beginning of the first centuries of the Chirstian era, Buddhist culture was flourishing in Ceylon so that serveral centuries later, Chinese pilgrims found it famous in other Asian Buddhist countries.

During the third and fourth centuries A.D., Mahāyāna influences reached the country, but its partisans did not enjoy royal favor for very long. During the reign of the fifth century king Mahānāma, three Buddhist scholars from south India came to Ceylon; one of these was the famous Buddhaghosa. His *Path of Purity* (Pali: *Visuddhimagga)* is an authoritative survey of Buddhist doctrine and meditative practice. By the end of this important period, the doctrine of the Theravādins was firmly fixed.

By the sixth century, the Theravādins had even expanded from Ceylon along India's western coast, and Abhidharma study flourished. But magical practices (chanting protective *paritta,* spells) also appeared. Mahāyāna continued with the support of one monastery; by the eighth and ninth centuries, Prajñā-pāramitā and Buddhist Tantra had a place on the island too. Hindu influences also persisted, so that by the eleventh century, King Vijayabāhu had first to liberate his island from Coḷa occupation and then revive the state religion, restoring a valid ordination succession (that is, a proper right to ordain as received from a country with an unbroken line of ordination) and appointing the first Saṅgha-director to oversee the Order.

Subsequent Hindu invasions continued to disrupt the country, endangering the Buddhist Saṅgha there. During this time (until the 1500s) land revenues declined, reducing support for Buddhist institutions; and, though the King and nobles continued their patronage, the Saṅgha was weaker financially. The old great monasteries were disbanded, schisms and lack of discipline split the Saṅgha, and the kings had to purge it of undesirables. Hinduism influenced Buddhist institutions and thought, worship of Hindu gods became a part of popular Buddhism, and Brahmanical gods were worshipped by kings and lay folk in elaborate festivals. In the north and east of the island, Hindu Tamils were in power.

Later, the Portugese (1505-1658) seized the lowlands, destroyed monasteries, and forcibly converted people to Catholicism. The Siṅhala kings withdrew to Kandy in the mountains, where they ruled from 1592 until 1815, supporting Buddhism insofar as their circumstances and resources would permit. The Dutch, ardent Calvinists, and finally the English, followed the Portuguese in dominating the island. The long period of European rule harmed the Buddhist cause greatly. Under the treaty by which they took over from the Siṅhala monarchy, the British were bound to protect Buddhism, but evangelical Christian missionaries proceeded to attack it. Before long, Buddhist spokesmen replied, lay associations were formed, training centers for monks were established, and a revival was under way. Two Westerners who aided the cause of Buddhism are especially revered in Ceylon: Henry Olcott, an American Theosophist who traveled around the country exhorting the people to revive their historic religion; and T. W. Rhys Davids, founder of the Pali Text Society, who, by rendering Gautama's teachings admirable in European eyes, gave confidence and pride to the peoples who had preserved them.

Since Olcott's and Davids's time, Buddhists in Ceylon have contributed a great deal of valuable scholarship to the Buddhist world and, since the achievement of Independence in 1948, have taken an active role in the affairs of their own country and Asian Buddhism. In 1950, they founded the World Fellowship of Buddhists, trying to unite Buddhists of all nations.

BURMA

Burma, possessing both ports and overland trade routes, was India's trade gateway to Southeast Asia. Sometime around the third century B.C., Indian merchants began bringing Indian cultural traditions (religious ideas, political and legal forms) along with their wares to the people who had settled along Burma's rivers. These reshaped native society, art, and thought, combining with the special character of the people to create a dignified culture that was Burmese and Buddhist.

The Buddhist element came when Aśoka sent monks as missionaries to the commercial center of Thaton, where they founded a monastic settlement. By the second century B.C., Ceylonese chronicles report that Burmese monks attended an important religious ceremony on the island. With the great expansion of commerce with India during the first century A.D. and following, many Indians came to Thaton not as colonists and exploiters but as friendly traders. Buddhism was well received and soon was firmly established around Thaton, which became as a result a great Buddhist center. Missions came also from south Indian Buddhist centers and, by the third century, overland from east India. Local spirit cults (of the *Nats)* were brought into Theravāda; art, including the making of Buddha images, fell under Indian influence, and stūpas were built. Soon, Burma was a flourishing center of Buddhist life, even spreading its Buddhist culture to other areas and enjoying a prosperity that allowed devout Theravāda practice to flower. Education and discipline were available to monks and laity alike in monasteries and convents.

Later, diverse influences appeared in the area. By the time of the founding of the Pagān kingdom (849-1287), Mahāyāna was coming via overland trade routes from south China, while Bengal in India was a source of Mahāyāna and Tantrism, as well as an aggressive Hinduism.

At the time of the Pagān dynasty's greatest king, Anawrahtā (1040-1077), Buddhism in Burma changed its character by turning to Ceylon for inspiration, particularly in response to growing non-Theravāda movements. Tantrism was asserting its practices, the neighboring Khmers were converting en masse to Hinduism, and Mahāyāna gained strength in areas closer to China. A Theravāda monk, Shin Arahan, considered Hindu influence excessive in the south so he fled Thaton and went to Pagān, where he converted Anawrahtā to

Theravāda. The king became its champion. He defeated the northern Mahā-yānist kingdom of Nanchao, converted those tribes who had returned exclusively to spirit cults, and conquered Thaton on the pretext of obtaining Theravāda texts denied to him by its king. Though Anawrahtā patronized Theravāda lavishly, archeological evidence indicates that Mahāyāna and Tantric monks whom he opposed continued to pursue their doctrines alongside the Theravādins, but it was really Theravāda's day. During this time Burma became the most thriving center of Buddhism in the world since Buddhism was everywhere else under attack or failing. King Anawrahtā had relics brought from Ceylon, and he transformed his capital of Pagān by magnificent religious building programs. By the time of the Ceylonese king Vijayabāhu, Burma was the most prosperous Theravāda country, sending monks in 1065 to Ceylon itself to restore the ordination line that was in danger of extinction there. Later, the Khmers were brought into the Theravāda fold by Burmese efforts.

Pagān was a fabled kingdom (also a city and a dynasty), known even in the West via Marco Polo. The people were prosperous and had splendid monasteries and temples. In a united Burma, Burmese made themselves masters of Buddhist thought so that Pagān was a center of Buddhist culture. The people had made Buddhism their way of life, monks taught children in the villages, spreading Buddhism far and wide; and for three centuries, the city of Pagān was a splendid city with over 9,000 pagodas (stūpas) and temples.

But Pagān was sacked by the Mongols in 1287 and abandoned. Wars and small kingdoms followed, dividing the country. Mahāyāna dwindled but Theravāda survived. King Dhammazedi of Pegu (later fifteenth century) reformed the Burmese Sangha along Ceylonese lines and made his capital a center of Theravāda culture. A new dynasty emerged, ruling a reunited Burma from 1752 until the British deposition of the king in 1886, when Burma was annexed to India. Previously, under the monarchy, the Sangha was favored and grew in spite of a petty controversy over whether a monk should wear his upper robe over both shoulders or only over the left. The issue bitterly divided the Sangha until 1784, when the king decreed that the both-shoulders faction was right. Pali studies flourished in the nineteenth century and Sūtras were translated into Burmese. The king appointed a hierarchy headed by his chaplain to regulate the affairs of the Order. After the British took over, they declined to appoint a new director of the Sangha when the old one died but eventually arranged for the whole Sangha to elect a superior for itself. When outside authority was thus removed, discipline in the monasteries deteriorated. Monks played a prominent part in the early days of the Independence movement, later faded into the background, and emerged after Independence was won following World War II as an ecclesiastical lobby.

Burmese Buddhism, like that of Ceylon, did much to preserve Theravāda orthodoxy. Scholarship was extensive in fields related to doctrine; Burmese authors rewrote versions of the Buddha's previous lives (the *Jātakas)* in Burmese, and they became very popular. The Sangha remained accessible to the Burmese people. Monasteries and shrines were built close to where the laity resided, giving access to monastic education and training for all who desired it. Today, Buddhism's place in Burma is secure and paramount.

CAMBODIA, THAILAND, AND LAOS

The boundaries of the contemporary countries of Cambodia, Thailand, and Laos do not necessarily correspond with those of the ancient kingdoms of the area. The peoples associated with them—Khmers, Thais, and Laos—were not necessarily the first in the area to practice Buddhism, but they often left the first records. Cambodian history traditionally begins in the first century A.D.,

A votive figure of a person adoring the Buddha. (Cambodian wood figure; sixteenth century.)

with the rise of the Kingdom of Funan on the India-China trade route. Buddhist traders and brahmins settled the area, bringing Indian religions, including a Sanskrit variety of Hīnayāna, as well as political and artistic culture. By the end of the fourth century, the region was thoroughly Indianized, with Indian influence extended to the population at large. Sanskrit inscriptions show that Hinduism and Mahāyāna Buddhism existed together by the fifth century A.D. A century later another strong Indianization took place. Though Funanese rulers were Hindu in these centuries, Buddhism was diffused throughout the kingdom and even enjoyed moderate royal patronage. A Chinese embassy came between 535 and 545 to seek Buddhist texts and teachers.

Khmer power increased in the late seventh century, but the accompanying prosperity favored both Hinduism and Buddhism. By 800 A.D., a unified Cambodian state was established with a god-king at the head of the state religion, which was distinctly Hindu of the Śaivite sect. Later rulers built monasteries for both Śaivites and Buddhists, and Hindu cults coexisted with Buddhism through the tenth century. Śaivism remained the main royal cult but Buddhism received continued patronage too. Some rulers in the eleventh century favored and promoted Buddhism, others blended various sects of Hinduism together, and still Buddhism, primarily Mahāyāna, continued.

It was during the late twelfth century that a monk from Burma introduced Theravāda into Cambodia. Later it was supported by Khmer kings and eventually supplanted Mahāyāna. Theravāda Buddhist monks were at the capital by the end of the thirteenth century, by which time the Cambodian state had dropped Hinduism for Theravāda. This situation remains today.

In the thirteenth century, small Thai states developed on the Indochinese peninsula. Previously, Cambodia and other Indianized states had influenced the area. When two Thai states gained dominance, they accepted influences from Burma and the Khmers. Most importantly, the Thais accepted Theravāda Buddhism from Burma. The king, Ramkham-haeng (late twelfth and early thirteenth centuries), was a patron of Theravāda, and inscriptions tell us that all the people were Buddhists, too. Bronze images of the Buddha produced in Thailand have been some of the finest in history.

Later, Thai kings in the fifteenth century borrowed Cambodian ideas of the ruler as god-king, used court brahmins and Brahmanical ceremonial, and adopted Hindu law. But Theravāda continued and, despite the court Brahmanism, Thais of all social classes considered themselves Buddhists. Buddhism at the popular level included monks who practiced magic and the Saṅgha filled a valuable social role in education and religion. Ceylon was the source of renewed Theravāda contacts for the Thais; the situation was reversed, however, in the eighteenth century, when Ceylon turned to Thailand for renewal of Buddhist knowledge and the ordination line. A Thai mission visited Ceylon to perform ordinations for monks and novices. Since that time, Thailand has remained Theravāda.

The Lao people emerged by the fourteenth century when, with the help of Khmer power, the first Laotian state was founded and Khmer missionaries introduced Theravāda. Previously, Mahāyāna was also in the area. Later kings defended and supported Theravāda Buddhism, which became the official religion of Laos by the fourteenth century.

INDONESIA

Indonesia was Hinduized by the fifth century A.D. after a long period of sea contacts with ports to its west. By that time Buddhist missionaries were also coming to the island, but brahmins had already brought the worship of Śiva. It was Śaivism that had royal patronage and prestige, and its devotionalism and forms of worship harmonized with preexisting Indonesian religion. In 671 A.D., the Chinese Buddhist pilgrim I-ching, on his way to Nālandā, stopped at Palembang in the kingdom of Śrivijaya. He found over one thousand monks, mostly Hīnayāna, and studied there before continuing on to India. Inscriptions also indicate that Mahāyāna Tantrism was practiced in Palembang before the close of the seventh century, grafting local Malay magical practices onto the imported Tantric methods of attaining power.

On the island of Java, the rulers of the Śailendra dynasty combined

Mahāyāna and Śaivism, with Tantrism linking the two. One of them, in about 800 A.D., built the greatest and most glorious of all stūpas, the one at Borobuḍur. This was a giant maṇḍala in stone, its bas-relief representing the pilgrim's search for enlightenment. Its circumambulation path leads past two

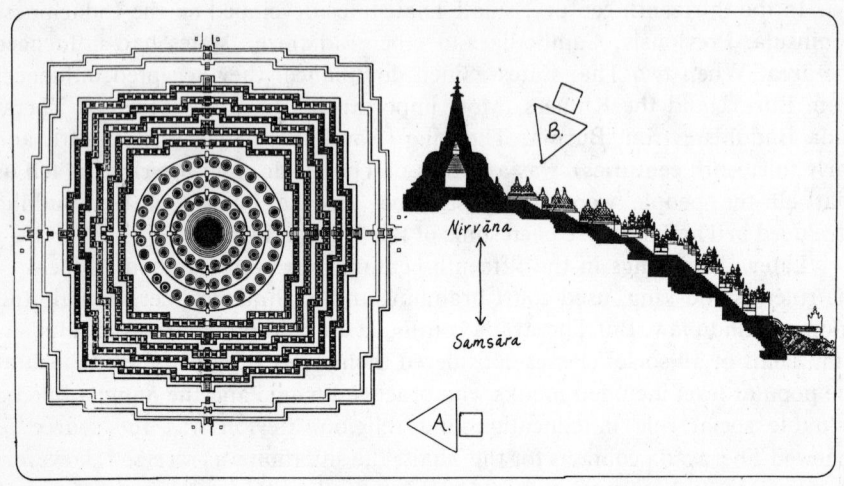

The Borobuḍur stūpa, a) ground plan, revealing its maṇḍala pattern, and b) cross-section of the ascent out of saṃsāra to nirvāṇa; Java, circa 800 A.D.

thousand and more reliefs depicting scenes from Śākyamuni's life, the Jātaka tales, and the Mahāyāna Sūtras. The ascent is a ritual journey through the material world, out of saṃsāra and into nirvāṇa. Only a half a century later, another Śailendra king constructed a great Śiva temple, indicating that both religions had been accepted as showing a way to salvation. The two shrines were also funerary monuments, symbolic of the dead kings' divine ascent to salvation. This form of Buddho-Śaivism continued until, by the end of the fourteenth century, Islām came to the islands and gradually converted all but those who took refuge on the eastern island of Bali. There a Hindu-Buddhist mysticism survives still today.

FROM CLASSICAL TO MODERN THERAVĀDA

We can understand the Buddhist religion only within its historical context. This survey of Theravāda history shows that it was not always in the ascendency in Southeast Asia, but that it succeeded when and where it received support from ruling hierarchies and wealthy patrons. Classical Theravāda has its roots in traditional agricultural forms of society. The world around it is rapidly changing into industrialized societies. The Saṅgha, which presupposes that everything changes, faces radical new changes in that world.

An advertisement for a Śrī Laṅka (Ceylon) bank. (From the publication *World Buddhism.)*

There are indications that Theravāda Buddhism is entering this new world. The World Fellowship of Buddhists has opened up greater avenues for lay participation in the Saṅgha, and fosters a Buddhist ecumenical movement that unites monk and laity, Hīnayāna and Mahāyāna. The sixth Buddhist Council, the most important event in recent Buddhist history, was held in Rangoon, Burma from 1954 to 1956. Scriptures were reedited and Buddhists thought about their Dharma together, as they had in the past. Within separate nations, movements such as the Buddhist Sunday School Movement (begun in Thailand in 1958) and lay meditation groups (originating in Burma and Thailand) indicate some renewed interest in bringing traditional Buddhist activities into the modern world. In Thailand, Buddhists have undertaken modernization, and in Ceylon and elsewhere monastic education has been improved. Buddhist politicians (U Nu and the late U Thant of Burma, Norodom Sihanouk of Cambodia) have indicated willingness to become involved in secular affairs, and Buddhists have generally supported neutralism and peaceful coexistence in Southeast Asia.

Curiously enough, the story of contemporary Asian Buddhism does not end in Southeast or East Asia. Bhimrao Ramji Ambedkar of India, late leader of Maharashtra's Untouchables, was responsible for leading 600,000 of his followers into the Buddhist fold in a mass conversion in 1956. Though identified with political strategy and the attainment of equal rights by Untouchables, this means that some Indians have become Buddhist again, at least in name.

THE RELIGIOUS LIFE OF CONTEMPORARY THERAVĀDA BUDDHISM

Recently, excellent empirical studies have described the Buddhist religion as it exists today in the Theravāda countries of Southeast Asia (see bibliography). A short summary of some of their findings will counteract the tendency to think of Buddhism only as a system of thought as it is preserved in its textual tradition, or solely as the practice of recluse monks who have cut themselves off from the world to cultivate exclusively their own spiritual growth. Buddhism exists as a religious practice in which lay and monastic Buddhists take equal part. By studying this empirical material, we see that Buddhism has a life of its own in the practical everyday world beyond what we have been able to describe in this book using ancient textual sources. We should keep in mind the whole religious life of Buddhists.

Another reason for describing contemporary Theravāda religious life is that in some respects it is probably remarkably similar to ancient Buddhism, which we today cannot observe directly since it has disappeared from the Indian scene. When the Chinese pilgrim Hsüan-tsang counted monks in the seventh century in India, he found that those of the Hīnayāna sects (of which Theravāda was one) outnumbered those of the Mahāyāna by 440,000 to 80,000, or almost six to one. Thus, whatever we can learn about the traditional (that is, nonurban) Buddhism of Southeast Asia can tell us something more of the practice of a major Hīnayāna sect, the longest surviving of any in history, and of ancient Indian Buddhism too. India and Southeast Asia are united to some extent by a common, ancient cultural substratum, an original indigenous religious practice which now has a mixed Buddhist and Hindu overlay. Its culture bears the stamp of Indian social and religious customs and conceptions that would have also been part of early Buddhism's environment.[1]

ABSOLUTE NIRVĀṆA AND RELATIVELY REAL SAṂSĀRA

In an anthropoligical description of village Buddhism in Burma, Spiro (1970) found not one Buddhist religious practice, but four.[2] Calling the Buddhism of the ancient texts normative or "nibbanic [nirvāṇic] Buddhism," he concludes that this religion of "radical salvation" (attainment of transcendent nirvāṇa) really is not practiced by most Burmese Buddhists. Spiro's evidence indicates that they do not search for cessation of rebirth (absolute deliverance) but for a better rebirth in the next life, expressed as a wish to continue living as a transmigrant individual in saṃsāra's Wheel of Life. He describes this as a shift to "kammatic [karmic] Buddhism," a religion of proximate (or worldly) salvation. Its followers seek to achieve, through the mechanisms of karman and merit, rebirth as wealthy humans or inhabitants of heavenly realms; or they consider nirvāṇa a superheavenly, blissful state. Two other attitude shifts correlate with this basic change. First, the self is not considered impermanent, on the contrary, its persistence in future rebirths is primary to Burmese Buddhists, who rely for this view on an older, pre-Buddhist notion of the "butterfly self." The second shift sees the solution to the problem of suffering not in the elimination of desire, but in eliminating the frustration of that desire through merit-produced, better rebirth states to come. Since donation and morality yield merit and thus more favorable rebirths, they are this Buddhism's principal soteriological acts, which may account for why very few Burmese in Spiro's sample actually meditated.

How are we to look at these conclusions? Spiro admits that they probably did not characterize ancient Indian Buddhism, pointing out that its adherents came from classes of people whose desires were largely satisfied, not frustrated, as witness the case of the Buddha himself. Thus, what Spiro describes may best be thought of as a popular worldly or samsaric Buddhism. Saṃsāra is not unreal or a total illusion, but only relatively real (which is enough). This denies as false the disjunction which most philosophers would maintain, claiming that reality must be either real or not-real, an Aristotelian conclusion. A relatively real saṃsāra is (or can be) relatively enjoyable. If rebirths will continue endlessly, and merit will lead to better and better positions on the Wheel of Life, why not aspire to better fates? The nirvanic Buddhist criticism of such relative soteriological aspirations would be that lives, however enjoyable, are endless and always end in painful death. Such a Buddhist would claim that many will take a much longer time to realize this, trying all the while to resolve the problem of suffering within the physical realm by eliminating desire's frustrations, and not desire itself. For them, though, such a project can never be successful anywhere within the Wheel of Life, even in the highest heavens. But for those in lower human rebirths, the karmic burden is so great that most will not be able to realize their mistake (seeking to do away with frustration rather than desire) until much more experience (including better rebirths in which they may be able to obtain more self-insight) teaches them the truth. Such arguments, however, mean little to most people.

Spiro found two more "Buddhisms" practiced in the Burmese village he studied. One, "apotropaic Buddhism," concerns itself with problems of this existence—health, enough rain for crops, and personal escape from calamity. It tries to influence developments by specific magical acts which create power to change the course of events immediately, or to enlist the help of divine forces to do so. This is a religion of magical protection, using Buddhist means (devotions, rituals, morality, and scriptures) to effect its ends. The other form is esoteric Burmese Buddhism, which Spiro calls a religion of chiliastic (awaiting a King) expectations. It syncretizes occult traditions from India, China, and indigenous sources with Buddhist doctrine. These esoteric sects require special initiation, as opposed to exoteric Buddhism. Some of these sects are eschatological; aspirants practice alchemy to prolong life until the future Buddha, Maitreya, arrives, when they can attain nirvāṇa in that much more favorable time. Other sects Spiro found were millennial, awaiting a Future King; still others, messianic.

THERAVĀDA BUDDHISM IN ITS RELIGIOUS ENVIRONMENT

Buddhism is only the dominant system of Southeast Asian religion. We have already seen that it is a heterogeneous religious practice in itself, including absolute and relative soteriologies. Two other religious orientations are present in Buddhism's environment. One derives from the indigenous cultural substratum of the particular area. In Burma, for example, a thriving cult of spirits *(nats)* exists, actively followed by most Burmese. Ultimately, this cult is integrated into Buddhism. Secondly, various vestigial forms of Hindu influence remain, particularly in life-cycle rituals, which, as in ancient India, are not the concern of Buddhist monks. This remains true in Burma where all rites of passage are non-Buddhist, except for death and the initiation of boys when they are temporarily inducted as novice monks. Often, descendants of brahmins continue to perform these rites along with others to produce auspicious conditions. Probably Buddhism's relations with these is similar to its relations with such elements in ancient India.

THE THERAVĀDA MONASTERY

The life of Buddhist monks and the monastery is little changed from its ancient Indian models, already described. The ancient Vinaya rule continues to govern corporate Buddhist life, making contemporary Theravāda monasteries remarkably like their ancient Indian counterparts. Monks may travel anywhere except during retreat, but only for a serious purpose. The monastery is always located beyond the village boundaries, and monks are forbidden to enter the village except in pursuit of some religious duty (going for alms, to chant protective paritta verses (spells), or attend a funeral). The Buddhist monk makes no pastoral calls on members of the laity. There is relatively little interaction between monk and villager except when the former leads recitations of the precepts on holy days or attends special occasions (funerals or crisis events at which he chants protective verses). Several times a year he officiates at initiation ceremonies, and on special occasions the laity come to the monastery to feed the monks a special meal. The monk also preaches the Dharma, either at the monastery or in the village chapel, especially during Buddhist Lent (the rainy season). Layfolk sometimes come to the monastery for advice.

Daily life in the monastery begins at five in the morning (before dawn), when monks or novices sweep the compound (the only physical labor allowed Theravāda monks apart from going to seek alms). The monk then says his daily devotions and for an hour has tea with his novices. Around seven they all leave to beg for alms, eating their main meal of the day between nine and ten after returning and bathing. Free for a while because his novices are studying, the monk may walk or study, nap or talk with a visitor. He takes his last meal of the day before noon, not eating again until the next morning. At liberty again until the middle of the afternoon, he next teaches boys attending the monastery school. Traditionally, in Burma, monks have been the school-masters for the village children. After the students leave, he has another free interval until five or six, when he studies with or teaches his novices. They say their devotions around eight in the evening and by nine have retired.

PSYCHOLOGICAL OBSERVATIONS OF BURMESE BUDDHIST MONKS

Though we know something of the externals of the monk's life in ancient India from texts and other literature, particularly the Vinaya, we have no objective psychological observations on ancient Buddhist monks. Spiro offers some examination of village Burmese monks from his descriptive, scientific point of view. He distinguishes monks who entered the Order directly, after being monastery students and not returning to lay life, from those who entered after adult experience of the world. Those who became monks after lay life gave three sorts of reasons for leaving the world to join the Order: desire to leave a difficult life, desire to be relieved of social and family responsibilities, and personal tragedy and frustration. These are conscious, stated motivations that monks reported in interviews. Spiro further considers unconscious motivations to be at work on determining which lay people, in the face of the kind of worldly difficulties that everyone is likely to experience, retire to a monastery and which do not. He found that three sorts of characteristics, present both in monks and nonmonks, could be more easily satisfied in the monastery than outside it. These are: (1) the need for dependence, desire to be taken care of by others (monks are served by their novices as well as by the laity) and to be released from responsibilities for self and others; (2) narcissism or self-absorption, and preoccupation with self; and (3) emotional timidity, the desire to live alone (despite the boredom) and not form social relationships.

His evidence also led him to conclude that Burmese Buddhist monks possess psychological traits similar to those of nonmonks. He found that the typical situation was that monastic life did not transform the monk from a worldling to someone less worldly. Most monks see salvation in kammatic rather than nibbanic terms. Thus, despite their normative commitment to radical self-transformation, most monks retain many of the characteristics and values of nonmonks. Finally, he did find that monks were remarkably true to their vows and monastic rule. He discovered no deviation from sexual prohibi-tions. The monk partakes of the relatively comfortable and carefree life of the monastery in exchange for giving up marriage, that "blessed bond of board and bed," and its responsibilities.

POPULAR RELIGIOUS LIFE

Popular religious life for the faithful includes devotions at the household shrine at the beginning and end of each day, and public devotions every evening in the village chapel after dark. Buddhist sabbath, or duty, days fall on the full and new moons and eight days after each of these, following the Indian custom. The devout lay sabbath observer may spend the day at the monastic compound which would be located close to the village. Such attendance would be merit-producing since it is a time to renew the vows upon which merit depends, and to communicate with the monks.

The annual religious cycle is fairly standard throughout Southeast Asia, following the seasonal agricultural (rice) cycle. The New Year is celebrated in April with a festival of three or four days, often involving water in various ways. Buddha Day (ancient *Vaiśākha)* comes in May, commemorating his birth, Enightenment, and death. The beginning of the rain retreat for monks in July initiates the period of Buddhist "Lent." The three months until October are a time of increased solemnity and piety. Marriages are not performed, many young men enter the monastery as novices (but stay only for the one season), and villagers specially visit the monastery. There they listen to sermons and rigorously follow their precepts, often adding to the five prescribed for the laity the next three usually followed only by monks. It is a time of piety and asceticism.

The Lenten season ends in October, beginning a period of festivals and the special time of the year for merit-winning by the laity through donation to the monks. At this time the monks of the village monastery are provided with most of their material needs for the following year in elaborate ceremonies, thus gaining merit for the donors.

Popular worship throughout the year includes attendance at stūpas or shrines (Burma: pagoda; Ceylon: dāgäba; Thailand: wat, 'temple'); taking the Three Refuges (in the Buddha, the Dharma, and the Saṅgha); making offerings to the Buddha, his relics, and symbols; and pilgrimage. Offerings venerate and honor the Buddha as worship did in ancient India. In the daily devotions before the Buddha image, and during attendance at the temple, shrine, or stūpa, offerings of candles, incense, food, flowers, and water are made. Before any image or reminder of the Buddha, physical prostration is appropriate; as in India, before entering any sacred area, footwear is removed. Various forms of verbal behavior, petitions, incantations, and devotions are used. The diverse kinds of stūpas that fill Southeast Asian sacred areas are the most important physical structures in this worship. The cult of Buddha relics is popular, especially the cult of the famous sacred Buddha tooth at the Temple of the Tooth in Kandy, Ceylon. Buddha images of great beauty are worshipped throughout the area and, indeed, are testament to the generous support and enthusiastic piety of Buddhism's laity.

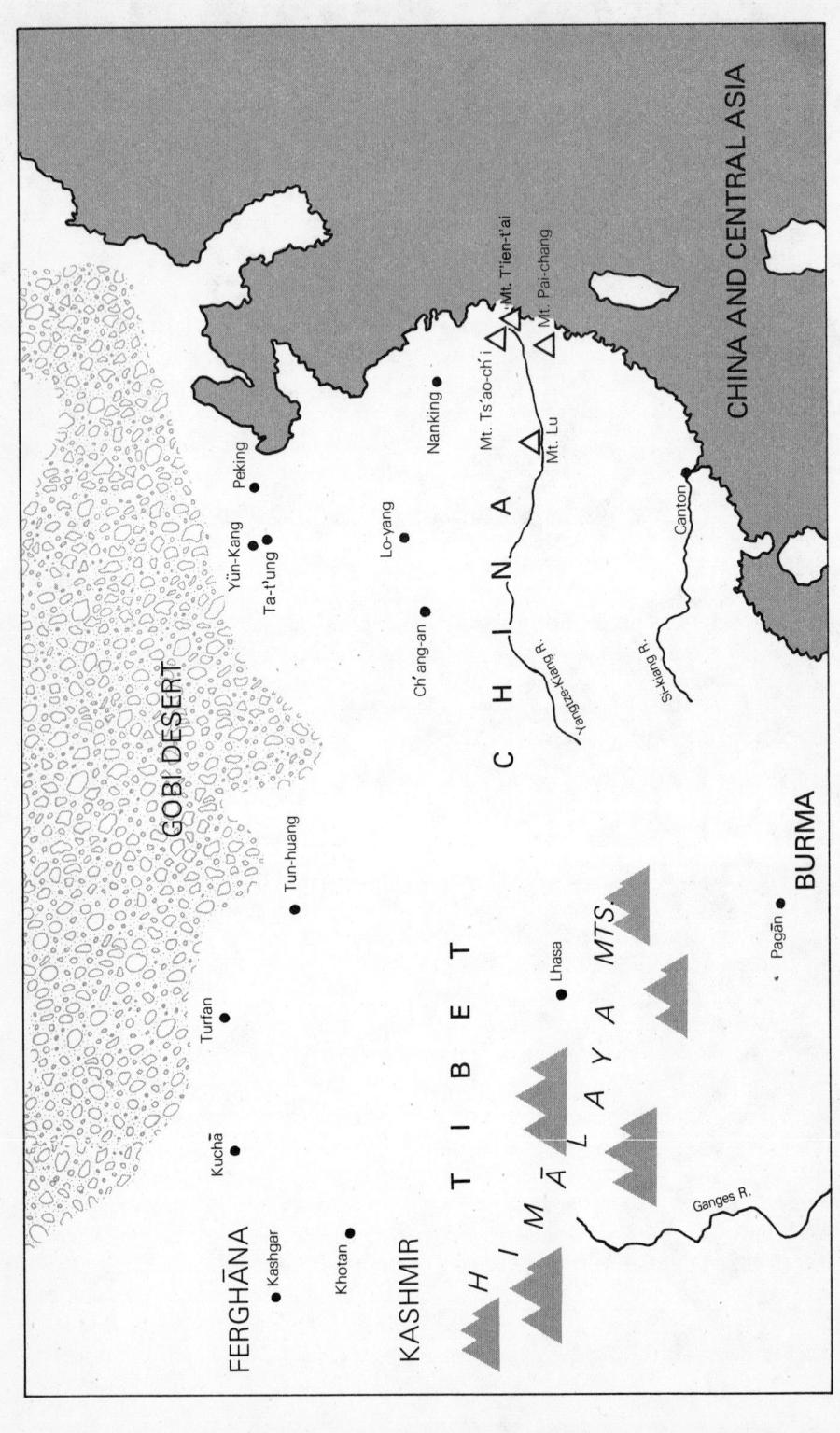

9.
The Buddhism of East Asia

INTRODUCTION OF BUDDHISM INTO CHINA[1]

In the first century A.D., the new and strong Later Han dynasty extended Chinese power into Central Asia, where the various small kingdoms owed their prosperity to the silk trade between China and the West. Serindian (Central Asian) merchant colonies—Khotanese, Sogdians, Parthians, Kucheans, and Kuṣāṇas—settled in an arc of cities from Tun-huang in the northwest to the Huai valley. Their families often stayed in China for generations and became bilingual and bicultural. As some of these people were Buddhists, they welcomed and accommodated the monks who traveled with the caravans. The Chinese, despite their fabled antipathy to learning from foreigners, have always loved exotica; and no doubt the orange-robed monks filled them with the same kind of wonder as parakeets from Cambodia and horses from Ferghāna (Tadži-kistan, in Central Asia). China has also cherished throughout the ages an addiction to magic, and the men of Han promptly recognized the kinship between the bhikṣu and the indigenous shaman and wizard-hermit. By the mid-century, Chinese patricians were giving donation feasts, and monks were a familiar sight in the capital.

Translating Indian Ideas into Chinese

The first notable translator, the Parthian An Shih-kao, arrived in 148 A.D. at Lo-yang, the capital, where he worked for twenty years translating short treatises on meditation and Abhidharma. The first known Chinese monk was his disciple, and the beginnings of Buddhist literature in Chinese went hand in hand with the formation of a Chinese Saṅgha.

Lokakṣema, the first known Mahāyāna missionary, worked in Lo-yang between 168 and 188. He translated the *Small Perfect Wisdom Sūtra* and the *Sukhāvatī-vyūha*. The cult of Amida made no impression at that time, but Chinese familiar with the fourth century B.C. Taoist philosopher Chuang-tzu were intrigued by Prajñā-pāramitā thought and demanded fresh trans-lations of the Sūtras from each successive missionary, though it was not until the early fifth century that they really understood the Buddhist emptiness teachings. Chuang-tzu had prepared the Chinese intelligentsia, giving them a sense of the emptiness of the Absolute as well as the essential meaninglessness of conventional values. Also, his mystical emphasis on becoming one with the boundless Tao through contemplative exercises accorded well with Buddhist ideas concerning the ineffable attainment of nirvāṇa.

The Later Han regime fell apart during the latter half of the second century. As magic is commonly the resort of the desperate, many of the gentry soon followed the path the peasants had taken decades earlier and sought strength and security in the occult. Their interest in Buddhism at this time focused on meditation as a means of obtaining paranormal powers. Only some of these gentlemen became monks; others served as scribes and assistants to the foreign monks or practiced meditation as lay recluses.

The work of translation and evangelization continued through the third century and came to fruition in the period of the western Chin dynasty (265–316). Dharmarakṣa, "the bodhisattva from Tun-huang," worked in north China from 266 to 308. Born in China of Sycthian ancestry, Dharmarakṣa was one of the most important translator-monks during this formative period of Buddhism in China. Being skilled in Chinese as well as Central Asian and Indian languages, he was able to translate a large number of Sūtras. Under him the Chinese Saṅgha reached the takeoff point. His disciples established monasteries, lectured on the Sūtras, ordained monks, and proselytized vigorously. The sacking of the capitals at the end of the western Chin period served to disperse Dharmarakṣa's school to other parts of the country and thus disseminate a new vigorous and intellectual style of Buddhism. The process was repeated often during the centuries of political division. Monasteries and libraries were often burned, but what the Saṅgha lost in security it gained in mobility and communication.

The monks in south China under the eastern Chin dynasty (317–419) lived peacefully and gradually insinuated themselves into the highest gentry circles by their adroit use of literary wit and personal urbanity. In the north, monks lived dangerously under the rule of "barbarian" chieftains, among a mixed population of Chinese, Tibetans, and Altaic tribesmen. A monk of Central Asiatic origin, the brave and righteous old Kuchean wonder-worker, Fo-t'u-teng, arrived in north China around 310. He became a counselor to Shih Lo, leader of the Hunnish state of Later Chao, and served as court advisor for over twenty years, performing magic, involving monks in politics, mitigating the excesses of the barbarian rulers, and training a cadre of disciplined and enterprising Chinese monks.

Tao-an (312–385) was the most illustrious of Fo-t'u-teng's disciples. Though driven from place to place by the incessant civil wars, he lectured on the Prajñā-pāramitā Sūtras, collected copies of the scriptures and prepared the first catalog of them, invited foreign monks and supported their translation work, and promoted devotion to Maitreya.

His disciple Hui-yüan (334–416/417) ran a school for gentleman monks and scholars in which he reinterpreted the Confucian and Taoist classics in a Buddhist sense, encouraged the writing of Buddhist devotional poetry in a typical Chinese style, and founded a society for meditation on Amitābha. He settled on Mount Lu and spent the last thirty years of his life there, letting the world come to him (as it did), and the armies pass him by. He staunchly defended the autonomy of the Saṅgha against the state, insisting that the monk is not obliged to kowtow to the ruler.

Thanks to the efforts of Tao-an and Hui-yüan, a sizable intellectual elite in the Saṅgha was ready to receive the great Kuchean translator Kumārajīva (344-413) when he reached the capital, Ch'ang-an, in 401. Already famous as a Buddhist monk well versed in doctrine, Kumārajīva was a major figure whose works were instrumental in transmitting Buddhism, especially Mādhyamika, to China. With the patronage of the king of Ch'in, Kumārajīva and a large team of Chinese collaborators revised (or redid) the translations of the most popular Sūtras which had been done by his predecessors and translated four Mādhyamika treatises, introducing Nāgārjuna's teachings to the Chinese. His translations were elegant and intelligible, though not always accurate. To this day they are in general use, in preference to the more accurate translations of the later Buddhist pilgrim and translator Hsüan-tsang (circa 596-664).

The three generations of Chinese intellectual monks from Tao-an to Kumārajīva's disciples are called the Buddho-Taoists, because they discussed Buddhism in a Taoist vocabulary and sought in Buddhism solutions to Neo-Taoist problems such as the relation of the Holy Man to the world, whether he really acts, and whether he feels compassion. For example, Seng-chao, in his essay "Prajñā Has No Knowing," tried to communicate the Buddhist idea that the Holy Man acts, but without self-preoccupation or purposive emotion towards the beneficiary, in keeping with Mādhyamika ethics. To convey this idea to his Chinese readers, Seng-chao, another disciple of Kumārajīva's, quoted from Chapter 5 of the familiar Taoist classic of Lao Tzu, the *Tao Te Ching*, writing, "The holy man's good works are as mighty as Heaven and Earth, yet he is not humane." Any Chinese reader would have recognized the allusion in this last phrase, "is not humane," and understood the analogy it draws between the Buddhist Holy Man's compassionate but detached action and that of the Tao (Heaven and Earth) which acts without favor or special feeling for one or another of its beneficiaries. The last luminary in this movement was, in fact, Kumārajīva's young disciple, Seng-chao (374-414). His four surviving essays are outstanding expressions of Śūnyavāda in Chinese vocabulary and literary form. Kumārajīva's school was dispersed when the Ch'in kingdom fell. Some of his disciples fled south, and a few went west to the warlord state of Kansu.

The Chinese Saṅgha and the State

Throughout the fifth and early sixth centuries, north and south China pursued separate courses, the south under native dynasties and the north under "barbarian" rulers. Southern Buddhists continued literary activity, producing new translations, debating doctrinal issues, lecturing, and commenting on the principal Sūtras.

Northern Buddhism during the fifth century excelled in works rather than ideas. Intellectual laity and monks had mostly fled south when the northern Wei "barbarians" (386–534) conquered Ch'in and seized Ch'ang-an in 418. The founder of this dynasty favored Buddhism, forbade his troups to pillage the Saṅgha's premises, and ordered the officers in his capital to erect Buddha-images and provide dwellings for monks. He appointed a moral and learned monk to the civil service post of Saṅgha-director, thus establishing government jurisdiction over the monasteries in his realm. Unlike Hui-yüan in the south, the monk appointed did not fight for the independence of the Saṅgha from the state, but kowtowed to the emperor and justified this seeming contravention of the monastic rule by identifying the emperor with the Tathāgata!

Buddhism flourished and spread in northern Wei until excessive prosperity led to corruption within the Saṅgha and intrigues by jealous Taoists and Confucians. In 446, an edict decreed the destruction of Sūtras, images, and paintings, and the execution of monks. Many monks were able to go into hiding, taking Sūtras and images with them; but many temples and scriptures were destroyed, and some monks were put to death.

A new emperor decreed an end to the proscription in 454. From then on, northern Wei rulers patronized Buddhism lavishly and employed monks in responsible civil service posts.

Shortly after 460, the Saṅgha-director persuaded the emperor to undertake one of the world's great religious monuments, the cave temples of Yün-kang. Twenty grottoes were excavated in a limestone cliff several miles from the capital, Ta-t'ung. The earliest caves contain giant stone Buddha-images, while the walls of later ones are sculptured profusely with scenes from the Sūtras, the life of the Buddha, bodhisattvas, celestial beings, spirits, and human donors. The project was an act of expiation for the persecution of Buddhism, an indication of imperial favor to the religion, and an attempt to create an expression of the Dharma that would withstand the ravages of time and persecution.

DEVELOPMENT OF SCHOOLS (LINEAGES)

Chinese Buddhism, both northern and southern, became sectarian during the sixth century. It should be noted that, though Chinese *tsung* is translated "sect" or "school," it denotes a wider range of institutions than either English word. In the classics *tsung* means "clan shrine; clan." Buddhists borrowed the terminology. A tsung consists of people who trace their Dharma-descent to a common *tsu* (ancestor, founder, patriarch).

One sign that Buddhism was acculturating to China in the sixth century was the interest shown by great masters in tracing their spiritual and scholarly lineage back to Śākyamuni. To do this, they had to eke out and cobble together Indian lists and names, sometimes filling the gaps with outright fabrications. The felt need was evidently acute. In Chinese eyes, a teaching was vouched for not by guaranteeing the general manner of its transmission (as

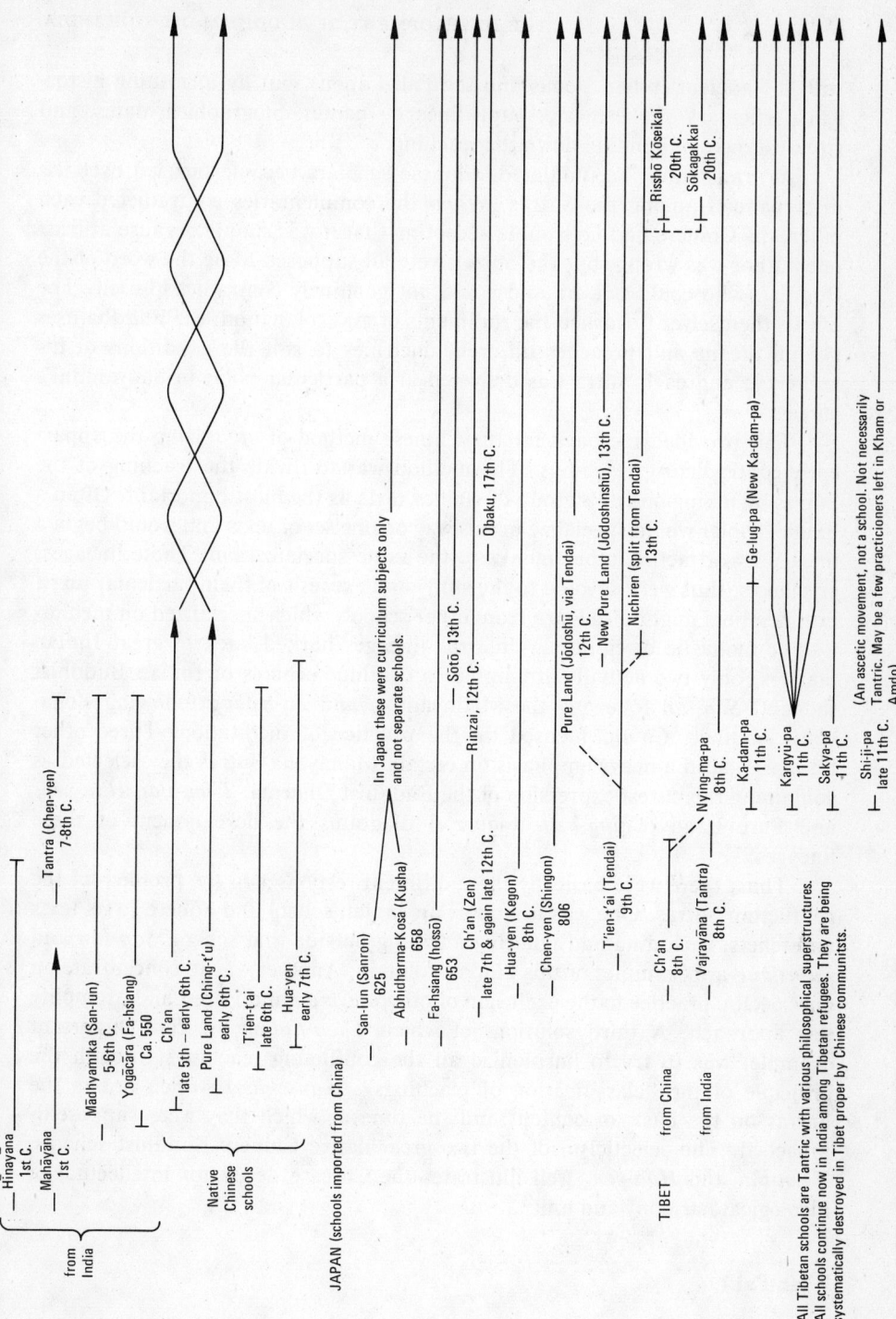

with the ancient Indian Vedas and the Pali Canon), but by furnishing historical particulars of the master-pupil lineage—names, biographies, dates, and
circumstances of handing down the teaching.

As translations accumulated, Chinese scholars became puzzled over the
discrepancies among the Sūtras. When the commentaries contradicted each
other, the Chinese had no trouble accepting that it was simply because at least
one author was wrong; but the Sūtras were all supposed to be the word of the
Buddha, who could not err and could not genuinely contradict himself. The
Sūtras themselves furnished the rudiments of an explanation: the Buddha uses
skillful means and preaches different doctrines to suit the conditions of his
audience, and each Sūtra was delivered at a particular point in Śākyamuni's
career.

This provided the basis for the Chinese method of organizing the apparently contradictory teachings. The method was to divide the teaching of the
Sūtras by taking one or a group of similar texts as the most important. Often a
monk-scholar would specialize in this way on one set of texts and would begin a
lineage by attracting other monks to the same specialization. These lineages,
or schools, thus were devoted to the study and exegesis of their particular texts,
but members might also learn from other schools which specialized on meditation or monastic discipline. While the lineages harked back to great Indian
masters, only two actually attempted to continue schools of Indian Buddhist
thought, San-lun following the Mādhyamika and Fa-hsiang following Yogācāra. Another, Ch'an, focused on the practice of meditation. Three other
lineages placed a heavy emphasis on certain Mahāyāna Sūtras they selected as
containing the purest expression of the Buddhist Dharma: T'ien-t'ai, Hua-yen,
and Pure Land (Ching-t'u). Figure 3 diagrams the development of these
lineages.

Thus, there were basically three different responses to the problem of the
conflicting Sūtras. One was to import an Indian school and adhere to its texts
and tenets, excluding and ignoring anything outside that school. San-lun and
Fa-hsiang are examples of this kind of solution. Another was to concentrate on
one specific practice to the exclusion of others. Ch'an and Pure Land exemplify
this approach. A third solution, of which T'ien-t'ai is the first important
example, was to try to harmonize all the conflicting teachings through the
principle of the "classification of teachings" (p'an-chiao), which orders the
Sūtras on the basis of content and the time at which they were supposedly
preached. The eclecticism of the two great native Chinese Buddhist schools,
T'ien-t'ai and Hua-yen, well illustrates the Chinese desire for intellectual or
ideological harmony and unity.

T'ien-t'ai

The T'ien-t'ai school took the *Lotus Sūtra* as the authoritative expression of
Buddhism, using it to harmonize and explain all the different doctrines found

in the Sūtras. It also brought into one system the two geographically-based divergent emphases in the developing Chinese Buddhism, uniting the northern penchant for practical action, exemplified in meditation and pious works, with the southern love of philosophical debate, discussion, and elitist intellectualism. A further harmonization it made was the incorporation of both sides of the "gradual" and "sudden" enlightenment controversy which had been flourishing for at least a century prior to this school's rise.

The goal to which all this was directed was enlightenment. The doctrine and practice are "expedient means" designed to direct one along the path, but when the goal is reached, path and goal alike vanish in the transcendent realm. This combines Mādhyamika (Nāgārjuna's metaphysics of emptiness) with soteriology. In the meantime, the great doctrinal synthesis, the classification and explanation of teachings, could well be described as a Chinese Mahāyāna Abhidharma.

This T'ien-t'ai quasi-Abhidharma was based on the idea of the threefold truth, which claims all dharmas are: (1) empty, since they arise because of causes and conditions and have no substantiality; (2) temporary, since they are transient; and (3) middle, since they are both empty but temporarily existent. The dharmas are particular and distinct because of (2), but are also one, a unity, because they are all empty (1). The system also considers that all worlds and all beings in the ever-changing Wheel of Life, from Buddhas to dwellers in the hells, are interpenetrating, constituting a single organic unity present in every single moment of thought. All beings have Buddha-nature and can be saved. The school emphasized meditation, therefore, to gain the insight required to perceive this ultimate truth of the emptiness of the dharmas.

The lineage of the T'ien-t'ai sect begins with Hui-ssǔ (515-576). He "went forth" (left his family and social position to join the Buddhist Order) when he was fifteen, and resolved at twenty that it was his vocation to save all mankind. He practiced asceticism and meditation, and attained the Dharma-Lotus samādhi, induced by weeks of alternately reciting and meditating on the *Lotus Sūtra*. After much fasting and meditation, he had a dream in which he sat in Maitreya's assembly on a giant lotus flower. He wept, thinking "In the Latter-day Dharma I have received the *Lotus Sūtra*, and now I have met Maitreya." This spurred him to even greater zeal, and many wondrous omens appeared.

The phrase "Latter-day Dharma" comes from the *Lotus Sūtra*. Indian texts distinguish three Dharma periods: (1) the True Dharma (0-500 A.N.), (2) the Counterfeit Dharma (501-1000 or 1500 A.N.), and (3) the Latter-day Dharma (expected to last 10,000 years). Sixth-century Chinese put the Nirvāṇa at 949 B.C., so they thought that the Latter-day Period began about 550 A.D. Most of the great sectarian patriarchs offered the advent of the Last Age as a reason why their teaching was necessary and timely. As preachers are always prone to do, they exploited the idea that the present age is sinful and degenerate in order to goad people into religious exertion. The *Lotus*, the *Diamond-Cutter*, and other Mahāyāna Sūtras say that people who uphold the True

Dharma in the Last Time will earn immeasurable merit. Chinese and Japanese followers of the *Lotus Sūtra* correctly discerned the intent of such passages and often felt that they themselves were called to the leading of holy lives in the last degenerate days of the Buddhist Dharma.

To escape the dangers of war, Hui-ssŭ moved south to a mountain where he spent the rest of his life. Secluded mountain monasteries had been institutionalized by famous monks of eastern Chin (317-420), especially Hui-yüan. Such an environment favored study and meditation more than the busy metropolitan monasteries that enjoyed imperial favor through their proximity to the court. Most of the great sects, or tsungs, started in the mountain temples and moved into the capital after achieving considerable success in the provinces. And most of the tsung lost their original purity and spiritual integrity amid the busyness and intrigue that accompanied fame and fortune. Schools that did not maintain a base in mountain monasteries perished when imperial disfavor, persecution, or internal degeneracy overtook them.

While Hui-ssŭ was the first of the T'ien-t'ai lineage, his disciple Chih-i is often recognized as the organizer of this school. Chih-i (538–597), "the great master of T'ien-t'ai," became Hui-ssŭ's disciple, practiced Dharma-Lotus meditation, and attained samādhi when reading a passage in the *Lotus Sūtra* about a bodhisattva who burned his own body in a sandalwood fire as an offering to the Buddha. Later the master appointed Chih-i to lecture on the Prajñā-pāramitā Sūtras and the *Lotus;* when Hui-ssŭ went south, he turned the leadership of the Community over to Chih-i (who was then twenty-nine).

Chih-i and his followers spent the next eight years in Nanking, the capital of the Ch'en dynasty. Disgusted with the dissolute and turbulent life of the capital, he then withdrew to Mount T'ien-t'ai, in Chekiang, from which the T'ien-t'ai-tsung takes its name.

Chih-i laid equal emphasis on meditation and doctrine study, on self-cultivation and propagating the Teaching. Though he insisted that he was a plain practicer of meditation and not a philosopher, his doctrinal system is an architectonic marvel. It is a vast syncretism designed to comprise and harmonize all Buddhist doctrines. He accepted Hui-ssŭ's thesis that the *Lotus* rather than the *Nirvāṇa Sūtra* contains Śākyamuni's highest teaching, and that each of the other Sūtras speaks on several different levels because it is addressing a mixed audience. T'ien-t'ai distinguishes five periods in Śākyamuni's teaching career; four methods of teaching in Sūtras prior to the *Lotus:* sudden, gradual, secret indeterminate, and explicit indeterminate; and four modes of doctrine: the Tripiṭaka teaching (= Hīnayāna), the pervasive teaching (= Śūnyavāda), the special teaching (= Yogācāra), and the round or perfect teaching (= the *Lotus* doctrine).

The Community on Mount T'ien-t'ai prospered with patronage from the Sui imperial family for two decades after Chih-i's death, but declined under the T'ang rulers, who did not appreciate the sect's close connections with the preceding dynasty. In the eighth century, T'ien-t'ai revived under the great master Chan-jan (711–781), who inspired some notable lay disciples to encompass Buddhism and Confucianism within one syncretic system. Out of this enterprise arose the Neo-Confucian school, which, ironically, became the most enduring and destructive of all Buddhism's enemies.

San-lun

The Mādhyamika school from India was continued in China in San-lun, the Three-treatise sect. The four Mādhyamika treatises translated by Kumārajīva were studied by a few scholars throughout the fifth century. For example, Chih-i drew heavily on the fourth, the *Great Perfection of Wisdom Treatise,* for his early lectures on meditation, and composed a commentary to it. But for Chih-i, Mādhyamika, the doctrine of emptiness, was just one ingredient among many, and he had little relish for dialectic, which is the heart of Nāgārjuna's system.

The greatest master of the San-lun (Three-Treatise) school was Chi-tsang (549–623). In distinction from other masters of Chinese lineages, he rejected "classification of teachings" as a wrongheaded enterprise. Otherwise, the Three Treatise doctrine is quite simply a restatement of Nāgārjuna's teaching in a new vocabulary, with a few additional theses on matters such as the Two Truths where Nāgārjuna was too brief and vague.

The Three Treatise lineage died out after Chi-tsang. He was not a meditation master, and the Chinese were not prepared by their type of education to pursue enlightenment through the therapeutic exercise of dialectic.

Fa-hsiang

Yogācāra was introduced to China by Paramārtha (arrived in 546), whose most influential translation was that of Asaṅga's *Compendium of Mahāyāna.* A

The Chinese pilgrim Hsüan-tsang, with his pack. (From a Chinese painting.)

school grew up around this text, and it was perplexity about certain points in it that prompted Hsüan-tsang (596-664) to go to India and study. He spent fifteen months studying Yogācāra at Nālandā, went on a tour through south India, came back to Nālandā and studied some more, was accorded an audience and much honor by the Emperor Harṣa, and returned to China with a large collection of Sanskrit manuscripts. He spent the rest of his life translating the texts he had brought back and teaching Yogācāra to his pupils. His disciple K'uei-chi (632-682) is reckoned as the founder of the Fa-hsiang (dharma-mark) school, which soon died out in China. However, it has survived in Japan and was revived in China about 1908 by Yang Wen-hui, the father of the Chinese Buddhist revival.

Hua-yen

The Hua-yen sect was started by Tu-shun (557-640). As a boy he worked as a laborer in a military service batallion. At eighteen he went forth and devoted himself to meditation, attaining miracle-working powers and becoming highly renowned. He concentrated on the *Avataṃsaka Sūtra (Hua-yen Ching)* just as Hui-ssŭ concentrated on the *Lotus Sūtra.* The third in line was Fa-tsang (643-712), the great architect of the school. In his young days he worked in Hsüan-tsang's translation bureau, and in his old age he assisted Śikṣānanda in the retranslation of the *Avataṃsaka.* He served as preceptor to four emperors and wrote voluminously. Two eminent masters followed Fa-tsang: Ch'eng-kuan (738/737-838/820), and Tsung-mi (780-841). The sect did not survive the general suppression of Buddhism in 845.

The Hua-yen "classification of teachings" assigns top place to the *Avataṃsaka,* and the school's metaphysics centers on the concept of the Dharma-realm expounded in the Sūtra. The Dharma-realm has two aspects: as noumenon *(li),* it is the realm of suchness, of transcendental and immanent Dharma. As phenomenon *(shih),* it is the realm of the dharmas, the conditioned world of rebirth. The Hīnayānist sees the Dharma-realm of phenomena. Mādhyamika and Yogācāra, says Hua-yen, see the Dharma-realm of noumena. T'ien-t'ai and the *Awakening of Faith* (a Chinese Yogācāra text falsely attributed to Aśvaghoṣa) are said to consider a Dharma-realm where phenomena and noumena do not impede each other. The Hua-yen teaching claims to see a Dharma-realm where phenomena do not impede each other but enter into, and are identical with, each other.

The Hua-yen doctrine is not so much a rational philosophy as a galaxy of concepts arrayed for contemplation. This kind of intellectual discipline is a very hard road to samādhi, and in any place or time very few are ready for it.

T'ien-t'ai and Hua-yen succeeded better than San-lun and Fa-hsiang, because they were Chinese adaptations rather than Indian transplants. They did not engage much in formal arguments and proofs, for which the native Chinese tradition had little fondness. In China, gentlemen refrain from argument. Another strength of T'ien-t'ai and Hua-yen was that they gratified the endemic Chinese penchant for harmonizing things, that they assured unity in doctrine while permitting a full panoply of individual options. Since the third century B.C., Chinese thought has usually considered unity in ideas as a factor of sociopolitical unity and has abhorred dissension in either realm.

The all-inclusiveness of T'ien-t'ai and Hua-yen diffused the energies of the individual and of the sects. Furthermore, they required a high degree of education and much book study. Starting from similar origins—mountain monks studying one Sūtra and meditating on it—there arose several popular sects during the sixth century, each of which radically simplified its statement of doctrine and advocated the exclusive and intense pursuit of some one practice. Some of these cults professed pessimism about the latter-day world, but they all fostered hope, enhanced faith in the efficacy of devout action, and released a torrent of religious energy. The two chief popular sects were the Ching-t'u-tsung (Pure Land) and the meditation school Ch'an-tsung (Japanese: Zen).

Pure Land

T'an-luan (476–542), the first master in the Pure Land lineage, got his religious vocation when, convalescing from a grave illness, he saw a vision of a heavenly gate opening to him. Deciding to seek everlasting life, he sought it first in Taoism, which professed to have recipes for lengthening this life into an immortal one. Then he met the Indian Bodhiruci, who told him that Buddhism possessed a superior method of gaining everlasting life and taught him the Amitābha texts. T'an-luan was convinced, burned his Taoist books, and concentrated on getting to the Pure (Happy) Land. He organized societies for recitation of Amitābha's name, and propagated the Pure Land cult with great success. He also laid the foundations of sectarian doctrine. He declared that even those who have committed evil deeds and atrocities are eligible for rebirth in the Western Paradise if they sincerely desire it. But he maintained that those who revile the Dharma are excluded, for one thing, because blasphemy is not conducive to aspiration, and for another, because the retribution for blasphemy is repeated rebirth in the lowest hell. T'an-luan asserted that even the merit one seems to earn for oneself is facilitated by the overarching power of Amida's vows, and that birth in the Pure Land and attainment of Buddhahood there are due to vow power. His stress on Other-power led him to advocate faith and recitation of Amitābha's name rather than meditation.

The next great Pure Land master was Tao-ch'o (562-645). He was born twenty years after T'an-luan's death, and as a young monk happened across the latter's epitaph, the reading of which deeply affected him and turned his course to the Pure Land teaching. He was the first Pure Land master to stress latter-day pessimism. Like T'an-luan, he adopted the terms "easy path" and "path of the saints." He believed that the Buddhist Dharma was in the last degenerate phase and thus argued that human beings did not have the capacity to follow the path of the saints. Consequently they had no recourse except the Pure Land teaching.

The religious practice that Tao-ch'o proclaimed for ignorant people in the age of decay was *nien-fo,* which he interpreted not as "Buddha-contemplation" (the usual technical meaning of the term) but as "Buddha-invocation," calling the name of Amida. He asserted that reciting the Buddha's name with undistracted mind would overcome all evil, erase all sins, and ensure rebirth in the Western Paradise. His disciples engaged in recitation marathons, one monk setting the record of a million times in one week.

The Chinese Pure Land sect received its definitive shape at the hands of Tao-ch'o's great disciple Shan-tao (613-681). In doctrine, he denied two ideas then prevalent: (1) that the Happy Land is an inferior apparition-land where ordinary beings can attain rebirth, and (2) that the Happy Land is a superior and transcendental Buddha-field inaccessible to ordinary people. Shan-tao clarified his predecessors' ideas as to the means of attaining rebirth. He classified religious acts that lead to rebirth (in Sukhāvatī or the Pure Land) as primary (nien-fo) and secondary (chanting Sūtras, meditating on the Buddha, worshipping Buddha-images, and singing praises to the Buddha). He insisted that both primary and secondary means should be practiced and did so himself. It is said that he attained the Buddha-recollection samādhi.

Shan-tao was a zealous and skilled evangelist. He preached for over thirty years to monks and laity in the capital, and convened big gatherings to chant "na-mo a-mi-t'o-fo" (salutation to Amida Buddha). He wrote out thousands of copies of the *Amida Sūtra (Smaller Sukhāvatī-vyūha)* and gave them to his innumerable disciples. He painted numerous pictures of the Pure Land and distributed them, causing the subject to become extremely popular in mid-T'ang painting. To promote singing Amida's praises, he wrote liturgical manuals. Famed for his tireless activity and his strict observance of the Vinaya, Shan-tao was a holy eccentric. It is said that for more than thirty years he had no special sleeping place, did not take off his robes except to bathe, never raised his eyes to look at a woman, and gave no thought of fame or gain. When he recited the Buddha-name, a radiant splendor issued from his mouth. Legend says that in 681 he climbed the willow tree in front of his temple, jumped from it, and died. According to one view, he did this to get rid of his body and go to birth in Sukhāvatī. The Japanese Pure Land *(Jōdo)* schools consider that Shan-tao was an apparition-body of Amitābha. Shinran (see p. 177) says, "Shan-tao alone understood the Buddha's true intention."

The Amitābha cult was further promoted by Tz'u-min (680-748), who became converted to it while sojourning in India from 704 to 716. On returning to China he propagated the nien-fo (Buddha-invocation) practice among the common people, and vigorously denounced the Ch'an sect for practicing meditation to the exclusion of morality. He advocated the combined practice of meditation, scholarship, morality, and Buddha-invocation. This is at variance with the exclusive nien-fo of Shan-tao, and a forerunner of a later syncretism between Pure Land and Ch'an.

The last great Pure Land master of T'ang times was Fa-chao (late eighth ⑤ century), who advanced the cause of Amidism against competition from great masters of Ch'an, T'ien-t'ai, Chen-yen (an eighth century Buddhist Tantra school) and Hua-yen. He started out in T'ien-t'ai and carried its syncretistic outlook over to his Pure Land doctrine. He was a noted composer of hymns. It is alleged that he received revelations from Amida and, through that Buddha's supervening power, performed miracles.

By the ninth century the Amida cult was so fully formed and so widely diffused that it ceased to need great masters. Only Ch'an withstood its influence. Yet by the sixteenth century, Chinese Ch'an was permeated by Pure Land practices, and nowadays "na-mo a-mi-t'o fo" is chanted regularly in the daily liturgy of Ch'an monasteries.

The two chief Chinese departures from early Indian Amitābhist doctrine ✓ were reciting the name rather than meditating on the Buddha, and affirming that sinners, too, can go to the Pure Land. It has been noted that reciting sacred names was a popular practice in India, and it was certainly not a part of pre-Buddhist Chinese religion. T'an-luan's motive in explaining away the *Sukhāvatī-vyūha Sūtra's* statement that grave sinners are excluded from the effect of Amida's vow was the conviction that all living beings possess Buddha-nature. This idea originated in India, but it found such favor in China precisely because no native Chinese philosophy (except Moism, which became extinct before Buddhism was widely accepted in China) preached universal love and the worth of every person regardless of family or class.

During the eighth century, the Amida cult attracted emperors and slaves, scholars and women, artists and soldiers, monks and laity. The common hope for rebirth in the Pure Land united the otherwise disparate segments of society. From the twelfth century, Neo-Confucian gentlemen disdained to share a cult that was both "vulgar" (since the common people had it) and "foreign"; but thier wives continued to recite "na-mo a-mi-t'o fo," and mandarin boys as they grew up had to expunge the devotion learned from their mothers if they wanted to keep their Confucian orientation pure. No native Chinese god has ever commanded the universal worship that Amitābha has received.

Ch'an

Meditation texts were among the earliest translations, because lay disciples of the second-century A.D. translator An Shih-kao were practicing meditation and needed manuals. Their purpose was to get the superknowledges, especially the mundane ones; and if we are to credit the tales in their biographies, some of them succeeded. The pre-Han Chinese Taoist texts credited to Lao-tzu and

Chuang-tzu mention various meditative techniques, and popular Han Taoism developed and enriched the repertory so that Buddhist meditation found a well-oriented clientele.

Most of the early missionaries and eminent Chinese monks were proficient in meditation. The *Lives of Eminent Monks,* completed about 530 A.D., contains biographies of twenty meditators and twenty-one wonder-workers, besides the translators and commentators who were also noted for meditation. So it is clear that Indian methods of meditation were effective and popular in China. Nevertheless, meditation was just one practice among many in the large monasteries and the famous sects of the late sixth century. The student was involved in lectures and reading, rituals, and sundry pious works to such an extent that he had little time and insufficient encouragement to practice contemplation.

The Ch'an sect arose to meet the demand for a well-grounded and lasting tradition specializing in meditation. It began, like the other Chinese sects, as a lineage of masters devoted to one text, in this case the *Laṅkāvatāra Sūtra.* Its early history is obscured by legends fabricated in the eighth century and later. It seems a fact that Bodhidharma, an Indian meditation master and champion of the *Laṅkāvatāra,* arrived by sea in Canton about 470, stayed briefly in south China, then went north and stayed there until about 520. Legend says that while in the south, Bodhidharma met the pious Emperer Wu of Liang, who asked him: "Have I earned merit by my lifelong temple building, donation, and worship offerings?" Bodhidharma said: "No merit at all." The emperor, disappointed, banished Bodhidharma. The tale is anachronistic, as Bodhidharma was already in the north by 483, and Wu did not become emperor until 502. The story, though, points up a cardinal idea of Ch'an, that true merit is not that which stems from good works and leads to mundane good luck, but that which springs from insight into the Dharma-body, which is one's own true nature. This is the distinction between finite or relative and infinite or absolute merit that is made repeatedly in the Prajñā-pāramitā Sūtras.

The legendary Bodhidharma. (From a painting by the Japanese Zen master Hakuin.)

Bodhidharma settled in a mountain temple near Lo-yang, where he acquired at least two disciples and taught them the *Laṅkāvatāra*. Legend says that in this monastery he spent nine years gazing at a wall, that he sat continuously until his legs fell off, and that he cut off his eyelids so that his gaze would never falter. The term "wall gazing" occurs in an early pamphlet attributed to Bodhidharma, and the earliest biography says that he taught "wall contemplation." This was probably a kind of "formless meditation" like that recommended in *The Awakening of Faith,* and the Japanese *shikan-taza* (just sitting) practice.

Ch'an (and Zen) teachers have used physical trials as part of their meditation training for disciples. These practices emphasize the need for great effort and severe spiritual training to break the disciple's habitual attachment to ordinary ways of thinking and acting. Bodily mutilation is a frequent theme in Ch'an legends. It serves several purposes: by example to encourage intrepid striving, to counteract ordinary timidity, and to arouse energy by fixing the imagination on intense physical pain. It is a manneristic exaggeration of the common Buddhist meditation on suffering.

The Second Patriarch in the *Laṅkāvatāra* lineage and the Ch'an sect is Hui-k'o (487–593). In youth he studied Taoism, the classics, and Buddhist doctrine. When a mature man, he met Bodhidharma and studied with him for six (or nine) years, at the end of which Bodhidharma designated him his successor. Hui-k'o led a wandering life after his Master's death, was persecuted by hostile monks, and hid in the mountains during the persecution of 574. After the restoration of Buddhism, he returned to the capital and lived out his old age in peace.

A fragment of Hui-k'o's doctrine has been preserved in *The Lives of Further Eminent Monks.* It expresses succinctly the fundamental Ch'an teaching:

> The deep principle of the True is utter nondifferent. From of old, one is confused about the Gem and thinks it is a piece of tile. When suddenly oneself wakes up, there is the real jewel. Ignorance and wisdom are the same and without difference. Know that the myriad things are all identical with suchness. When you regard the body and do not distinguish it from the Buddha, why go on to seek [nirvāṇa] without remainder?

All these ideas we have seen in the Indian teaching of emptiness and Tantra—the identity of saṃsāra and nirvāṇa, the womb of Tathāgatahood as the gem of intrinsic Buddhahood, this body as the Buddha-body, and the futility of seeking for nirvāṇa as if it were another thing among things. The Ch'an masters, like the Tantric poets, did not invent new concepts but extracted the most powerful religious ideas from a diffuse literature and presented them in concentrated, forceful form.

The Third Patriarch, Seng-ts'an (died 606), is relatively unknown. He was an intelligent boy and grew up to become one of Hui-k'o's disciples. He studied with him for six years, received the Dharma-seal from him, and fled along with him to the mountains in the persecution of 574. Seng-ts'an is credited with authorship of a long poem, *The Inscription of Faith in Mind,* which has remained immensely popular to this day.

The Fourth Patriarch, Tao-hsin (580–651), went forth when he was seven, studied six years with another teacher, and then came to Seng-ts'an and stayed with him for eight or nine years. He was famed as a miracle-worker. When he visited a city beseiged by bandits, the dry springs flowed with water, and the bandits dispersed when he chanted the Prajñā-pāramitā Sūtras. In 624, he took up residence on a mountain in Hupeh and stayed there the rest of his life. It is said that he foresaw his imminent death, that he died to the accompaniment of natural prodigies, and that three years after death his body was incorrupt. He had a number of disciples.

The Fifth Patriarch, Hung-jen (601–674), went forth as a child and was soon recognized for his talent by Tao-hsin. After spending a whole night in meditation, he attained enlightenment without reading the Sūtras. He became a Master with a community of disciples who learned spiritual practice from him. The *Platform Sūtra* gives a vivid glimpse of Hung-jen's community, said to number over a thousand disciples, in Huang-mei County, Hupeh, on East Mountain, so-called because it lies to the east of the Fourth Patriarch's mountain. Not much is known about his teaching, but he seems to have drawn on the *Avataṃsaka* and the Prajñā-pāramitā Sūtras as well as the *Laṅkāvatāra;* and the *Platform Sūtra* may be right in stating that Hung-jen especially encouraged his followers to recite the *Diamond-Cutter Sūtra.*

That the Ch'an movement was growing and not just perpetuating itself in the seventh century is indicated by the branching of successions. The Fourth Patriarch, Tao-hsin, had two eminent disciples, Hung-jen (601–674) and Fa-yung (594–657). Fa-yung's branch prospered and survived at least until the eighth generation; it was taken to Japan about 800. Hung-jen, the Fifth Patriarch, had eleven notable disciples, of whom the most important were Shen-hsiu (606–706) and Hui-neng (638–713).

Shen-hsiu was the chief of Hung-jen's Community when the boy Hui-neng, widely recognized as the Sixth Patriarch, arrived to seek admission. His branch, later called Northern Ch'an, became very popular in Lo-yang and received imperial recognition.

Hui-neng was, like many other great Dharma-masters, the son of a gentry family that had fallen on hard times. His father was demoted from office and banished to Kwangtung, where he soon died. Hui-neng sold firewood to help support his widowed mother. One day he chanced to hear a man reciting the *Diamond-Cutter.* He experienced an awakening and asked the reciter where he came from. The man referred him to Hung-jen, so the boy took leave of his mother and went to call on the Fifth Patriarch, who said: "If you're from Kwangtung, you're a barbarian. How can you become a Buddha?"

Hui-neng answered, "There is no north and south in Buddha-nature. Although my barbarian's body and your body are not the same, what difference is there in our Buddha-nature?" Hung-jen sent the bright boy to work as a lay brother, pounding rice in the mill.

The *Platform Sūtra* tells a suspect tale of how Hui-neng received the Dharma-succession from Hung-jen. After the boy had been working in the mill for eight months, the Patriarch ordered his disciples each to exercise his insight and write a stanza, announcing that he would give his robe, Dharma, and succession to anyone who revealed enlightenment. Shen-hsiu wrote his verse secretly on a wall at midnight:

> The body is the Bodhi Tree,
> The mind is like a bright mirror-and-stand.
> At all times wipe it diligently,
> Don't let there be any dust.

The Fifth Patriarch, say the partisans of Hui-neng, told Shen-hsiu privately that he had arrived at the front gate but had not entered it and sent him away crestfallen to try again. Hui-neng heard a boy reciting Shen-hsiu's verse, composed his own reply, and had someone write it up on another wall:

> Bodhi really has no tree;
> The bright mirror also has no stand.
> Buddha-nature is forever pure; (or: Really no
> thing exists)
> Where is there room for dust?

The Fifth Patriarch, so the story goes, said in front of the crowd that the verse showed incomplete understanding, but summoned Hui-neng at midnight and expounded the *Diamond-Cutter* to him. Hearing it once, Hui-neng awakened right away, and the Fifth Patriarch conferred upon him the patriarchal insignia without anyone else's knowing it. The master then ordered his disciple to go away immediately lest jealous people harm him.

This story shows several distinctive features of early Ch'an. The Chinese character *wu* (read *satori* in Japanese) means to awaken, to understand. It translates Sanskrit *budh,* the root of *Buddha* and *bodhi.* In Ch'an it signifies an opening of insight, a change to a higher level of understanding similar to the "recognition" that Kauṇḍinya experienced when he heard the First Sermon and to what the audience in a Mahāyāna Sūtra experiences upon hearing a Dharma-discourse. Hui-neng had his two awakenings upon hearing the *Diamond-Cutter.* This is in accord with the general Indian notion that hearing is the proximate cause of attaining insight. It also shows that early Ch'an acknowledged degrees of awakening and a progression from lower to higher. Hung-jen's question and Hui-neng's answer show that the school took seriously the Buddha-nature of all beings and sought supreme, perfect enlightenment in this life.

Shen-hsiu's verse expresses the Ch'an tenet that this very body is the Buddha. "Mirror-knowledge" is a synonym for enlightenment in Pali and Sanskrit texts, and the mirror is a widespread symbol for the psyche. The Ch'an meditator, like every other meditator, continually wipes away distractions as well as random and meandering thoughts, until finally no more dust alights on his mirror. Hui-neng's verse plays one-upmanship by switching to the absolute standpoint, a familiar gambit in Prajñā-pāramitā Sūtras. It does not refute Shen-hsiu, but, by the conventions of the game, Hui-neng is one up.

That the crowd was covetous of the Dharma and prepared to do bodily harm to someone in order to get it must have seemed thoroughly plausible to eighth-century readers. Vicious intrigues within the Saṅgha are well attested for this period. The rivalries between Shen-hsiu's and Hui-neng's branches were prosecuted with slander, fabrication, competition for official favor, and political machinations to get rivals banished or dispossessed.

Hui-neng is represented by his later school as an untutored genius, illiterate and unschooled in the scriptures. The myth serves a purpose: the school opposed book-scholars' pretensions and called the laity and uneducated people to attain awakening simply by using their native talent. The *Platform Sūtra* shows Hui-neng as illiterate, which may be less than true; but it also shows him quoting the Sūtras, handling a large technical vocabulary, and giving sermons that, though not high prose by T'ang dynasty standards, are far from uncultivated.

The private interview with the master has remained a crucial part of Ch'an procedure ever since that between Hung-jen and Hui-neng. Dialogs that occurred in these encounters form a substantial part of later Ch'an literature. They are terse, often witty, sometimes bizarre and obscure. The master usually had a lot of students, and only two or three short periods a day were set aside for interviews, so the chance was precious. In addition, the student's hopes and fears were usually keyed up by long waiting and intense striving so that the meeting had the sudden-death quality of a duel. The master diagnoses the student's problem and treats it. Sometimes he simply explains or advises. Sometimes he provokes, shocks, or otherwise manipulates the student. The Ch'an strategy is to catch a person at the critical moment and do the appropriate thing that triggers awakening. The Buddho-Taoists, amalgamating the general Indian doctrine that the Buddha adapts his teaching to his hearers' capacity and the Taoist ideal of going with the grain of the Tao, had said repeatedly that the Holy Man accords with things, teaches according to the critical situation, responds to appeals. Ch'an follows Taoism in recognizing the uniqueness of each natural specimen. No two trees, rocks, tigers, or people are really the same. Chinese law, unlike Hellenisic and European law, was a respecter of persons, and never maintained that what is fair for one is fair for all. Ch'an masters similarly treat each case as *sui generis,* acting and expecting responses with spontaneity and without preconceptions or premeditation.

Hui-neng's first sermon (as given in the *Platform Sūtra)* deals with the relation between wisdom and meditation. He says that they are not two things, but one. Meditation is the substance of wisdom, and wisdom is the function of meditation, just as the lamp is the substance *(t'i,* "body") of light and light is the function of the lamp. The "one-course samādhi" is coursing in a sincere mind at all times, whether walking, standing, sitting, or lying. As the *Vimalakīrti-nirdeśa Sūtra* says, "A sincere mind is the bodhi-ground. A sincere mind is the Pure Land." In other words, meditation is having an earnest and concentrated mind. It is to be carried out in all postures and is to suffuse all one's activities.

Hui-neng was said to have received the Dharma from Hung-jen in 661. He went south again and stayed in hiding. One day in 676 he showed up at a monastery in Canton where the master Yin-tsung was lecturing on the *Nirvāṇa Sūtra.* He attracted the attention of the master and delighted him, says the story, with a profound discussion of the *Nirvāṇa Sūtra,* whereupon the master first conferred ordination on Hui-neng (who had been a layman until then), and then became his disciple. In the spring of the next year, Hui-neng went to Mount Ts'ao-ch'i (in Kwangtung), where he is said to have delivered as an inaugural address the first sermon in the *Platform Sūtra,* and where he spent the rest of his life, acquiring several thousand disciples, including both monks and nonclericals. He announced his approaching death to his disciples a month before it happened. It is said that, for two days after his coffin was interred on Mount Ts'ao-ch'i, a bright light arose from it up into the sky.

After Hui-neng's death, his school remained in obscurity for two decades while Shen-hsiu's school enjoyed popularity in Ch'ang-an and Lo-yang. Then in 732, Hui-neng's disciple Shen-hui organized a big conference in which he launched an attack on Shen-hsiu's successor, asserting that Hui-neng was the true Sixth Patriarch. In 745, he was appointed to a temple in Lo-yang from which he carried on his campaign against the rival school and enjoyed brilliant success as a preacher. After eight years, a powerful official who favored Northern Ch'an accused Shen-hui of sedition, and the emperor banished him. But after the rebel An Lu-shan drove the emperor into exile in 756, Shen-hui was called back and put in charge of an ordination platform amid the ruins of Lo-yang, where he performed ordinations and raised money, through the sale of monk certificates, for the loyalist war effort.

Shen-hui was considered the Seventh Patriarch by his followers, but other houses in the Hui-neng line gave him no special honor.

The acrimony, the threats, the charges of violence that marked the dispute over the patriarchal succession seem as sordid as the mutual calumnies and assaults of Lenin and his left-wing confreres, and sprang from similar causes. The Ch'an people were in life-and-death earnest. They had forsaken the comfortable dilletantism of the all-embracing sets such as T'ien-t'ai. They wasted no time on "classifying teachings," on arranging pretty smorgasbords of doctrine. The roots of the movement were in the back-country mountain temples, where life was rough and rigorous, where isolation and exclusive concentration on one quest tended to foster extremism. The Ch'an movement, too, was undoubtedly inebriated by its successes, its ability to lead the seeker to enlightenment in this life, the presence of men who were virtual Buddhas, and by the way that earnest people from all classes of society rallied to the Ch'an teachers. Like the builders of other popular Chinese sects, they were convinced that the robe of destiny had devolved on them; and this seemed to justify drastic expedients, as well as to render purity of teaching extraordinarily momentous.

In 796, the emperor called a council to decide the true Ch'an teaching and to settle the controversy about the lineages. Afterward an imperial decree designated Shen-hui "Seventh Patriarch," thus confirming that Hui-neng, not Shen-hsiu, was the Sixth. Posthumous imperial honors were conferred on Hui-neng, and the controversy was over.

The characteristics of early Ch'an are well shown in the interviews with Hui-neng related in the *Platform Sūtra*. A monk named Fa-ta (Dharma Penetration) had been reciting the *Lotus Sūtra* for years but was confused and

Hui-neng, the Sixth Patriarch, tearing up a Buddhist Sūtra—since enlightenment is not in knowing the words but having the experience. (From a Chinese Southern Sung painting by Liang K'ai.)

in doubt about what the Sūtra meant. He called on Hui-neng, who asked him to recite the text and then interpreted it for him, telling him, "Listen to the one Buddha-vehicle and do not seek the Two Vehicles. . . . If you awaken to this Dharma, in one instant your mind will open, and you will become prominent in the world." In other words, the One Vehicle is the Sudden Teaching. The master then said that if your mind is right, you recite the *Lotus,* but if your mind is wrong, the *Lotus* recites you. When Fa-ta heard this, he had a great awakening and broke into tears. From that day, he understood the profound meaning of the *Sūtra,* and continued to recite it.

One of the basic features of Ch'an is "not setting up the written word as an authority." Otherwise phrased, it is "not clinging to written words and not separating from written words." Hui-neng had no objection to the recitation of the scriptures; he owed his own first awakening to an itinerant Sūtra-chanter. But he disparaged the all-too-common practice of mere reading without comprehension: "If you cling staunchly to your recitation and regard it as an achievement, you do not differ from a yak that loves its tail." Real and efficacious practice is illumined by prajñā.

Hui-neng's explanation of the *Lotus* is straightforward and intelligible, like most early Ch'an teaching and unlike the sayings of many later masters. He regularly contrasts the conventional meaning of a doctrine with its "true" or absolute meaning. This is a frequent device in the Śūnyavādin Sūtras. Its purpose is not to contradict conventional truths on their own level, but to jolt the hearer out of the habitual and conventional. Fa-ta's failure to understand the central idea of the *Lotus* was probably due to lack of education. Many novices in China were trained simply to recite one Sūtra, which they learned by rote and without explanation. Often it was the only book that they had read or could read. They made their living reciting it in the streets, or at funeral and memorial rites. Hui-neng and Shen-hui expounded the Prajñā-pāramitā teachings to monks and laity who had known only the religion of merit, who had been blindly performing pious acts without knowing their meaning and purpose. No wonder that men like Fa-ta broke into tears of amazement and gratitude.

The awakening that climaxes the Ch'an interview tale is triggered by the master's words, but usually seems much stronger than the mere words would warrant. This is equally so with Śākyamuni's First Sermon and Kauṇḍinya's awakening. One factor is the spiritual aura, the charisma, of the master. Ch'an is said to be "a special transmission outside doctrines," a direct transmission from mind to mind. Another factor is that the master's instruction was directed to the specific condition of the inquirer, which the ordinary reader is unlikely to duplicate. Ch'an is for those with keen faculties, and the teaching is given only to those who are ripe for it. A third factor is the interaction between master and disciple. The tense, expectant inquirer feels strongly that he is in the presence of a wise man who can read his character and prescribe for him. He is relieved and thankful to have someone concentrate on him, know him as he really is, and "point directly at his nature." And the student is humiliated, disappointed, and stimulated to greater effort when the master candidly criticizes him.

The early Ch'an contemplative exercise was simply striving constantly to have no notions, and to see one's nature and become a Buddha. It meant playing a simple, difficult, and fascinating game of cat-and-mouse with one's "fundamental mind." Interviews with the master were a crucial adjunct. As generations passed, sayings and dialogs of the old masters were collected and came to be used as themes for contemplation. The "old case" or "public document" *(kung-an,* Japanese *kōan)* literature and exercise were fully developed by the early twelfth century. Though kung-an meditation is especially associated with the Lin-chi (Japanese Rinzai) subsect, it is also practiced by the other branches.

Tao-i (707–786) was the greatest disciple of Huai-jang, the disciple of Hui-neng. Also called Ma-tsu, he was born in Szechuan. He went forth under a local Ch'an master, then went to Huai-jang at Mount Nan-yüeh in Kiangsi. One day Ma-tsu was sitting in meditation, and Huai-jang asked, "What are you doing?"

"I wish to become a Buddha."

The master picked up a tile and began grinding it with a stone.

"What are you doing?"

"I am polishing this tile to make a mirror."

"But no amount of polishing will ever make a mirror out of a brick."

"And no amount of sitting cross-legged will ever make a Buddha out of you."

"What am I to do then?"

"It is like driving a cart. When it doesn't move, do you whip the cart or the ox? Are you sitting cross-legged to practice meditation or to become a Buddha? If it is to practice meditation, that does not consist of sitting or lying down. If it is to become a Buddha, the Buddha has no fixed form. You cannot take hold of him or let him go. To think that you can obtain Buddhahood by sitting is simply to kill the Buddha, and until you give up the idea that you can so obtain it, you won't come near the truth."

Ma-tsu became Huai-jang's Dharma-heir (designated successor), traveled around for a while, then settled and taught at a temple of his own in Kiangsi. His appearance inspired amazement and awe: "He strode along like a bull and glared about him like a tiger. If he stretched out his tongue, it reached up over his nose; on the soles of his feet were imprinted two circular marks." He used shouts and blows to shock the student into awakening.

Ma-tsu's chief successor, Huai-hai of Mount Pai-chang (749–814), created a new Vinaya and gave Ch'an community life its classic and distinctive form. The chief innovation in his rule is the requirement that all monks do manual labor: "One day no work, one day no food." Other Buddhist monasteries owned much land which was tilled by serfs. The Ch'an monks had taken to manual labor to support themselves as early as the Fourth Patriarch. Huai-hai, also called simply Pai-chang, made labor mandatory. The T'ang Ch'an masters acquired considerable tracts of mountain and waste land and developed them by means of work parties of monks. They grew rice, cut bamboo, and developed tea plantations. These enterprises made the monks less dependent on donors and their whims and obviated the charge that they were parasites on society. But physical work also served as an integral part of the spiritual discipline. The exercise counteracted the lethargy and depression that can come from sitting in meditation. Also, hoeing the fields and picking tea leaves were performed mindfully as part of day-and-night meditation.

When Pai-chang was old and feeble, his monks took his garden tools away from him, but he refused to eat until they let him go out and work again.

The most decisive catastrophe in the history of Chinese Buddhism was the proscription of 845. The external causes were rivalry between the Buddhists and the Taoists, and factional strife at the imperial court between the administrators on the one hand and the eunuchs on the other. In addition, the

Sangha had accumulated a disproportionate share of the nation's wealth; had taken out of use large quantities of bronze and iron to make images; and had acquired tax-exempt status for some 260,000 clerics, 100,000 temple serfs, and a host of lay employees. The Taoists' malice and bureaucratic concern for the national economy sufficed to persuade the emperor, who, in 841, ordered that clerics who practiced magic, kept women, or otherwise violated the Discipline should be laicized, and that money and real estate owned by monks or nuns should be confiscated by the government. This is no more than a devout Buddhist monarch would do to purify the Sangha. But in 845, the emperor, after first ordering a census of the clergy and its property, decreed the destruction of all except a few designated temples, confiscation and melting down of metal objects, return of monks and nuns to lay life, and confiscation of the Sangha's lands and serfs. This proscription, unlike the previous ones, was effective throughout all of China. But the emperor died in 846, probably poisoned by the longevity pills his Taoist mentors had been feeding him. The new emperor started by executing the Taoist leaders who had instigated the persecution, and soon gave permission for the restitution of Buddhism.

Many sects perished entirely during this short, severe persecution. Only Ch'an prospered after the restoration. It had suffered like the other sects, but survived because it was less dependent on libraries, images, and the pomp and circumstance of temple cult. Even so, the city-based line of Shen-hui died out, and subsequent growth came in the lines of southern mountain masters.

One of Pai-chang's successors was Ling-yu of Kuei-shan (771–853). When twenty-three he came to Pai-chang, who recognized his talent and took him as an attendant. One day the master said, "Who's there?"

"It's Ling-yu."

"Poke and see if there's still some fire in the stove."

Ling-yu poked around, and said, "There's no fire."

Pai-chang got up, went to the stove, poked quite a bit, managed to stir up a small glow, and said to his pupil, "Isn't this fire?" Ling-yu was awakened, knelt down, and bowed in gratitude to the master.

This kung-an (kōan) is readily intelligible. Fire stands for Buddha-nature. The disciple had not found his "nature" because he had not searched hard enough. Pai-chang commented to Ling-yu that seeing Buddha-nature depends on the right moment, the cause (the student's inherent Buddhahood), and the accessory cause (the master's direct pointing at the mind). The beauty of kung-an language is that it coins its vocabulary freshly and impromptu, avoiding scholastic terminology and using natural symbols. But the kung-an is mastered not when the symbols are identified with technical terms but when, for example, Buddha-nature is experienced as directly as the glowing coals.

Ch'an has been accused of iconoclasm and antinomianism (avowed rejection of the usual). In the eighth century, a lay follower of T'ien-t'ai charged that "those who travel the Ch'an path go so far as to teach the people that there is neither Buddha nor Dharma and that neither sin nor goodness has any significance." He alleged that ordinary people took this as license to sin and were drawn to destruction like moths to a candle. Then there is the tale of T'ien-jan (died 824) who on a cold night took down the wooden Buddha-image in the shrine hall and made a fire with it. When he was accused of sacrilege, he said, "I was only looking for a Buddha-relic." "How can you expect to find a relic in a piece of wood?" "Well then, I am only burning a piece of wood, after all."

It may well be that some people took Ch'an teachings as an excuse to sin, just as some have so taken the Pure Land and Christian teachings that sinners may attain paradise. But the Ch'an masters required strict discipline from their clerical followers and sound morality from lay disciples. T'ien-jan's burning the image was indeed an act of sacrilege, and his companions' reaction is sufficient proof that Ch'an at that time did not condone the destruction of sacred objects. He got away with it and it was reported, because he gave his act a transcendental significance and handled the repartee with wit.

Ch'an has kept the monastic system and has not discarded rituals, images, or the pantheon. Its style and language are distinctively Chinese, but its essence is the core teaching of Indian Mahāyāna. In some ways, too, Ch'an runs counter to major Chinese values. The Chinese as a whole have always loved magic, but the lives of the Ch'an masters contain very few references to the magic powers the meditation expert is supposed to attain. Confucian gentleman and Taoist adept both consider themselves above manual labor, but Ch'an trainees and masters toil like coolies. The glory of the Ch'an-tsung is not that it made Buddhism thoroughly Chinese, but that it extracted, concentrated, and made efficacious the essence of the Dharma.

From Sung to the Present

The story of Chinese Buddhism from 900 to 1900 is one of a golden later summer (900–1300), an Indian summer in the fifteenth century under the early Ming dynasty, and a fall shading into winter thereafter. No generation was without eminent monks, and yet the place of Buddhism in national life declined under government restrictions on entrance to the monastic orders, curtailment of monasteries' activities, and relentless anti-Buddhist propaganda from the Neo-Confucians, who controlled the education system and the imperial examinations.

A modest revival began in the late nineteenth century, stimulated initially by the need to rebuild monasteries and reprint scriptures destroyed in Central China during the T'ai-p'ing rebellion (1850–1864). The rebels, who fervently professed a kind of Christianity, looted and burned most of the great monasteries in the areas they occupied. The shock stimulated both monks and laity. Soon scripture-printing societies and study clubs were active. Some young monks who acquired modern ideas through lay-initiated schools became revolutionaries and participated in the overthrow of the Manchu dynasty in 1911. However, these radicals were not approved of by the majority of the

Saṅgha, who considered that a monk should stay out of politics and should study the scriptures rather than modern secular subjects.

The most famous of these radicals was the modernist monk T'ai-hsü (1890–1947). He was never accepted by the abbots of the great Ch'an monasteries of central and south China, who held the real power in the Saṅgha, and who were carrying out extensive revitalization of their institutions along traditional lines. But he set up schools; introduced Western-style classroom instruction; taught secular subjects and foreign languages including Tibetan and Pali; and revived the study of the scholastic treatises, especially of the Fa-hsiang school. T'ai-hsü and his followers opened up relations with coreligionists abroad and promoted the idea of a world fellowship of Buddhists. They announced an ambitious program of eduation, preaching, welfare, and economic development work, and attempted to implement it insofar as their resources and the troubled state of the country allowed.

The Nationalist regime in Mainland China fluctuated between mild hostility and mild support for Buddhism, but by and large allowed proponents of the Dharma a freedom they had not had during two-and-a-half centuries of Manchu rule, when all private associations were under suspicion of treason. When the Communists took over the mainland in 1949, they were committed to wiping out all religion as soon as it could be done expediently. First, they declared that the clergy were parasites on society. Then, in 1951, they confiscated the land holdings of the monasteries and so deprived the monks and nuns of the means to carry on religious activities. Young monks and nuns were returned to lay status, and the older clerics were put to work farming, weaving, running vegetarian restaurants, or teaching school. They were subjected to brainwashing to cleanse their minds of non-Marxist ideas. Then, in 1953, a Chinese Buddhist Association was organized so that the government could supervise and manipulate the still sizable Buddhist community, and so that China could reap the diplomatic advantages of representation at international Buddhist gatherings. Famous and beautiful old temples were maintained at government expense, Buddhist art works were safeguarded, and sites such as the Yün-kang caves were designated national treasures. Then, when the Great Cultural Revolution got under way, Red Guards proceeded to destroy Buddhist buildings and monuments along with other reminders of China's past.

In 1930, there were said to be 738,000 monks and nuns and 267,000 Buddhist temples in China. This was by far the largest clergy in China, or in any national church in the world. The majority did not live in strictly run monasteries, but at least 50,000 did. There was much idleness and laxity, but also much diligence and rigor. Buddhism was not a prominent force in national life, but insofar as Republican China was religious, it was more Buddhist than anything else.

Many monks have fled from Communist China to Hong Kong and Taiwan, where Buddhist associations operate freely and show a certain amount of vitality. Both as a popular religion and as a monastic vocation, Buddhism on Taiwan has recently entered a period of genuine renewal. In addition, Buddhism has some following among expatriate Chinese communities in Malaysia, Singapore, the Philippines, Vietnam, and San Francisco.

KOREA

The earliest Korean religion was shamanism, which survives today as a cult of spirits. As early as the first century B.C., Chinese colonies were established in the north, bringing Chinese thought and institutions with them. According to tradition, Buddhism was brought to the northernmost Korean kingdom (Koguryŏ) from China in 372 A.D. by the monk Shun-tao. A short time later a Serindian (Central Asian) monk took the teaching to the kingdom of Paekche in the southwest. It was not until the fifth century that it was accepted in the third Korean kingdom of Silla. By the sixth century, however, it was well enough established so that emissaries from Paekche took Buddha statues and texts to Japan, officially introducing the Dharma there.

From the time of these beginnings, the fate of Buddhism hinged on its association with politics and the aristocracy. For the latter, Buddhism provided support for autocratic monarchy, the common people being most attracted to Pure Land teachings of bliss in the next world. Confucianism was followed by lower level aristocrats. Over the following centuries, Buddhism flowered in Korea, producing great works of art and fine temples. Regularly, Korean monks went to China to study, bringing back with them the teachings of the Chinese schools. During the period of unification under Silla rule, in the eighth and ninth centuries, Buddhism became a major institution, and Ch'an (Korean: *Sŏn)* was introduced from China, becoming the most popular form of Buddhism and absorbing other sects.

In the following period, from the late tenth century through the fourteenth, Buddhism flourished, with government patronage resulting in new monasteries and works of art. Aristocrats followed both Buddhism and Confucianism, the former for its personal, spiritual aspects, the latter for its political and ethical content. The government built new institutions for both. In the twelfth century Buddhism was suppressed by bureaucratic forces not satisfied with Buddhism or its internal corruption, turning instead to Neo-Confucianism.

Under the Yi dynasty, which lasted until the early twentieth century, Confucianism became the sole official state religion. Buddhism was suppressed, reducing the number of sects and monasteries, and state support for Buddhism ended, all of it funneled to Confucian developments. By the nineteenth century, Buddhism, once the state religion of Korea, was at a low point in its history. The Sŏn, or meditation, school dominated what was left of the Saṅgha there, following ancient Korean and Chinese forms of monastic practice.

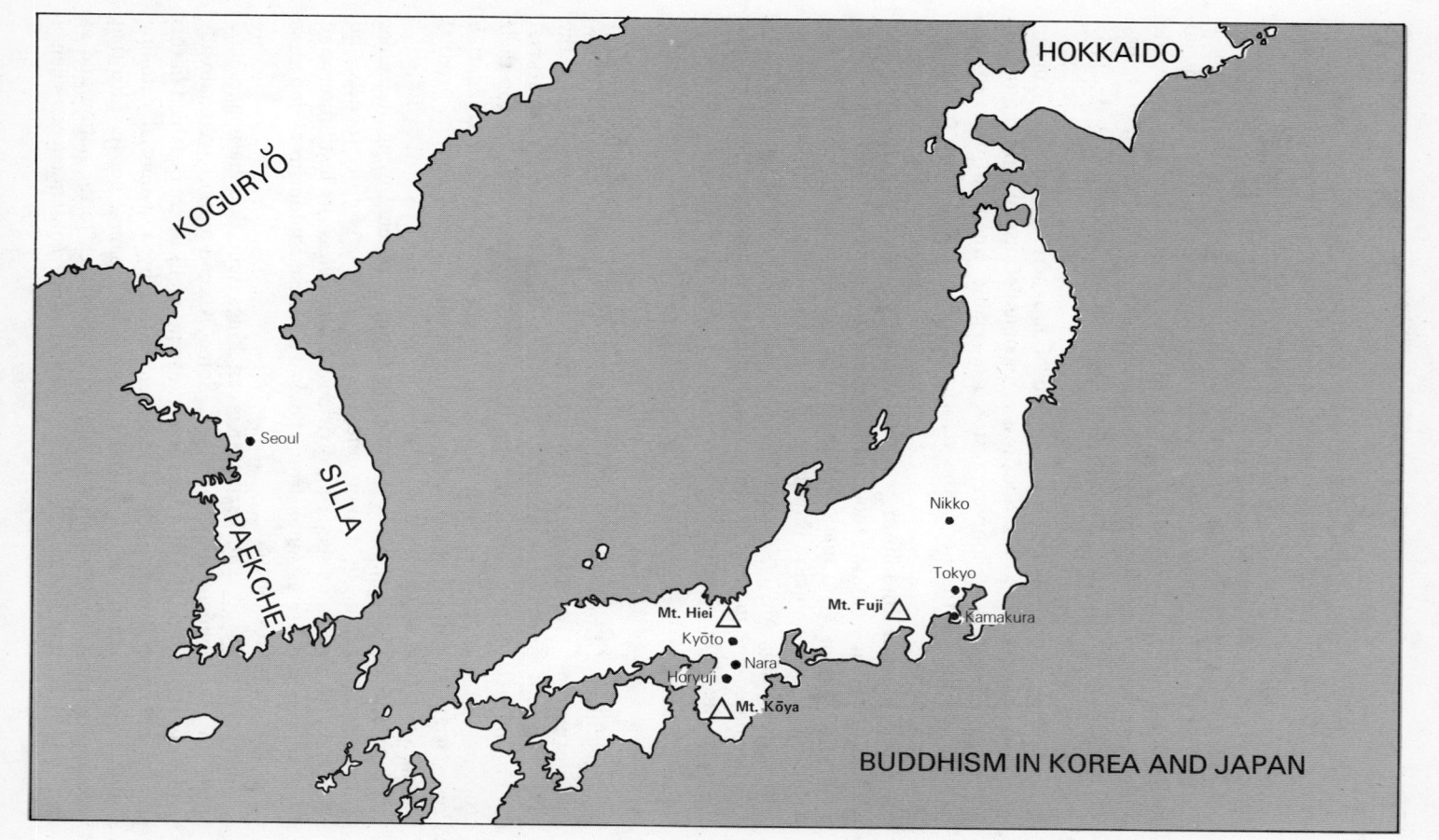

KOGURYŎ

HOKKAIDO

SILLA

• Seoul

PAEKCHE

Nikko
•

Tokyo
•

Mt. Hiei △

Mt. Fuji △

Kamakura

Kyōto •
Nara •

Hōryuji •

△ Mt. Kōya

BUDDHISM IN KOREA AND JAPAN

The policy of severe restriction by the government, however, began to ease near the end of the last century. In 1895, monks were no longer banned from the capital. With the advent of Japanese control, Korean Buddhism began to enjoy a renewal, but Japanese direction often went against Korean practice. The Japanese imported their own forms of Buddhism, eventually causing a split in the Korean Saṅgha between those who followed the more traditional Korean practice of not allowing monks to marry and those who, like the Japanese, accepted married priests. Japanese policy in the decades to follow did not favor the Korean monks who were more nationalistic. By 1935 however, a single sect united Buddhists in Korea.

Following World War II and the end of Japanese control, the Korean Saṅgha was threatened with serious loss of income because of land reform. In the south, government support restored a viable financial base to the monasteries, but in the north the reform probably ended the presence of Buddhism there.

South Korean Buddhism was still disturbed by dissension over the problem of married monks, though the issue was somewhat resolved in 1962. Some progress has been made by virtue of a national organization and the leadership of two councils. Buddhists have become active recently in education, youth groups, and lay organizations. Today, the Buddhist Canon is being fully translated into modern Korean, and Buddhism is beginning to take a new role in the life of the country.

JAPAN

The Buddhism of Korea and Vietnam is Chinese in its origin, sects, doctrines, and institutions. To this day, Korean and Vietnamese monks read the scriptures in Chinese. The religion has taken on a pronounced national coloring in each of these countries and has played an interesting part in their histories, but has departed from Chinese models no more than Hungarian Presbyterianism and American Lutheranism have deviated from the original churches of Calvin and Luther.

Japanese Buddhism,[2] too, follows its Chinese parent, using the older culture's language for its Canon and drawing from it for its models and inspiration, as well as its sectarian divisions. Nevertheless, its institutions and social character differ as much from those of Chinese Buddhism as Japanese society differs from Chinese.

Between 550 and 600, various Korean kings sent Buddha-images and Sūtras to the Japanese imperial court. Some Korean monks were already resident in Japan, and the first Japanese nuns and monks were ordained in this period. The first Korean gifts were accompanied by a memorial extolling Buddhism as productive of merit and wisdom. The Japanese got the idea that worshipping these foreign deities would bring good luck to the nation and at first judged the new religion entirely on short-range consequences; when a plague broke out, the Buddha-image was dumped into a moat, and the first temple was razed. When another plague broke out later, images were again thrown into the moat and the nuns were defrocked. When the plague still did not stop, the emperor agreed to permit the Buddhist cult to be practiced freely.

Japan was in process of consolidating a centralized monarchy out of a federation of tribes when Buddhism arrived, bearing the high culture of China and motivated to convert and civilize. Confucians did not like to go abroad and teach among "barbarians," so in Japan the Buddhists had the field to themselves for centuries. Desire for mundane fortune and cultural prestige made the Japanese hospitable to the Dharma, and from the first it was accepted that religion is primarily an organ of national life, and only secondarily a ministration to the individual's needs. Buddhist missionaries were also Chinese, which meant that they brought with them a number of Chinese values; these, along with Buddhism, became part of the fabric of Japanese life.

During the seventh century, under a series of devout emperors, Buddhism was developed as part of the state apparatus. Temples were founded, monks ordained, and public ceremonies sponsored, all for the well-being of the nation. Four Chinese sectarian systems were imported. In 625, a Korean who had studied under Chi-tsang introduced the study of the San-lun (Japanese, Sanron) and the Hīnayāna Ch'eng-shih (Jōjitsu) treatise. In 658, two Japanese monks who had studied under Hsüan-tsang introduced the study of Vasubandhu's *Abhidharmakośa (Kusha)*. A Japanese monk went to China in 653, studied the Fa-hsiang (Hossō) teaching under Hsüan-tsang for over ten years, then returned and introduced it to Japan. Other Koreans as well as Japanese returned from abroad, and reinforced the initial transmissions. Kusha, Jōjitsu, and Sanron were never more than curriculum subjects, but Hossō became a wealthy ecclesiastical corporation and has maintained an institutional existence to the present day. In 1948, it had about eighty temples and a thousand clerics. These scholastic treatises must have puzzled early Japanese students, whom we can imagine reading them with the same attitude of knowledge-is-good-for-you-especially-if-it-hurts with which their modern compatriots often tackle Hegel, Heidegger, and Tillich.

In the eighth century, when the capital was fixed at Nara, the Hua-yen (Kegon) sect was introduced by several teachers—Korean, Chinese, and Indian—and rapidly acquired great influence. The Hua-yen world view was adapted to political ideology by equating Vairocana with the emperor and the fourth Dharma-realm, that of phenomena not impeding each other, with Japanese society. The implicit metaphor of the spider and her web fits to perfection the society that the Japanese have created over the intervening centuries, and a study of Kegon renders more intelligible the peculiar Japanese blend of individualism and collectivism. Abstract philosophy was beyond the grasp of Nara intellectuals, but Kegon presented a concrete world vision giving spiritual elevation and political orientation.

In 752, a colossal bronze image of Vairocana was dedicated at the Tōdaiji

(Eastern Great Temple) in Nara, where two years later the Chinese Vinaya master Ganjin established an ordination center. The Japanese government permitted ordinations only at approved centers, which were kept few, and so it maintained some control over the Saṅgha. This system, though, gave certain sects a monopoly, enhanced their power, and led to the typically feudal sectarian structure. In such an arrangement the branch temples were ritually dependent on the head temple to provide properly ordained monks since only it could perform legitimate ordinations. On the other hand, the local temples sent money or goods to the head temple. If the latter had sufficient income of its own, then it depended on the client temples for its living. The Great Buddha is still in Nara, but his network has been small for many centuries. The Kegon sect now counts about 125 temples and 500 clerics.

Buddhism strongly influenced Japanese social customs and material culture during the Nara period (710-784 A.D.). Arts and crafts—architecture, sculpture, painting, carpentry, metal-casting, calligraphy, and papermaking— were stimulated to bigger and better production by the demand for cult articles. Artisans were brought from China and Korea, and Japanese craftsmen were trained. Monks also introduced the Chinese mundane sciences and wizardry: calendar-making, astronomy, geomancy, and magic. Buddhist ritual permeated court observances. The public bath and cremation, two of the most notable features of Japanese life, were introduced under Buddhist influence at this time. Monks served as scribes and clerks, providing the literate skills necessary for the Chinese-style administration that the imperial regime was trying to institute. They also acted as engineers in building roads, bridges, dikes, and irrigation systems. Wandering monks explored distant parts of the country and drew the first Japanese maps.

During this period, the imperial authority was virtually the only large entrepreneur in the country which did not yet have either an independent landed aristocracy or a sizable merchant community. As part of the colonization process, the emperor ordered each province to build a seven-storied pagoda, a monastery for twenty monks, and a convent for ten nuns. Copies of the *Golden Radiance Sūtra* were distributed to each province. Before this the monks and court officials who could understand the scriptures in Chinese were a tiny elite. The copying and distribution of Sūtras did much to spread a knowledge of Chinese, even though the immediate aim was to create talismans rather than to acquire knowledge.

The capital was moved to Heian (Kyōto) in 794 in order to rusticate the corrupt and politically meddlesome Nara sects. Six years earlier, in 788, a young monk named Saichō (767-822) had built a little temple on Mount Hiei, northeast of Kyōto. He soon received the patronage of the emperor, who sent him in 804 to study in China. During his year there, he studied T'ien-t'ai (Japanese Tendai) and on returning to Japan he propagated this teaching and so founded a new sect. Saichō kept his monks in seclusion on Mount Hiei while they underwent a twelve-year period of study and meditation. Some of his graduates stayed on the mountain, while others left to serve the state as scribes, engineers, and teachers. Saichō tried hard to get an ordination center established on Mount Hiei; but, due to the opposition of the Nara clerics, the center was only authorized by 827, five years after his death. He received the posthumous title Dengyō Daishi (Great Master Who Transmitted the Teaching).

Mount Hiei flourished. In its heyday there were 3,000 buildings in the temple complex, and 30,000 monks. Initially the court asserted its superiority to the mountain, but eventually the monasteries took to enforcing their demands on the government by mass demonstrations in the streets of the capital, and kept armed retainers to lend force to their claims. Even when Mount Hiei became worldly, thought, art, scholarship, and devotion continued to flourish there. The founders of all the new sects of the twelfth and thirteenth centuries were Tendai monks, which testifies to the vitality of Saichō's lotus even after it had begun to rot.

Another Buddhist school that was organized in the early Heian period was *Shingon*. It was founded by a well-educated man, Kūkai. Whereas Saichō was a good monk and a fine teacher, Kūkai (774–835) was a genius. Born a Nara aristocrat, he studied Buddhism, Confucianism, and Taoism during his teens. He sailed for China in 804, and there studied the Chen-yen (Japanese Shingon) sect, a Tantra system introduced to China about 720. Chen-yen ("True Word") translates mantra (spell). The sect's practices include not only mantras, but initiations, ritual gestures, *maṇḍalas,* and contemplations as well. Kūkai returned to Japan in 806, and was granted many honors by the emperor. In 816, he founded a monastery on Mount Kōya which eventually became the headquarters of the Shingon sect. Brilliant disciples flocked to take initiation from Kūkai. He wrote prolifically and systematized the doctrines that he had received from his teacher in China. He accorded a high place to the arts and so furthered the aestheticism that distinguishes Japanese Buddhism and general culture. Famous as a calligrapher, he set up a popular school, and is said to have invented the cursive syllabary *(hiragana)* of forty-seven signs in which, alone or mixed with Chinese characters, Japanese is written. Kūkai died in 835 on Mount Kōya, where he lies buried. There is a folk belief that he is merely sleeping and will rise up again someday. His posthumous title is Kōbō Daishi (Great Master Who Propagated the Dharma).

Shingon became even more popular than Tendai. Mount Kōya is said to have had 990 temples in its heyday. Shingon teaching was received even on Mount Hiei, which rivaled and soon bested Mount Kōya as an esoteric center. By the eleventh century, superstitions and heresies had contaminated Shingon and brought esotericism into disrepute, thus setting the stage for the resolutely exoteric popular sects of the Kamakura period (1192–1338).

By the end of the Heian period, in the twelfth century, Tendai was coming apart at the seams. Saichō had drawn all the Chinese sectarian teachings into a catholic synthesis, and his successors reached out to encompass even Japan's

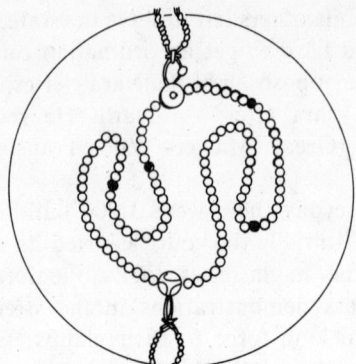

A Shingon Buddhist rosary.

native Shintō by identifying its deities with figures in the Buddhist pantheon. But being so all-sided consumed a lot of energy and slowed the student's progress. So earnest monks desiring realization in this life, or at least assurance of rebirth in Sukhāvatī, took to exclusive pursuit of one or another path. Thus, Japan in the twelfth and thirteenth centuries underwent the same sort of fission into sects as China in the sixth and seventh.

The chief social cause for the rise of new sects about 1200 was the shift in balance of power between the capital and the provinces, with a new class of provincial small landowners and samurai claiming their share at court and on the battlefield. They were inclined to support their local temples but were reluctant to give lavishly to the head temples in the distant capital area. Moreover, the new samurai class provided an effective link between the old aristocracy and the peasantry. For the first time the higher culture was diffused to the lower classes throughout the country, and some aristocrats, including the founders of most of the new sects, took the task of popularization seriously.

The cult of Amida was encompassed in the Tendai synthesis. Very early, though, a few Tendai monks became evangelists of the Pure Land teaching exclusively. One of these, Kūya (903–972), danced in the streets singing simple Japanese hymns about Amida, organized self-help projects among the common people, and even spread the Amidist gospel among the Ainu. Another Tendai monk, Ryōnin (1072–1132), similarly spread the practice of *Nembutsu* (nien-fo) in song and attracted followers in court and countryside. Yet a third, the learned Genshin (942–1017), wrote an enormously influential treatise, *The Compendium on Rebirth.* He favored the Nembutsu way, not because he considered other paths wrong, but because it was open to all, whether saint or sinner, monk or layman, man or woman, emperor or peasant.

Hōnen (1133–1212), founder of the Jōdo-shū (Pure Land sect), might have followed the same course as Genshin within the Tendai fold if hostile reactionaries had not forced him and his followers into secession. Orphaned in boyhood, he went forth at fifteen and during the next decade, spent on Mount Hiei, he excelled in the wide erudition esteemed by Tendai. Yet he was distressed that he and the people of his age were not able to reach enlightenment or become free from their sins. When he was forty-three, he became convinced through studying Shan-tao and Genshin that only complete reliance on Amida would save him. He wrote a treatise setting forth his faith, but when it was published, monks from Mount Hiei seized and burned all available copies and the printing blocks. Hōnen continued to teach his message humbly and without ostentation, and converted an emperor, a regent, noblemen and ladies, monks and commoners. Old-line monks intrigued against him until, in 1206, when he was seventy-four, they had him exiled to a remote area from which he was allowed to return only a year before his death. The Jōdu-shū lineage remains strong and active today, but not as much as the school founded by Shinran.

Shinran (1173–1262), founder of Jōdo-shin-shū (the True Pure Land sect), was one of Hōnen's disciples exiled when his master was. His early career resembles Hōnen's. His parents died while he was a child. He went to Mount Hiei as a novice and studied there for twenty years, gradually despairing of finding a passable way through the jungle of scholasticism and syncretisms. At twenty-nine, he left Mount Hiei and the Tendai teachings to follow Hōnen. Kwannon (Avalokiteśvara) appeared to him in a dream and told him to marry. With Hōnen's approval, he married a young noblewoman, demonstrating that monasticism was not necessary to salvation, and showing by example that the family should be the center of religious life. Shinran described himself as "neither a monk nor a layman," which aptly categorizes the married clergy of the sect he founded. They continued to live in temples and perform religious services, but they led a family life and expected the eldest son to take over the temple from his father. But Shin-shū (the shortened form of Jōdo-shin-shū) has not proclaimed the household life as an arena in which the great bodhisattva surpasses monks in wisdom and holiness. Shinran considered himself a sinner and thought of his marriage as an admission of weakness, a recognition that he could not save himself through his own power but must depend on Amida's grace.

Shinran was exiled to the northern province of Echigo, where he propagated the Nembutsu among the common people. Although he was soon pardoned, because Hōnen was dead he did not return to Kyōto but traveled through the towns and villages of east Japan (Kantō), spread the teaching, and founded temples. During this period he composed his chief work, *Teaching, Practice, Faith and Attainment,* which was published in 1224. In 1235, he returned to Kyōto and lived quietly there until his death.

Shinran interpreted, elaborated, and in some ways modified Hōnen's teaching. Hōnen had eliminated the element of meditation and merit-gathering from the Nembutsu in order to deepen one's devotion. He held that a single sincere invocation suffices for salvation. Subsequent repetitions are just expressions of gratitude to Amida for assured salvation. The power to exercise faith, says Shinran, is a gift from Amida and not an intrinsic possession of man.

The last point is the general Mahāyāna idea that religious initiative is possible only because the germ of Buddhahood is innate to living beings and is irradiated by the grace of the Buddhas. The radical feature of Shinran's teachings is his utter rejection of the cult of merit, and his apprehension lest the deliberate pursuit of virtue or wisdom either prevent faith or impair one's gratitude to Amida.

Shinran was not a saint in the usual Buddhist sense. He did not keep an austere regimen, was not celibate, did not practice meditation, did not exercise superknowledges, and used his great erudition only to reinforce the simple Nembutsu faith that he propagated. Nevertheless, he is revered by his followers with as much fervor and more sentiment than Tantra accords its great preceptors or Zen its famous masters. He was a good and humble man, compassionate and sentimental, sincere in his words and candid about his feelings. Though an aristocrat by birth, he made common cause with the lower classes, shared their way of life, and forewent the display of upper-class learning.

At Shinran's death, there was no Jōdo-shin sect because he had never tried to organize one. He left behind many loose associations of followers, whom his blood descendants organized into a sect. Rennyo (1415–1499) defined the religious position of the school more clearly and shaped its adherents into a feudal domain with armies and territorial control. They fortified their temples and in the sixteenth century, withstood Nobunaga's siege of their temple in Osaka for ten years before surrendering, only to be slaughtered by the perfidious Shōgun.

Another Buddhist sect was founded by Nichiren (1222–1282), who also studied at Mount Hiei but became dissatisfied with traditional Buddhist methods. Nichiren was the son of a fisherman. While still a boy he entered a local monastery, and at twenty was studying on Mount Hiei. Like Hōnen and Shinran, he was appalled at the corruption around him and frustrated with a teaching that offered all paths to all men yet rendered none of them effective. His solution, though, was to return to the root of Chih-i's and Saichō's teaching, to the *Lotus Sūtra*. He left Mount Hiei after ten years and went back to his native district. In 1253, he launched his campaign to conquer Japan with the pure *Lotus* gospel. He began chanting "Namu myō-hō-ren-ge-kyō" ("Salutation to the *Lotus Sūtra*"), which formula he held to be a sufficient means of salvation. Anyone who pronounced it would attain Buddhahood, acquire moral virtue, and become on this earth an embodiment of paradise. Nichiren identified himself as an incarnation of the Bodhisattva Superb Conduct, a leader of the bodhisattva hosts whom Śākyamuni summoned out of the earth, and whom he commanded to worship the *Lotus Sūtra*. He was convinced that it was his mission to save the Japanese nation from social and political disorders which he viewed as the consequences of wrong religion. He condemned Shingon because it worshipped Vairocana and neglected Śākyamuni. Amidism he castigated for worshipping Amida rather than Śākyamuni. His criticism of Zen was that it revered only the historical Śākyamuni and not the eternal Buddha of the *Lotus Sūtra*. When he went to Kamakura (the seat of the Shōgun's government) and broadcast his virulent denunciations of all other sects, the government was shocked and the religious world outraged. He was twice exiled and once narrowly escaped execution. Each suffering was in his eyes a glorious martyrdom: "Indeed every place where Nichiren encounters perils is a Buddha-land." He achieved recognition as a prophet when the Mongol invasion that he had predicted in 1260 and 1268 was attempted in 1274. Many followers were attracted by his courage, his single-minded zeal, and his vision of Japan as an earthly Buddha-land from which the revived and purified Dharma was to spread throughout the world.

Ch'an (Japanese: Zen) was introduced to Japan as early as the seventh century, and taught by a few masters in the eighth and ninth; but it did not catch on until the early Kamakura period, when concentration on a single path came into fashion. Eisai (1141–1215), a Tendai monk and a scholar of Mount Hiei, went to China and trained in the Lin-chi (Rinzai) house, established this sect in Japan upon his return in 1191. He won the favor of the Shōguns and forged the alliance with the military class which has ever since been the social foundation of Japanese Zen. By compromising expediently with Tendai and Shingon, he managed to win acceptance for Zen without exacerbating sectarian strife. He appealed to nationalist interests to get Zen accepted, writing a tract, *Propagate Zen, Protect the Country*. He is also venerated as the father of Japanese tea culture. Chinese Ch'an monks engaged in tea planting and also drank tea, as a stimulant to aid meditation and as a social alternative to wine. Kūkai is said to have brought tea from China, but it was Eisai who brought the seeds, planted them in the temple grounds, and fostered the use of the beverage. Fifteenth-century Zen people developed the tea ceremony as a social art and a spiritual discipline. Like flower arrangement, archery, jūdō, and kendō, it is a secularization of Buddhist ritual and contemplation. The goal in these arts is to realize a perfect fusion of aesthetic perception and noumenal awareness, of stillness and motion, utility and grace, conformity and spontaneity.

Dōgen (1200–1253), who established the Ts'ao-tung (Sōtō) house of Ch'an in Japan, is revered to this day by Buddhists of all sects and by many non-Buddhists as a great thinker, an admirable man and a gifted contemplative. His early life is much like that of the other sect-founders of his time. He was born to a noble family, lost his father when he was two and his mother when he was seven, and was awakened religiously by this encounter with suffering and impermanence, reinforced by his mother's deathbed plea that he become a monk. At twelve he left home, and a year later he became a novice on Mount Hiei, where he studied hard until he became engrossed in an enigma: if all living beings have Buddha-nature, then why do the Buddhas and Bodhisattvas all aspire to bodhi and engage in practices? He went around seeking an answer, and so came in 1214 to enter a Zen temple in Kyōto under Eisai's successor. He and his teacher set out for China in 1223, where he trained under two eminent masters. Dōgen returned to Japan in 1227 and soon settled in a small rural temple where he would be free from the intrigues and contention of temples in Kyōto. He taught _zazen_ (sitting meditation), wrote, and attracted so many followers that he had to move several times to more spacious temples. Rather than do battle with the hostile and envious monks of Mount Hiei, he moved to east Japan, was for a while the Shōgun's guest in Kamakura, and settled in the nearby mountain temple, Eihei-ji, which was built especially for him. He was ill for several years with a lung disease, and died at the comparatively young age of fifty-three.

During the Ashikaga period (1333–1568), when the country was divided among powerful feudal lords and, after 1400, rent by civil wars, the two Zen sects were the only major religious bodies that did not resort to arms to defend themselves and to further their cause. Zen monasteries were peaceful havens for thinkers, teachers, and artists. But the monks were also business entrepreneurs. They engaged in trade with China, maintained their own ships, and sold their imports. Zen monks devised new methods of accounting. Other Zen monks managed academies which taught not only Buddhism but Neo-Confucianism and classical Chinese literature as well. At the same time, Zen masters wrote tracts in colloquial Japanese, using the forty-seven sign syllabary so that they could be easily read and easily understood when read aloud. Provincial temples disseminated these tracts and their teachings to the people at large.

The Shōgun Nobunaga put an end to Buddhist militancy by destroying all fortified monasteries. He razed the temples on Mount Hiei in 1571, burning the libraries and chapels and beheading or taking captive all the inhabitants. The Tokugawa Shōgunate (1603–1868) gave Japan peace, but at the price of civil and religious liberty. Christianity, which had made headway in the late sixteenth century, was stamped out brutally in the early seventeenth century. As part of the anti-Christian proceedings, every family was required to register as adherents of a Buddhist temple. This "altar-family" system divided the territory and the population into parishes and incorporated the Buddhist clergy into the state apparatus as census takers, registrars of vital statistics, and government informers. Sects were forbidden to proselytize; conversion from one sect to another was obstructed by bureaucratic means. The government did not contribute financially to the temples, however, but laid the burden on the parishioners. The Buddhist sects became "established" churches, protected from both growth and collapse, spiritually discredited in the eyes of the populace.

Nonetheless, there was a great deal of scholarship, and the sects kept their traditions alive. The temples ran primary schools for children, and deserve much of the credit for the comparatively high rate of literacy with which Japan ended the Tokugawa era. A new Zen sect, the Ōbaku, was introduced from China in the seventeenth century. This stimulated a reform movement within Sōtō Zen in the late seventeenth and early eighteenth centuries. Japan's greatest poet, Matsuo Bashō (1644–1694) was a lay disciple of Zen. In his lapidary haiku,[3] he secularized several salient Buddhist insights and stamped them indelibly into Japanese culture—transiency, loneliness and silence, compassion

Matsuo Bashō (Banana Tree), foremost of Japan's Buddhist poets.

for living things, awareness of the transcendental in the mundane and natural. Hakuin (1685–1768) revitalized Rinzai Zen, teaching peasants and children and founding a line of eminent meditation masters.

The Meiji Restoration of 1868 was inspired by a Shintō nationalism hostile to Buddhism. After a brief spell of persecution and the expropriation of temple lands, the Buddhists were roused to assert themselves, recovered much of their prestige, and took steps to modernize, such as founding schools and universities and giving the clergy modern educations. The Meiji government decree that the clergy of all sects be allowed to marry has been observed so well that nowadays there are very few monks in Japan except for young men in training. The various sects have taken on a panoply of modern lay organizations, Sunday schools, Boy Scout troops, meditation clubs, and young people's societies. There are many popular Buddhist magazines, popular books on Buddhism and translations of the Sūtras are found in every neighborhood bookstore, and a plethora of scholarly books and journals continues to be published. Busloads of tourists visit the old temples of Nara. Kōya-san and Hiei-zan, the ancient centers of the Shingon and Tendai schools, are accessible by cablecar; women are no longer excluded from their premises. The old sects possess an impressive number of temples, clerics, and lay followers. They are apprehensive about the new lay movements such as Sōkagakkai and Risshō-kōseikai, which appeal to some Buddhist texts and insights but bypass the old ecclesiastical apparatus and often use aggressive methods that are offensive to traditional Buddhists. These new sects have attracted millions of members and have placed Buddhism in the central arena of national life for the first time since the sixteenth century. But they are not likely to jeopardize the future existence of the historic sects. Since the Nara period, no sect that acquired independent institutional status has ever become extinct.

VIETNAM

Buddhism came to the area of Vietnam from both Chinese and Indian spheres of influence, but it was the Chinese Mahāyāna forms that finally prevailed.

Chinese civilization was a major force in shaping Vietnamese development, with secondary influences coming from the Indianized states of Funan, Campā, and the Khmers.

Indian colonists helped found Campā on the east coast in the late second century A.D., and under them Buddhism came to the area, along with economic and cultural ties with India. Judging by a bronze Buddha-image in a south Indian style, Theravāda Buddhism was probably present by the third century. In the later centuries, Mahāyāna and Tantra monks came. By this ninth century, Buddhism was receiving royal patronage, but the dynasty probably supported Hindu Śaivism as well, creating a syncretistic Buddho-Śaivism similar to that of Cambodia. Mahāyāna continued in Campā up until the fifteenth century, when Annamites, formerly settled in Tonkin, invaded, bringing with them Chinese forms of Buddhism more characteristic of the north. These eventually replaced earlier forms, except for Theravāda survivals on the Cambodian border.

In the north, successive Chinese invasions led to long centuries of Chinese domination after the first century B.C. The Chinese brought their state Confucianism and imposed their culture by force, stressing Taoist and Confucian learning. Even though Chinese rule continued until the tenth century, Chinese Buddhists did begin coming to the area in the second century A.D. In following centuries other missionaries arrived by sea from India and overland through China from as far away as Central Asia. Hīnayāna and Mahāyāna were both represented. Due to the proximity of China, Ch'an (Vietnamese: *Thien)* became dominant. It was introduced by the famous Indian meditation master Vinītaruci at the end of the sixth century. Chinese emperors also sent Buddha relics to be enshrined in stūpas, and temples and shrines were constructed in the countryside. Amidism (Pure Land) came to dominate village-level Buddhism while monastic institutions remained Thien. The split continued after Vietnam became independent from the Chinese in the tenth century. Amidism spread among the people and Thien monasteries produced an illustrious line of Buddhist scholars, poets, and meditators. Thien monks gained prestige due to their literacy in Chinese, and rulers vigorously patronized Buddhist learning, especially during the eleventh century. Several sects of Thien Buddhism flourished, producing venerated teachers and lay leaders to support them. Amidism continued at the village level, incorporating the gods of the older, pre-Buddhist religion. The two schools were integrated at the monastery level during the centuries that followed, and this mix characterizes Vietnamese Buddhism today.

EAST ASIAN BUDDHISM IN THE TWENTIETH CENTURY

In countries that have become Communist, official party policy discourages any observance of the Buddhist religion. What this will mean for the future of Buddhism in North Korea, Vietnam, China, and Tibet is not apparent at the present time. Some scholars see the end of Buddhism in China and Tibet. The Chinese New Constitution of 1965 included strictures against Buddhism designed to hasten its disappearance from Chinese life. The Buddhist community was the target of severe repression during the Red Guard movement (1966–69) in China and Tibet. Committing genocide against the Tibetan people, the Chinese have effectively ended Buddhism there. It survives only in India, where the Indian government gave fleeing refugees a place to settle in a country that, in 1956, had just celebrated the 2,500th anniversary of the Buddha. The official policy of Communist government is that religion perpetuates social injustice and that religious thought and culture do not serve the people's proper (material) needs. Given this climate the survival of Buddhism is in considerable doubt.

The situation in contemporary Japan is paradoxical. Though no official policy condemns the Buddhist religion, Japan's Western-style modernization has turned many of its people away from their temples, leading especially to neglect of such important practices as serious meditation. Zen meditation halls lack full contingents of participants, even though they are open to the laity; and priests leave their hereditary positions in the temples for secular pursuits. On the other hand, the laity is gaining a greater role in Japanese Buddhism. Secular meditation groups and new sects like Sōkagakkai give laypeople new opportunities to act within a Buddhist context. Japan, like Ceylon and Thailand, has shown interest in sending missions abroad, and emerging Japanese sects (Tenrikyo, The Religion of Heavenly Wisdom; Nichiren Shoshu, The Church of World Messianity; and Seicho-no-le, The House of Growth and Perfect Liberty) are gaining converts especially on the West Coast of the United States. It is perhaps significant that Japanese Buddhist scholarship is voluminous and substantially furthers the cause of Buddhist studies the world around. Recently, major philosophers in Japan, such as Nishida Kitarō, have been Buddhists.

The Buddhist experience in the Vietnamese war is too recent to assess. All the world remembers the newspaper and television images of Buddhist monks burning themselves to death. In all, over thirty self-immolations took place. Actually, the Buddhist Saṅgha did not become involved in politics there until partisan Roman Catholic anti-Buddhist leaders abused it. Militant Buddhists responded by supporting the coup against their oppressor, Diem, in 1963, though during the war Buddhists were split between moderate and militant factions. Buddhist calls for peace were thought treasonous by the Saigon government's tough anti-Communist leaders, a stand that precluded real Buddhist participation in peace-making efforts, which remained in the hands of the military. It is still too early to know what Communist policy towards Buddhism will bring in the two Vietnams, as well as in Laos and Cambodia.

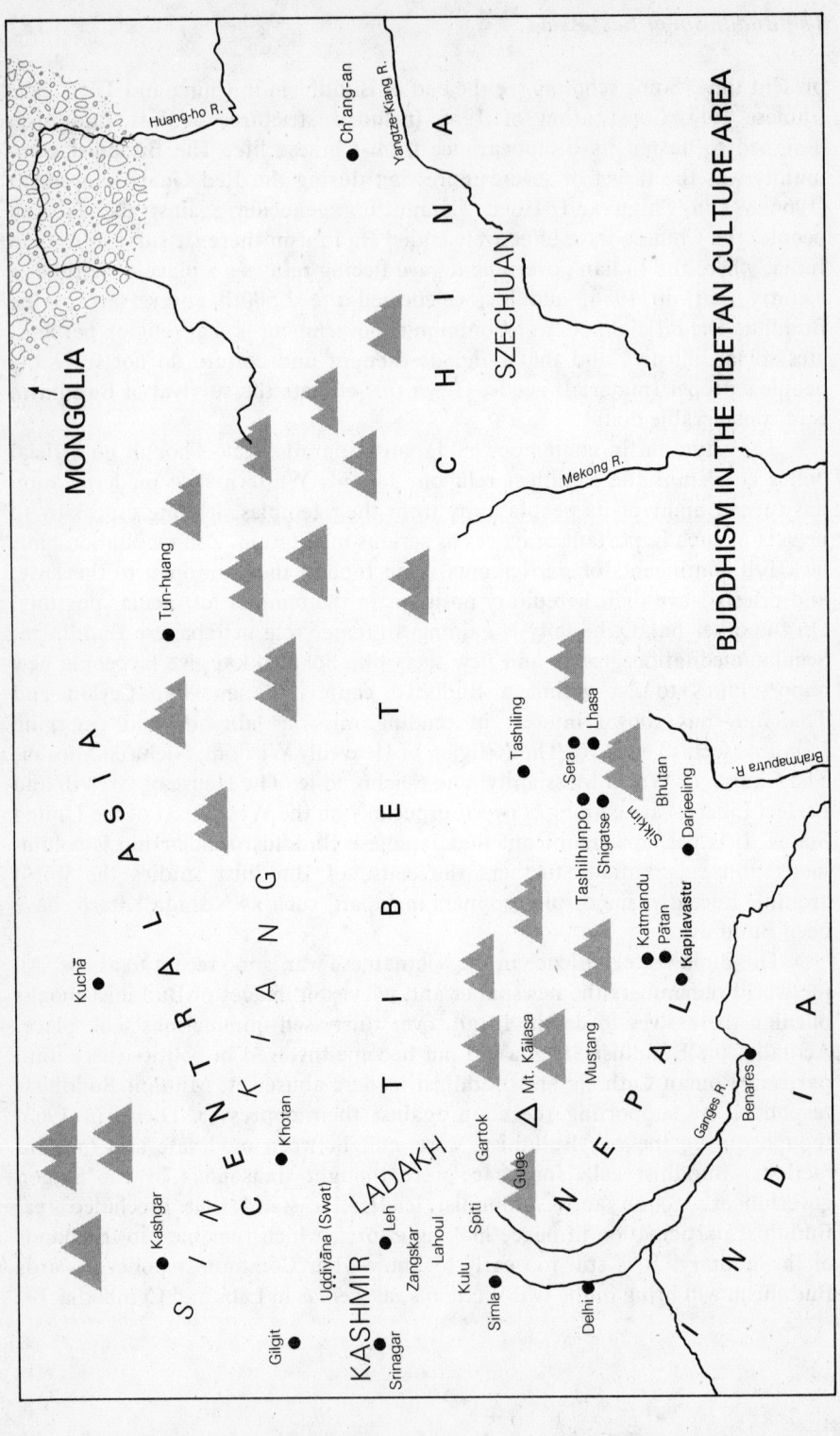

10.
Buddhism in the Tibetan Culture Area

NEPAL

Nominally, Nepal has the unique position in Buddhism's history of being the birthplace of its founder. It was within the boundaries of contemporary Nepal that the Buddha was born, in the Lumbinī Grove about fifteen miles from his father's capital of Kapilavastu. Legend says that the Buddha returned home after his Enlightenment to declare the new path, converting his own son. In the third century B.C., the emperor Aśoka visited the area, and his daughter reportedly married a Nepalese nobleman, bringing Buddhism with her. Thus, it probably has existed in Nepal from a very early time, but we know almost nothing of its history there before the seventh century.

A Tibetan Yabyum (father-mother) figure, symbolizing the union of wisdom and compassion.

In the early centuries the Buddhism of Nepal most likely developed along the lines of north India. In the fourth century Vasubandhu visited Nepal. Pātan, a Buddhist center of learning, resembled those of eastern India. Royal favor supported it in the seventh century, and during the two centuries that followed, Nepal developed strong ties with Tibet as many Tibetans came to study in Nepal. Tradition says that king Aṃśuvarman gave his daughter in marriage to the first important Tibetan king, Song-tsen-gam-po (617-650). She took the cult of Tārā, indicating Tantra was present in Nepal by then.

After the Muslims invaded Bihar and Bengal, in the late twelfth century, many Buddhist monks and scholars took refuge in Nepal, bringing with them

Tantrism and large numbers of manuscripts and images. Some of the documents survived until this century, when they were retrieved by scholars, adding to our small stock of extant Indian Buddhist manuscripts, most of which were eaten by white ants or otherwise destroyed in their homeland. However, the decline of Buddhism in India paralleled its waning in Nepal. It eventually suffered a fate similar to that of Indian Buddhism, primarily through the weakening of its monastic system. After 1000 A.D., royal patronage sustained the Saṅgha for some time, and the country remained a center of Buddhist culture. Nepal, however, was primarily Hindu, especially the laity, so that once the flow from India stopped, Buddhism gradually became a part of Hinduism. Around the fourteenth century, Buddhist monks became high Hindu caste called *banras* (worthy ones), gave up celibacy, and lived in their monasteries as metal workers. Others became *vajrācāryas* (so-called diamond masters), ceremonial specialists who served the ritual needs of the laity, performing rites of birth, death, and other sacraments as hereditary monastery or temple functionaries. Buddhist scholarship declined accordingly during this period. Buddhism finally became syncretized with Tantric Hinduism and today no longer exists as a separate religion in Nepal, except for small minorities who still consider themselves Buddhists. Its vestiges (prayer wheels and flags, stūpas) are found today in the country's popular religion.

KASHMIR, TIBETAN BORDER VALLEYS, CENTRAL ASIA, AND MONGOLIA

The history of Buddhism in the sub-Himālayan vale of Kashmir probably began earlier than its third century B.C. annexation by the Emperor Aśoka, but his efforts strengthened it greatly. He had monasteries built and may have donated the valley to the Saṅgha. In the first centuries of the present era, the fate of Buddhism was dependent upon royal patronage. Kings were often

The Buddha touching the earth for witness to his merit. (Bajo Monastery, Bhutan, 16th or 17th century.)

Hindus who favored Śaivism and repressed Buddhism. However, Kashmir came to be a great center of Buddhist learning, and Kashmiri monks spread the Word to Central Asia, China, south India, and even Java.

At the time of the Hun invasion (515 A.D.), monks were persecuted, but soon the new Buddhist ruler and his followers renewed the royal patronage of Buddhism. A later era of prosperity, in the seventh and eighth centuries, brought another revival, but one which syncretized Buddhism with Hindu Śaivism. This continued when Buddhist Tantra and devotionalism brought it even closer to Śaivism. In the ninth century, many Buddhist monks went to Tibet; after the year 1000, even more went there as well as to the remote Himālayan valleys closer to western Tibet. By the fifteenth century, Muslims had repressed Buddhism and, as in Nepal, only its vestiges survive in the Hinduism of the area.

Between Kashmir on the west and Bhutan in the east, along the long crescent bordering western and central Tibet, many valleys have remained Buddhist to this day because of their remoteness from the plains. These include Ladakh, Zangskar, Lahoul, Spiti, Guge, and the Nepalese valleys more accessible to Tibet, as well as, to the east of Nepal, the Indian protectorates of Bhutan and Sikkim. In the seventeenth century, a Tibetan lama introduced Buddhism into Bhutan, while about the same time others were bringing it to Sikkim. The Buddhism in all these areas is Tibetan in form.

Central Asia was Buddhist from the second century B.C. on, influenced by the Indo-Greek Bactrian kingdoms. Its establishment in Khotan, Kuchā, and Turfan meant that Buddhism could soon spread along the silk trade routes into China. Also, thanks to the favorable climate, many Indian manuscripts and a rich Buddhist art have survived to the twentieth century, becoming invaluable records for scholars. In the seventh century, Central Asia again linked India with the great T'ang dynasty of China. Tibetans influenced the area for some time between the seventh and tenth centuries, but open to diverse religious influences, the region gradually became Islamic after 900.

Finally, the Mongols, whose original religion was shamanism, were twice brought under the control of Tibetan Buddhism, in the thirteenth and later in the sixteenth centuries. After the first conversion, Tibetan Buddhism shared the power of the Mongol Empire and established many monasteries in China, especially in Peking, exerting great power there during the Yüan dynasty (1260–1368). On the whole the people were not won over in this period. Following the second conversion, however, Buddhism adopted for political reasons, became very popular, this time gaining the support of the people. Mongolia became a site of great Buddhist monasteries and a center of learning. It is from this period that the term Dalai (Ocean, All-encompassing) Lama comes. A Mongol king, Altan Khan, gave it to a Tibetan prelate who claimed primacy in Tibet over his rivals. Buddhist scriptures were translated into Mongol. In time support waned, however, and in the twentieth century a Communist government has taken over.

TIBET

Tibet entered history in the seventh century A.D., when a line of kings became firmly established, enlarged their domain, and came to the notice of Chinese historians. About 632, according to tradition, King Song-tsen-gam-po (Srong-btsan-sgam-po)[1] sent an emissary to Kashmir to learn writing and devise a script for Tibetan. Buddhism seems to have entered Tibet from Kashmir and Khotan during this king's reign. For some time the new religion made little progress. In the mid-eighth century, there were faction fights between pro- and anti-Buddhist nobles at the court. When the Buddhists won, the king and his ministers brought in the Indian master Śāntarakṣita (775–795 A.D.), who stayed a while, went to Nepal, and came back later for a more successful second visit. At the same time a famous but historically vague figure, Padma-sambhava, arrived from Uḍḍiyāna (Swat), a noted Tantric center. He ranks as one of the eighty-four Siddhas (Tantric saints), and is credited in Tibetan tradition with fabulous wonder-working. The sect of the Nying-ma-pas (Rnying-ma-pa, "Ancient One") claim him as their founder, though he stayed in Tibet just long enough to cofound with Śāntarakṣita the Tibetan Saṅgha and the country's first monastery (787). A Chinese Ch'an master named Mahāyāna came to the court and made many converts. In 794 or thereabouts, a debate was held before the king in which Śāntarakṣita's school vigorously attacked the Ch'an faction and succeeded in getting the king to banish the Chinese. Despite continual intercourse with the Chinese, Tibetan Buddhism has ever since been based on that of India.

The development of Tibetan Buddhism has been an interaction between scholar-monks leading a conventional celibate life (typified by Śāntarakṣita) and wonder-working yogins wandering freely, often not wearing the monastic robe and not bound to celibacy (typified by Padma-sambhava). Spiritual masters of both types are called "lama." "Lama" is just the Tibetan translation for *guru* (preceptor), and either an eminent monk or an outstanding householder yogin may bear the title.

The work of translating scriptures went forward rapidly in the early ninth century and under the patronage of the pious King Ral-pa-can. A commission of Indian and Tibetan scholars standardized the technical terminology and published a Sanskrit-Tibetan glossary. It was decided that, with few exceptions, texts would only be translated from Sanskrit, and works previously translated from vernacular versions were retranslated from Sanskrit. The Tibetan language was stretched, bent, and molded to express a wide range of alien contents and styles. Tibetan translations are often opaque, but they are marvelously consistent and usually match the original point for point.

The king's chief minister, a monk named "Virtue," was first slandered and then executed. Pro-Buddhist nobles murdered the king, whose vicious brother Lang-dar-ma (Glang-dar-ma, 836–842) succeeded him and by persecution eliminated organized Buddhism from central Tibet. Lang-dar-ma himself was murdered by a monk, but the damage to Buddhism was not repaired for generations. The line of kings terminated, and the religion survived as mundane magic practiced by itinerant yogins. Refugee monks spread Buddhism in other parts of the country, notably in east Tibet (Kham). A descendent of Lang-dar-ma established a strong kingdom in west Tibet in the tenth century, and his successors undertook to promote the Dharma. They chose twenty-one Tibetan boys and sent them to India to learn Sanskrit, study doctrine, and persuade Indian masters to come to Tibet. All but two of the boys died from heat and disease on the Indian plains. Of the two who survived to become scholars, the more famous was Rin-chen Sangpo (Bzang-po, 958–1055). The illustrious Bengali scholar Atīśa (982–1054), after much persuasion, came to west Tibet in 1042. He was well versed in exoteric and esoteric teachings, and his career crowned the renaissance of doctrine studies in Tibet. He is also famed for the most gracious of all recorded first reactions to Tibetan buttered tea: "This cup contains the elixir of the wish-granting tree."

By this time, central Tibet had recovered from the Buddhist persecution. Monks had come in from Kham and rebuilt the monasteries, and a new line of kings (also descended from Lang-dar-ma) were furnishing patronage. Atīśa's chief disciple, Drom ('Brom), persuaded him to go to Lhasa, where he spent the rest of his life conferring Tantric initiations and translating. Drom, though a layman, was Atīśa's spiritual heir, and founded the Ka-dam-pa (Bka'-gdams-pa) lineage, the first Tibetan sect whose historic beginnings (unlike Nying-ma-pa) are clear.

Drok-mi ('Brog-mi), a contemporary of Atīśa's, studied in the Tantric university of Vikramaśīla for eight years, then returned to Tibet, where in 1073 he founded the monastery of Sa-skya, whose abbots possessed great learning and temporal power during the twelfth and thirteenth centuries. Clerics from this monastery, Sa-kya-pa (Sa-skya-pa) abbots, are permitted to marry, and the succession passes either from father to son or from uncle to nephew. The abbot 'Phags-pa (1235–1280), continuing the relations his uncle had established with the Mongols, became prelate to Kublai Khan, from whom he received temporal jurisdiction over all of Tibet.

Another lineage of Tibetan Buddhism, the Kargyüpa, began in the eleventh century with Mar-pa (1012-1097). Mar-pa was a disciple of the great Bengali adept Nāropa, under whom he trained at Nālandā. Returning to Tibet, he took a wife whom he called Nairātmyā, as she also served as his prajñā in the rites of Hevajra (see p. 122). Mar-pa was a man of strong character and strong passions, wrathful and possessive. Only when his own son died did he stop denying the spiritual succession to his long-suffering and gifted disciple, Milarepa (Mi-la ras-pa, "the Cotton-clad Mila").

Milarepa (1040–1123) is the most popular saint and the greatest poet of Tibet, as well as the Second Patriarch of the Kargyüpa (Bka'-rgyud-pa) sect founded by Mar-pa. As a youth, he learned magic in order to take revenge on a wicked uncle who had dispossessed and maltreated Mila's widowed mother.

The Cotton-clad Mila, his ear cupped to hear the teaching of his teacher or to listen to Nature's secrets. (From a Tibetan image.)

Having destroyed his enemy, he was seized with remorse and sought first to expiate his bad karman and then to attain liberation. At thirty-eight he became Mar-pa's disciple. For six years the master put him through cruel ordeals before finally granting him the initiation he sought.[2] Milarepa spent the rest of his life meditating in the caves and wandering on the slopes of the High Himālayas (Kailāsa, Everest). He gradually attracted a following, converted many disciples, and worked wonders for people's benefit. His numerous songs express not only profound Dharma, but the unearthly atmosphere of his mountain home, and the cruel rigors and high ecstasies of the ascetic life as well.

The Kargyüpa line was continued by Gam-po-pa (Sgam-po-pa, 1079–1153), who at thirty-two heard of Milarepa from a beggar and acquired his teachings in thirteen months' study. After Gam-po-pa, the sect split into four branches, one of which converted the people of Bhutan in the seventeenth century, and another of which was favored by the Mongol and Ming emperors of China.

The Tibetan scriptures were collected and edited to form a Canon by Butön (Bu-ston, 1290–1364). This Canon consists of two collections: the *Kanjur* (Bka'-'gyur) which comprises the Vinaya, Sūtras, and Tantras, and the *Tenjur* (Bstan-'gyur) which contains treatises, commentaries, and works on auxiliary disciples such as grammar, astrology, and medicine. The first printed Kanjur was completed in Peking in 1411, and the first complete printings of the Canon in Tibet were at Narthang (Snar-thang)—the Kanjur (100 volumes) in 1731 and the Tenjur (225 volumes) in 1742.

The scene in the early fourteenth century was a welter of sects and subsects. Besides the Ka-dam-pas, the Sa-kya-pas, and the various Kar-gyü-pa branches, there were the Shi-je-pas (Zhi-byed-pa, "Tranquilizer" or "Peacemaker"), a sect of yogins founded in the late eleventh century by the Indian master Pha-dam-pa Sanggye (Pha-dam-pa Sangs-rgyas, "Holy Father Buddha"), and the Nying-ma-pas, revitalized by Guru Chö-wang (Chos-dbang, 1212-1273) who discovered (or claimed to discover) "hidden scriptures" deposited by Padma-sambhava and others. Except for the Ka-dam-pas, these sects were lax in discipline, and all were given to politics and magic.

Tsong-kha-pa (1257-1419) was a native of northeast Tibet, where he became a novice in boyhood and received Tantric initiations. Then sent by his teacher to central Tibet, he studied the exoteric Mahāyāna treatises for years and visited all the notable centers of learning there. He was particularly fond of Logic and Vinaya. He took full ordination at age twenty-five, began to teach, and through the good offices of a preceptor was able to "meet" Mañjuśrī. In 1393, he had just eight pupils. By 1409, he had a multitude of disciples and controlled the main temple of Lhasa. His new sect, the Gelukpa (Dge-lugs-pa, "Partisan of Virtue"), professed to continue the strict discipline of the Ka-dam-pas, laid equal stress on the exoteric and the esoteric teachings, and implemented a regular curriculum of systematic doctrinal studies leading to the degree of *Geshe* (Dge-shes, "spiritual friend"), equivalent to a doctorate in philosophy or divinity. Three large Gelukpa monasteries were founded near Lhasa in 1409, 1416, and 1419. Tsong-kha-pa was a brilliant scholar, an excellent organizer, and a reformer. His monks had to forego liquor, sex, evening meals, and long naps. He condemned worldly magic, and his sect practices the Tantras only as a means to enlightenment.

Tsong-kha-pa's third successor was his nephew Gendün truppa (Dge-'dun grub-pa), who took office in 1438. He was accepted as an incarnation of Avalokiteśvara, and so started the line of Dalai Lamas. Since they are incarnations in a continuing series, the intermediate stage must pass between the death of the last Dalai Lama and the birth of the next. It is believed to last forty-nine days. Therefore, a search party looks for a child born that long after the death of a Dalai Lama, guided by whatever indications the dying Incarnation has left concerning his next appearance, and by the pronouncements of the state oracle. The searchers look for certain physical signs on the infant, prodigies at the time of his birth (for example, a tree that blossoms in winter), and ability to recognize objects belonging to the previous Incarnation. Once the right child is found, he is brought to Lhasa and carefully educated for his future role. Meanwhile, regents rule on his behalf.

The third Dalai Lama (1543-1588) converted the Mongols for the second and last time. He is said to have met the pagan gods of the Mongols, converted them, and made them into Dharma-protectors. The fourth Dalai Lama (1589-1616) turned out, providentially, to be the grandson of the great chief of the Mongols. The fifth Dalai Lama (1617-1682) was a great scholar, surprisingly well versed in Nyingmapa literature. He was an energetic and shrewd politician, and, with the aid of Mongol armies, overthrew the enemies of his sect and became the temporal as well as the spiritual ruler of Tibet. His repressive measures forced many clerics of other sects to take refuge in outlying areas of Tibet, Sikkim and Bhutan. The new Manchu dynasty in China confirmed the

Dalai Lama's power and used him and his successors to keep Tibet quiet and safe for China, just as the Dalai Lamas used their status and their wiles to keep the Chinese out of Tibet as much as possible.

The sixth Dalai Lama (1683–1706) was a drinker and girl-chaser and the reputed author of a collection of love songs. He came from a family of Nying-ma-pas, and his apparent debauchery seems to have been part of an attempt to revive the old Tantric ways. Intense opposition to him sprang up. A conclave of lamas decided that Avalokiteśvara had abandoned the body of the incumbent and had entered another lama. Finally a Mongol army burst into Lhasa, killed the regent, and captured the Dalai Lama alive. He died in captivity, perhaps murdered. Subsequent Dalai Lamas were loyal Gelukpas, and kept out of trouble with the Chinese. The ninth through the twelfth Incarnations died in boyhood.

The thirteenth Dalai Lama (1874–1933) survived the perils of childhood only to get caught in international politics. He had to flee to Mongolia when the British sent an army to Lhasa in 1904, and in 1910 he fled to India to escape the Chinese, returning in 1912 after the Manchu dynasty fell. The fourteenth Dalai Lama (1935–) was enthroned in 1950, one year before the Chinese Communists marched in and occupied his country. He fled to India during the anti-Chinese uprisings of 1959. While he lives in exile and serves as *de facto* leader for the tens of thousands of Tibetan refugees, the Chinese grind away the remnants of a medieval culture and religion that, sordid politics notwithstanding, produced a brave, cheerful, and courteous people, many great scholars, and in each generation a few real saints.

THE RELIGIOUS LIFE OF TIBETAN BUDDHISM

Beyer (1973) has described the typical religious life of a Tibetan monastic community in his study of the cult of Tārā. Tārā is a Buddhist savioress who guards and protects all who call on her for help in danger. Her cult is widespread in Tibet, found at all social levels. Though it was imported from India in the eighth and eleventh centuries, it became thoroughly Tibetan.

"Glorious Divine Isle of the Wheel of the Law" was the name of this monastery, located in K'am (eastern Tibet). Within its walls were two temples or assembly halls; workrooms for the production of ritual artifacts; the living quarters of the monks; and outside, a monastic college for 300 monks, one of two run by the monastery. Before the main temple was an area used for the yearly masked dances (see Prologue, pp. 3–4). The monastery was supported by donations from wealthy patrons and the king of the district, as well as by its own trading activities. A storekeeper headed a committee responsible for monastic finances, and separate offices handled buildings, suplies for the monks, and the ritual functions of the monastery.

Ritual was the institution's foremost activity. Each monk had ceremonial responsibilities to the monastery, to the lay community and to its king, and, as a bodhisattva, to all sentient beings. The typical ritual day of a monk considered an Incarnation began before dawn, when, for an hour-and-a-half, he performed his private ritual contemplations and prostrations. He then spent two hours participating in the monastic assembly's morning evocations and prayers, and followed this by working in the library. After lunch he supervised craftsmen in the monastic workshops, followed by another two-hour assembly in the evening. After dinner he again performed his private prescribed contemplations.

The life of the monastery was totally devoted to ritual and ritual-related activities since in them power for good resided. In the monastery, ritual surrounded the monk on all sides and was his principal link to the lay community. The monastery's mercantile activities supported its devotional responsibilities; royal patronage ensured in return ritual protection for the district; the laity supported it for the benefit of its specialization in the control of divine power. The head lama performed rituals for healing, protection, and exorcism of evil spirits. The monastery was thus a "service organization" providing ritual services for those who needed them. This ritual power in turn derived from the monks' steadfast pursuit of enlightenment. The health of the total community depended on the monastic channeling of power for its protection and everyday well-being.

When a novice monk entered the monastery, usually around nine or ten years old, he became immersed in its ritual life immediately. Over a period of years, he underwent a complete training in ritual. First, during his earliest years there, he memorized the immense body of ritual texts he would later need and became familiar with the daily routine of the monastery, helping out by performing tasks for the older monks. Later, after training in the monastic college, he spent three years learning the necessary ritual hand gestures, chanting, making of maṇḍalas and offering-materials, as well as how to play ritual musical instruments and to perform religious dances, having already become acquainted with all of them during his younger days.

As soon as he could, the monk also spent a period—usually three years, three months, and three days—living in the monastery's yogic hermitage. There he learned the techniques which were to be the basis for all his future contemplations. His teachers were yogins who lived permanently in the

A Tibetan yogi in solitary meditation. (From a wood-block print.)

hermitage, engaged in constant meditation. First, he internalized through meditation the basics of Buddhist doctrine—that it is supremely difficult in the multitude destinies of the Wheel of Life to obtain this precious human rebirth in which release may be won, that all existence is limited by death and impermanence, that all actions have karmic consequences, that continued existence in the world is terrifying. After these meditations, he went through further ritual experiences to qualify him for his monastic vocation; these included formally going for refuge, accepting the bodhisattva vows to awaken the thought of enlightenment, and practicing Tantric visualizations of the deities and lamas associated with his monastery. By the end of this training period, he was infused with the attitudes of renunciation and benevolence necessary for his attainment and use of ritual, magic power.

The young monk spent the remainder of his training in the hermitage learning Tantric visualization skills in solitary contemplation. He learned the ritual service of the deities he would evoke both in his private meditation and for those who sought the help of the divine power he would adeptly control. He learned the mantras each visualization required, perfecting as many as he could, becoming the deity, as Tantrics do, to make the power of that deity his own and thus be capable of controlling divine power.

Upon leaving the hermitage, the monk was ready to join in the full life of the monastic cult as it unrolled according to the daily and seasonal ritual calendar of the monastery, and in his personal meditation. The monastic cult involved the evocation and worship of three categories of divine meditative objects: (1) the teachers of the monastery's lineage, primarily the "precious guru" Padma-sambhava; (2) the high patron deities; and (3) the protectors of the Law, or the "Lords." A special room, one of the most sacred in the monastery, was maintained for the worship of its special protector Lord. For twenty hours a day, a designated monk and his two assistants worshipped there to the accompanyment of drum, cymbal, and recitation.

In contrast to this monastic cult, the worship of Tārā was part of the religious life of all Tibetans, lay and monastic alike. A recitation to her was included in the morning monastic assembly but more, she was never far away from the attention of all. Her picture was on altars everywhere as she was a personal patroness to everyone rather than a specific monastic protector.

Tārā's popular cult was expressed in many forms. She was featured in folklore and her deeds were dramatized by native Tibetan troupes of wandering performers. Performed in the open air, their masked dances told of Tārā's bounteous protection. Tibetan poets composed verses to honor her and celebrated instances of the help she bestowed on her devotees. In eastern Tibet, during the summer, whole villages would go into the flower-covered hills. There, in a suitable valley, families would pitch their tents in a circle around a main tent set up for ritual and smaller ones used for cooking and games. They would first worship Avalokiteśvara for two days, and then Tārā for from three to six. This was not a monastic function but a popular festival. In the morning, from eight to ten, the ritual honoring the goddess would be held in the main tent, attended by all the layfolk, led by nonmonastic monks who lived in the village. During the afternoon, there were dances and games, conversation and eating. Men would race their horses and shoot at targets, and much native Tibetan beer would be consumed. It was a time of great religious devotion and exuberant socializing.

11.
Buddhism Comes West

Buddhism has come gradually to the countries of the Western world. At first the process was slow since contacts, upon which knowledge and the exchange of ideas depend, were few. Even though Buddhism is the East's main missionary religion (its missionizing posture is not aggressive), it was not until Westerners themselves went to the East that it began to make a significant impact on Europe and America. We have seen that, within Asia, Buddhism spread beyond India by following trade routes into Southeast Asia and, through Central Asia, into East Asia. Zealous missionaries accompanied traders, political and military expeditions, and adventurers, spreading Buddhism wherever they went. How has Buddhism expanded beyond the confines of Asia, to come to the West?

Before the journey of Marco Polo (1271-1295) and the subsequent colonial expansion of European powers into Asia, Western civilizations came into only minimal encounters with Buddhism. During periods of military or economic expansiveness, Europeans had some slight contact with India. Militarily, Alexander the Great brought Greeks and Indians together by crossing the Indus River in the spring of 326 B.C., but he and his successors returned with no substantial knowledge of Buddhism that we know of. There were also peaceful mercantile relations between the Hellenistic world and the Roman Empire on the one side and India on the other, but again Buddhism was not brought back with the peacocks and other exotica. Between that time and the dawn of European colonialism, only the Islamic expansion into India brought Eastern ideas to the West. Europe's knowledge of Buddhism increased only as Europeans themselves began going to Asia, when for various reasons—economic, political, and religious—East and West began to find themselves in close and continuous communication beginning especially in the nineteenth century. Early Christian missionaries returned with versions of Buddhist texts; and, as colonial powers began to learn about the peoples of the East, the secular, academic study of Buddhism also began, using texts and information brought back by officials, teachers and scholars, and travelers.

Sometime later, populations of Asians increased in some Western countries (such as Japanese communities in Hawaii and on the West Coast of the United States), bringing Buddhism with them. Buddhists also came in response to growing Western interest. In the twentieth century, vastly increased contacts were facilitated by improvements in travel and communications so that today many Westerners know something about Buddhism, and significant minorities among them now practice some form of the Buddhist religion. At least one Japanese sect, Nichiren Shōshū (Sōkagakkai) claims

The First Vietnamese Buddhist Temple

in the United States

requests the honour of your presence

at its Founding Ceremony

Sunday, the eleventh of January

nineteen hundred and seventy-six

at eleven o'clock in the morning

928 So. New Hampshire Avenue

Los Angeles, California

RSVP   487-1235
1:30-4:30 pm

Invitation to the Founding Ceremony of the First Vietnamese Buddhist Temple, January 1976, in Los Angeles, California.

groups of followers in North, Central, and South America; the Caribbean; and Oceania.

EUROPE'S EARLIEST KNOWLEDGE OF BUDDHISM

Little can be said of Europe's earliest acquaintance with Buddhism. There were certainly no extensive direct or accurate reports of Buddhism in the pre-

Christian or early Christian periods. Through the Middle Ages, Europeans remained ignorant of Buddhism. There may have been Indian influence on early Greek thought, expressed in Gnosticism and Manichaenism. Some wonder whether Plato's doctrine of the transmigration of souls and his notion of knowledge as remembrance originated in India. The Buddha's first night watch vision, crucial to his Enlightenment, has both these elements in it, but there is no certainty that it inspired Plato. Islamic civilization, the first to stretch all the way from Europe to the Indus since Alexander's empire, brought Indian tales to Christendom, but the influence was not important religiously. The Catholic saints Barlaam and Josaphat (that is, bodhisattva) may derive, curiously, from the Buddha legend. Professor Conze has even speculated that modern commercialism could scarcely have developed in the West without the Buddhist contribution of the idea of emptiness. It reached Europe via the Arabs, who brough the idea of the 'cypher' (Arabic *shifr* for śūnya, 'empty'), without which we might still be using an abacus. More concretely, in 725 A.D., a brilliant Chinese Tantric Buddhist monk, I-Hsing, cooperating with a military engineer, solved the problem of mechanical time-keeping; in short, they invented the clock, called by Lewis Mumford "the key machine of the modern industrial age." Thus, a Sino-Buddhist method of mechanically measuring time may have been known in Europe before Western inventors solved the critical problem nearly six hundred years later in the thirteenth century.

THE GROWTH OF EUROPEAN KNOWLEDGE OF BUDDHISM

Europe had no firm knowledge of Buddhism until Europeans actually went to the East and came into contact with it at first hand. Beginning in the thirteenth century and as a result of the Crusades, Europeans gradually began to travel to Asian Buddhist lands. But these were only occasional ministers to the Khan, or an adventurous merchant like Marco Polo. It was not until European exploration at the end of the fifteenth century, and the first journeys of missionaries in the sixteenth, that Europe began to learn about Buddhism. Catholic missionaries went to India, Japan, China, even Tibet, bringing back with them knowledge of Eastern languages and a few Latin versions of Buddhist texts. By the nineteenth century, scholars had brought back substantial materials from the various European colonies and the academic study of Buddhism began in France, the United Kingdom, and Germany, as well as in the United States, Russia, and Hungary. By the end of the century, Western knowledge of Buddhism, though sometimes incomplete and faulty, was nevertheless considerable, and Europeans were beginning to find Buddhism attractive as a religion. In the present century, the academic study of Buddhism has continued to develop, every decade bringing more adequate sources to the attention of specialists, students in colleges and universities, and the general reading public. Translations of Buddhist texts are today scientific and accurate, and Buddhism is studied as part of the curricula of universities in the United States, Canada, Europe, Australia, and Asia.

Although Buddhist ideas, however imperfectly transmitted, have had some influence on Western intellectuals, they probably have had very little on the public. European philosophers adopted a few ideas from the somewhat inadequate sources available to them in the nineteenth century. Schopenhauer thought he saw a pure pessimism in Buddhism and, in turn, influenced Wagner and Nietzsche. Though he refers occasionally to Buddhism, Nietzsche knew little of it, even though some of his later works have a Zen ring to them. Spengler was also influenced, and in the United States, Emerson and Thoreau were interested in Indian ideas, some of which had a Buddhist flavor.

Buddhism also affected European religious groups such as the Theosophical Society and, of course, others specifically founded to practice some form of Buddhism. In France, *Les Amis du Bouddhisme* (The Friends of Buddhism) was founded in 1929 in Paris. In the early part of this century, societies were established in the United Kingdom, including the Buddhist Society of Great Britain and Ireland (1907) and the Buddhist Lodge of the Theosophical Society (1924), renamed in 1943 the Buddhist Society. Various other groups formed after the Second World War, in London as well as in Germany.

BUDDHISM IN THE UNITED STATES

Asians were the first to bring Buddhism to the United States. In the beginning these were mostly Japanese immigrants who came to the West Coast and

The San Jose, California, Buddhist Church (1975).

established churches to serve their own communities. But they did not proselytize. In 1899, in San Francisco, Jōdo Shinshū (Western Branch) founded the Buddhist Mission of North America, which later became the Buddhist Churches of America. Since then, temples have been established belonging to several Japanese sects with American headquarters on the West Coast including Pure Land (called Jōdo Shū, in Los Angeles and Jōdo Shinshū in San Francisco and New York, with many independent churches and branches), Shingon (in Los Angeles, the Kōyasan Buddhist Temple), and Nichiren. Monks of the Rinzai and Sōtō Zen schools came to lecture and live in the United States as early as 1905, and Rinzai was settled by 1930 in New York City (the Buddhist Society of America, now called the First Zen Institute of America). Sōtō was more popular in Hawaii at first, but is now strong in Western states, too. The San Francisco Zen Center, a Sōtō group, now has an American-born *rōshi* (teacher). Caucasian Americans who have become Buddhists have also started founding organizations.

Today representatives of many Buddhist groups are active in the United States.[1] There is a Theravāda monastery in Washington, D.C., which is Sinhalese, and many groups practice Theravāda-style Burmese insight *(vipassanā)* meditation. Tibetan lineages (Nying-ma-pa, Kargyüpa, Gelukpa) are well organized in California, Colorado, Canada, and New Jersey under such teachers as Tarthang Tulku, Chögyam Trungpa, and Geshé Thupten Wangyal.

The Rinzai Zen teacher (rōshi) Kimura Kozan in samādhi. Photographed in his home in Los Angeles, California (1975).

Tibetan scholars teach in major North American universities, while Chinese, Korean, and Vietnamese Buddhists also have temples and growing organizations.

Clearly, most North Americans and Europeans no longer would define Buddhism as "false religion of India," which the French dictionary writer Bouillet did in 1826. The last century-and-a-half has brought an amazing change. The most important reason today for the growing North American acquaintance with Buddhism is the vastly increased communication we have with the East. We have available here everything from scholarly, accurate translations of Buddhist texts to Zen teachers residing in major cities ready to teach the Buddha-mind to anyone willing to take the time to meditate. Political

The contemporary Tibetan teacher Chögyam Trungpa, Rimpoche (1975).

events have brought many North Americans into direct contact with Buddhists, both in Asia and on this continent. The American involvement in the East since the advent of its great Asian wars has brought thousands into contact with Buddhism, and past misfortunes may be turning into new good fortune after all. The population of Asian Buddhists is beginning to grow in the United States, among them new groups of refugee Koreans, Vietnamese, and Cambodians; a few refugees have settled elsewhere as well. The Communist take-over of Tibet forced hundreds of that country's extraordinary scholars, teachers, meditators, ritualists, artists, and craftsmen into northern India, some of whom have migrated to the West to receive enthusiastic support from increasing numbers of followers. Now they are establishing independent bases of action, buying land and constructing new buildings for whole Buddhist communities.

Apart from the greatly enhanced communication between Americans and Asian Buddhists, important shifts in attitudes have also brought the Buddhist religion closer to at least some groups of Americans. Many people—from physiologists and experimental psychologists to businessmen, students, housewives, and Catholic contemplatives—are more and more interested in meditation. Machines and the scientific realism of twentieth century Western thought have pervaded every aspect of life, relieving us of great burdens of labor and much past superstition but bringing with them the socioeconomic problems of pollution, economic exploitation, overuse of natural resources, and overpopulation. To a Buddhist, these too are instances of ignorance which will lead inevitably to suffering. But many think that the West suffers also from a spiritual loss because the scientific world view denies reality to any category of spirit, saying as it does that material reality is all that exists and is all there is that we can really "know." Our own religious traditions have suffered the brunt of this scientific attack on spiritual knowledge systems, and many people are looking elsewhere for a means to revitalize their spiritual tradition. What these trends portend for the future of Buddhism in North America and the Western world no one can really say.

Self-realization, psychotherapy, meditation, and alternate (that is, non-scientific) reality movements in general have created whole new populations interested in Buddhism, just as long-playing record albums have allowed English rock groups to become popular in America. Small numbers of young Americans have been willing to support various leaders of Buddhist movements. Many others of all ages, less discriminating, seem to purchase every kind of book on Buddhism brought out by publishers. Presumably age groups other than those most visibly attracted to Buddhism are beginning to learn about it, teen-agers and old people alike. Some groups are busy founding meditation and study centers devoted to Buddhism, while others staff new academic centers and programs of study devoted to Buddhism (the University of Wisconsin, the University of California at Berkeley). Both academics and nonacademics are responsible for the increased dissemination of learning about Buddhism and for bringing more and more Asian Buddhists to live here.

Buddhism appeals to many Western intellectuals. As more and more scientifically minded intellectuals accept the presuppositions of the scientific world view, Buddhism with its emphasis on personal psychology and rational analysis and its claim that ignorance is the root of all evil (one of the foundations of the scientific method) becomes increasingly attractive. Perhaps Buddhism can provide these people with religious alternatives that do not directly clash with contemporary rationalism and that have not become identified with medievalism. Buddhists have been inveterate experimentalists, a penchant that appeals to the scientific tenor of our age. The great monk Kumārajīva cooperated fully with his barbarian royal patron when the king suggested that the monk's marvelous brilliance be passed on to offspring. The experiment relied on Buddhist assumptions about causality that modern science also holds. After all, the viability of a science of eugenics is still being investigated today. In any case, the king gave Kumārajīva ten women, each with her separate quarters. Preaching all the while that the lotus grows from the mud, and that his listeners should pay more attention to the lotus (purity) than the mud (the physical), Kumārajīva fathered sons, but neither sons nor grandsons ever were as exceptional as their original progenitor.

Buddhism can be quite practical too. An ordinary course of self-transformation, using a Western system of therapy such as Freud's, now takes up to five years and can cost an astronomical sum. Sitting with a qualified Zen teacher, though he uses different terminology of self, different metaphors and procedures (techniques of transformation), results if successful in similar therapeutic breakthroughs to knowledge of self. Did Freud just happen to decide that his patients should adopt a special posture for self-analysis, just as Buddhists had long before? To allow thoughts and unconscious motivations to rise above the limen of consciousness, a person has to quiet the distracting "noise" in the bodily systems generated by nervous energy, breathing, and motor activity. So Freud had his patients lie down, a technique as effective in its context as the lotus posture is for Asian meditators.

Buddhism was successful in Asia outside of India because it was able to communicate its ideas across formidable barriers of culture and world view. In part this resulted from Buddhism's ability to adapt to another world view. A Western Buddhist can discard the archaic Indian world view without damaging the practical or spiritual aspects of Buddhism, and thus need not give up cherished convictions which deny that death is recurrent and personhood forever continuing, or that life and the world will endure endlessly roughly as they are, or that realms of extra-human life exist somewhere in our world system. The empiricism of early Buddhist psychology and its emphasis on meditation and rigorous exercises in self-knowledge techniques is in tune with the mood of contemporary religion and psychology. Humanistic, Gestalt, and Freudian psychologies and therapies all espouse goals common in Buddhism, especially in their attention to introspective self-knowledge. Buddhism's emphatic stance requiring a person to face the realities of existence corresponds closely with the demand for authenticity and non-self-delusive confrontations with life and one's inner motivations that inspires Western existentialist (religious or not) concerns as well.

At this time, no one can say what will come of the immense amount of intellectual, emotional, and physical energy that is being spent in coming to grips with Buddhism in the West. The understanding arising from these beginnings can only be achieved, internalized, and evaluated with the passing of time. The fate of Buddhism in North America and Europe cannot now be predicted. The present situation is changing so rapidly that no one can reliably say what will be happening even a decade or two hence. Buddhism in

Asia, ironically, probably faces a bleaker future, since it is only beginning to face the challenges hurled at Western religions by scientific rationalism for the past two centuries. Perhaps Asian Buddhism will further weaken, as the attack has only just begun in most areas that are not today communist; and in countries now communist, the attack is already institutionalized as party doctrine. In Japan the process is more advanced, which may be one reason why Japanese teachers are leaving their temples for Western countries. A prosperous economic base is requisite for most cultural or spiritual achievement, but this is lacking in nearly all Asian Buddhist countries. Only one thing today is sure: that the forces determining Buddhism's future fate are no longer confined to Asia, because Buddhism has successfully come West.

12.
Past, Present, and Future

Buddhism, like the other higher religions, has been slow to perceive that modern civilization is radically different from that of any preceding age, that it is not just machines and techniques. Devout Buddhists have been loathe to give up hoping that this menace will go away and leave traditional religions alone if only they ignore it or make a truce with it or try to subordinate it by declaring their jurisdiction over spiritual matters and relegating science to the lower, worldly sphere. Yet the Buddhist responses to the waves of social and cultural change originating in Europe have been distinctive in some ways, and have conformed to patterns well instanced in the Buddhist past.

From the first, the Saṅgha has seen itself as parallel to the state, subject to the Dharma-king and claiming the adherence of people who also owe allegiance to the king of the land. Conflict of duties has usually been avoided by specifying which authority is to prevail in which sphere. Nonetheless, certain tensions in moral matters have been perennially unresolved. Strict observance of the precepts is incompatible with statecraft and with the life-styles of ruling classes. A few devout rulers have renounced war, for example, but no Buddhist state has ever given up the use of armies and police. Moreover, the rulers have often had to use force to quell violence and corruption in the monasteries themselves. Eventually, all Buddhist states established the post of Saṅgha-director so as to incorporate the church into the bureaucracy and prevent it from becoming a rival political power. Yet the chief source of disorder in the Order has been the patronage of princes, who, by giving more lavishly than wisely, have made the monastic life a haven for drones and a temptation to the ambitious. After the tax and rent collectors were through with them, peasants did not have enough surplus left to support a learned Saṅgha. Where commerce flourished, merchant guilds usually financed Buddhist activities; but merchants often practiced emulative donation, thus making the Saṅgha too wealthy for its own good. Besides, interregional commerce was allied with the kings, and did not constitute an independent counterbalance. When a strong state such as imperial China decided to exclude the Buddhist community from a major role in national life, there was no social bloc strong enough to insist on its inclusion. Under the circumstances, it is not only the reluctance of bhikṣus to dictate morals to the laity which has restrained the Dharma-masters, with a few notable exceptions, from denouncing the tyranny and licentiousness of rulers.

Colonial rule, secular governments, and land reform have stripped the Order of state patronage and economic self-sufficiency in almost every Buddhist country. The shock of losing their lands and privileges dissipated the monks' lethargy, and the need to find a new donorship base stimulated revivals that the Christian missionary and Western secular challenges then enhanced. The Saṅgha typically affiliated itself with the national bourgeoisie that rose in the early stages of modernization. Where there was no bourgeoisie, as in Tibet, there was no revival. Where the modernizing elite already had a secular ideology, as in Japan and China, Buddhism had to stand on the sidelines, where many of the old-fashioned gentry, forsaking a discredited Confucianism, rallied to the most "modern" and international element in their national heritage.

Everywhere, Buddhists have been staunch nationalists, taking part in anticolonial movements and claiming to be custodians of the national culture; they have longed to reestablish the old symbiosis between Saṅgha and state. In a secular age, this dream is not going to come true, but nationalist sentiment will undoubtedly maintain Buddhism wherever freedom of religion prevails. However, Buddhist doctrine is presently too weak, and the Saṅgha, too dependent, to exercise moral authority and restrain political excesses. Most citizens are nationalists first, and Buddhists second, if at all.

The traditional case for public donorship was that Buddhism protects the community from disasters and ensures prosperity. The original standpoint was that ethics is a better magic than magic, but in course of time meritorious deeds came to be prized more for their unseen effects than for discernible ethical consequences. The expectation of miraculous "advantages here and now" is still lively among the culturally disadvantaged, but when a modern government sponsors a Buddhist enterprise—publication of the Canon, or an international conference—it is thinking not of earning merit for the nation but of fulfilling cultural responsibilities and gaining popularity.

Modern educated Buddhists tend to jettison the magical component. They say that it is a separable accretion of superstition. This is historically true for many specific practices, but we have seen that the realm of the spirits and the preternatural operations of karman are integral to the earliest known Buddhist world view. Modern Buddhist thinkers (with some exceptions) are ashamed to believe something that is out of fashion in the West, yet they have not squarely faced the intellectual and practical consequences of rejecting the belief. Buddhism cannot be reduced to a humanism without radical structural changes. Apologists, tailoring their theses to needs and opportunities, have usually insisted that Buddhism is scientific, and have played down anything that does not fit the claim. This has widened the gulf between intellectuals and lower-class devotees, for whom the magical is the most meaningful part of the religion.

There has not yet been a cogent attempt to update the intellectual foundations of Buddhism. The Theravāda clergy has mostly adhered to a fundamentalist position, thus foregoing fruitful two-way interchange with the secular world of today. But things are changing, and in Ceylon lay scholars plus a few monks, for example, are pursuing historically critical and philosophically rigorous studies. Japanese Buddhist intellectuals adopted an eclectic modernism almost a century ago, and have striven to keep up with international fashions in religion and philosophy while avoiding decisive engagements with basic problems. Thus there has been almost no creative application of their massive historical scholarship. The "new religions" of Japan have developed their ideas by methods that were second-rate even in the thirteenth century, but in demonstrating that a radical break with venerable institutions can lead to success, they may be liberating as yet undetected creative energies.

Some decades ago, meditation was commonly neglected by Buddhists who were trying to become modern, because until recently Westerners have scorned it, alleging that quietism and subjectivism are morbid and sap the will to act. Political independence movements have lessened this accommodation to Western disapproval. And now that psychiatry has sparked a cult of self-awareness in the West, meditation is coming back into fashion in every part of Buddhist Asia that Marxism does not hold in thrall to nineteenth-century European attitudes. In Japan, where contemplative arts became secularized in the Middle Ages, lay meditation movements have made considerable headway, and have strengthened the still vigorous core of monastic meditation. The Theravāda meditation revival is an urban appropriation of a tradition that survived precariously among jungle hermits. The motive force is humanistic: to alleviate the tensions of urban and industrial life, and to find secure values by gaining insight.

A hundred years ago, the chief service role of the Saṅgha was performing ceremonies, especially funeral and memorial rites. Nowadays this function has dwindled greatly as ritual simplification keeps pace with declining belief in unseen forces. The second service role of the Order was elementary education, which has now been taken over by public schools. But as the old needs wane, new needs emerge. In some places, the Saṅgha has become an educational entrepreneur, running modern-style private schools and universities. Conversely, some public school systems include religions instruction and so give secular jobs to monks.

A need closer to the Saṅgha's proper role is that for relief from anxiety, agitation, and confusion. Though the secular palliatives—art and literature, philosophy, psychiatry, tranquilizers, and psychedelics—are moderately efficacious, some of them are pscyhologically very expensive, and all stop short of the moral, intellectual, and spiritual integration that is the goal of the Buddhist life.

In past ages, revitalization of Buddhism happened when a widespread demand was met by outstanding holy men. Today there is certainly a world-wide spiritual need. There is also an ever-growing study and dissemination of the Dharma. This is creating a clientele ready to respond if, out of season in this Last Age, a great holy man should appear.

Epilogue

IN THE INDIAN HIMĀLAYAS

In the early spring of 1962, an American college lecturer living in south India travels northward with a backpack from Delhi to escape the torrid plains. Reaching the green Kulu Valley, he hears of more valleys still beyond, over the Rohtang Pass, 14,000 feet high. The traverse, a trek through snowfields after reaching 11,000 feet, brings him into a narrow down-sloping valley called Lahoul on the map. The next day it strikes him that the people on the trail are different from those on the other side of the pass, Tibetan-looking; and in the villages he notices small shrines (stūpas, Tibetan *chö-ten*). Another stands at the confluence of two mountain rivers. Even more striking along the trail are the "mani-walls," great collections of flat stones sometimes twenty feet long and head-high, each stone carved with the Tibetan characters for the mantra, *"Oṃ maṇi-padme hūṃ"*—"Om in the lotus a jewel hail!" He notices that, as people pass these walls, they keep them on their right side.

Continuing along the following day, he sees a few buildings to the right, far up the bare mountainside. Following a little-used trail, he reaches a small Buddhist monastery after a stiff climb. Nearby, he meets a middle-aged shaven-headed woman plowing in a small field with a yak-like animal pulling her plow. Inside he is received by a monk, about the same age as the nun, who has the nun bring the foreign visitor some hot tea and flat bread that looks a bit green. Smiles and friendly understandings flow from their welcome to their American guest. Living here, far above the main trail and small villages, they have ample time, especially during the winter, to listen to the wind blowing in the cracks and to meditate "far from the madding crowd's ignoble strife"[1] on the insubstantiality of existence.

The lecturer is surprised to find Buddhists in the Indian Himālayas. Previously, he had trekked towards Tibet, paralleling the Hindustan-Tibet road from Simla, but for a hundred miles had seen only tiny Hindu villages of farmers or woodcutters. The Kulu Valley was also Hindu, but here were Buddhist monasteries in India! He had wandered into the Tibetan culture area by crossing the high pass, which actually had carried him beyond a 19,000-foot-high mountain barrier from Hindu India into India's Buddhist "Tibet."

Later, at the head monastery of the valley, he watches some solemn ceremonies attended by many of the village folk. All enjoy the chanting and drumming, the drama and pomp of the occasion. On still another day he visits a man who speaks excellent English. His host had been a wandering monk in Tibet for thirteen years but had also gone to Europe to teach. Over many full cups of *chang* (rice beer), he describes his life as a Buddhist, entertaining his guest with his humor and animated conversation.

After two weeks, the lecturer returns to the Hindu lands of India, again over Rohtang, the "Pass of the Dead," so named because many have died crossing it too late in the day and becoming lost in a sudden blizzard.

THE SMILE OF THE BUDDHA

"What do you see in his face?" the art historian asks her colleague. He looks for a moment, but unable to say what it is, ventures some careless comments.

"No, that's not it. You see that same feature on so many Buddhas, especially those depicting him as he touches the earth as his witness. Don't you see? Look carefully. You stand to learn so much of the Buddhist religion from its art."

He had looked before, too, in books on Indian, Southeast Asian, Tibetan, Chinese, and Japanese Buddhist art. He muses, "There is a composure in the facial features. They are meditative, peaceful. In this example, his eyes are half-closed, perhaps looking down."

"Still, you are not seeing what so many of the Buddha images represent as essential, provided to the artist by his tradition and called up before his mind's eye as he finished his work. See, it is the smile of the Buddha that points to the great mystery. It symbolizes his achievement of release, the moment when he was able to break with his past and become 'enlightened'. He smiled at the moment he was victorious over Māra, you remember. At that time, he touched the earth and smiled. Whatever is behind his smile must contain the secrets of Buddhist enlightenment."

WITH THE TEACHER

The graduate student eyes his coffee cup a bit nervously as his teacher talks on and on, fidgeting with his doughnut. The teacher watches the people pass through the Madison drug store and answers the graduate student's many questions.

"But how are we to interpret the Buddhist idea of transmigration? Is it to be understood literally, or rather symbolically, say as a psychological myth laying out the different types of mental states there are? Can a person ever really go beyond the sum total of his personal conditioning (karman) and be released from causality, even while living? Can what we find in Buddhist texts be subjected to critical scrutiny and not be found wanting by a person who accepts a Western, scientific world view? What concrete meaning can we give to such a goal as nirvāṇa, embedded as it is in an alien, archaic world view not our own? What does it mean when a Buddhist meditator claims he is able to 'see things as they really are'? What independent criterion of reality will we use to measure his claims against?"

The teacher welcomes these questions. He argues forcefully, as one well versed in philology as well as contemporary philosophy, skeptical but inquiring and not unwilling to admit appropriate belief too. He seems serious, then playful, developing his thought there amidst the noise and commotion of the drugstore crowds. It is cold outside so they enjoy the hot coffee and spend quite a while there, both silently wondering what the future is to bring as they examine their skepticisms and try their abilities to interpret and understand ideas and practices they deem most worthy of their attention.

NORTH OF SAN FRANCISCO, 1975

The professor stands on the rounded top of a hill dominating many around it in a verdant, mountainy area about one hundred miles north of San Francisco, and reached along winding back roads. In contrast to the noise of the city streets behind him, the spot is a silent setting for the cries of birds; crows and jays are heard occasionally in the distance. The sun is just setting across the hills to the southwest, where in clear weather, one can see the Pacific Ocean; crossing it you can reach the China and Japan Columbus never found. Sunlight streaks through the trees on the next ridge, sending shafts of light around him, silently, in all directions.

He is standing by an odd, octagonal skeleton of steel, anchored solidly in newly laid concrete, that crowns the hill. Now at the beginning of the rainy season, puddles of water scattered on the gray cement reflect the somber blue sky of dusk. He knows that this is to become the meditation retreat of a Buddhist yogi from China. Two devoted supporters of the yogi from Berkeley, an artist-musician and a dancer, found and purchased the land several years before, and have spent every spare moment and dollar since to plan and build this ideal residence-retreat. Downstairs, where today he sees only puddles and bare concrete, will be the yogi's living quarters; upstairs, will be a single large hall for meditation, where now only steel and wooden beams score the evening sky.

One Asian Buddhist come to the United States has found lay patrons, and is about to move into his new quarters.

Notes

Prologue

1. I am obliged to Stephan V. Beyer for showing me his excellent and detailed color slides and for explaining this Tibetan ritual dance. The craft community has now moved to Palampur, Himachal Pradesh. This particular dance is held in early July.

Chapter 1

1. For a longer account of the religious significance of this civilization and of the important Brahmanical background to Buddhism, see Thomas J. Hopkins, *The Hindu Religious Tradition* (Second Edition), in this same series.

2. In this book the following convention is observed in transliterating terms relating to the derivatives of the Sanskrit term *brahman:* for a member of the priestly class (brāhmaṇa), the English term brahmin is used; for the pre-Hindu religion of the brahmins, Brahmanism and Brahmanical; for the sacerdotal literature of Brahmanism, the Brāhmaṇas; to designate the Brahmanical notion of the Absolute, the term Brahman; and for the demiurge, creator god of Hinduism and Buddhism, Brahmā.

3. See "Note on Linguistics," for guidance in pronouncing Sanskrit terms.

4. The Upaniṣads were speculative texts growing out of the Vedic literature. They served as transitions to more classical orthodox Hindu writings such as the Bhagavad Gītā.

5. For more information on Jainism, see Padmanabh S. Jaini, *The Path of Purification,* in this same series to be published in Fall, 1977.

Chapter 2

1. The chronology of Gautama's life hinges on the date of his death, which in turn is variously assigned by the regional Buddhist traditions. Modern scholars, calculating back from the dates of the emperor Aśoka, have agreed within a few years: Thomas, 563–483 B.C. *(The Life of the Buddha);* Filliozat, 559–478 *(Inde Classique,* nos. 375, 376, pp. 2178, 2209).

2. See Beyer, *The Buddhist Experience: Sources and Interpretations,* in this same series, pp. 165-169, which gives another version of these events.

3. See Beyer, pp. 169-174.

4. See "Note on Linguistics."

5. See Beyer, pp. 186-191.

6. See Beyer, pp. 191-197.

7. See Beyer, pp. 85-86, 107-108.

8. See Beyer, pp. 87-89.

9. See Beyer, p. 194-197; discussion of precondition 12 begins on line 12 of p. 194.

10. See Beyer, pp. 15-17, 29-38.

11. See Beyer, pp. 13, 20.

Chapter 3

1. See Beyer, pp. 95-98.
2. As defined by Frederick J. Streng in *Understanding Religious Life* (Second Edition, 1976) in this same series, p. 7.
3. See Beyer, pp. 89-99.

Chapter 4

1. See Beyer, pp. 6-9.
2. See Beyer, pp. 65-69.
3. See Beyer, pp. 69-73.
4. See Beyer, pp. 81-83.
5. See Beyer, pp. 55-64.

Chapter 5

1. "Hīnayāna" originated as a Mahāyāna pejorative for those who did not accept the new Sūtras and their doctrines. As the conservatives answered the Mahāyāna propaganda and polemics with silence, they did not adopt any name for themselves *vis-à-vis* Mahāyāna. Consequently modern European, Japanese, and Indian scholars have given them the name their enemies gave them, "Hīnayāna," though without implying any deprecation. Modern Theravādins do not like being called Hīnayānists, but there is no other current term that designates the whole set of sects that arose between the first and the fourth centuries after the Parinirvāṇa. Continued usage may expunge all derogatory connotations of the term. "Quaker," "Mormon," and even "Christian" started out similarly as labels sarcastically attached by outsiders.
2. See Beyer, pp. 215-217.
3. See Beyer, pp. 199-206.
4. See Beyer, pp. 10-18, 215-217.
5. See Beyer, pp. 212-215.
6. See Beyer, p. 19.

Chapter 6

1. See Beyer, pp. 217-225.
2. See Beyer, pp. 40-43, 101-115.
3. See Beyer, pp. 43-45.
4. See Beyer, pp. 111-115.
5. See Beyer, pp. 229-235.
6. See Beyer, pp. 116-124.
7. See Beyer, pp. 116-124.

Chapter 7

1. See Beyer, pp. 130-139.
2. See Beyer, pp. 140-153.
3. See Beyer, pp. 258-261.
4. See Beyer, pp. 124-130, 154-161.
5. See Beyer, pp. 214, paragraphs 6 and 7.
6. See Beyer, pp. 174-184.

7. As well as in such important matters as ritual, worship, mythology, and art. See Thomas J. Hopkins, *The Hindu Religious Tradition,* in this same series, *passim.*

Chapter 8

1. For a contrasting portrait of a Mahāyāna religious context, see below, "The Religious Life of Tibetan Buddhism," pp. 192-195. Also, *Japanese Religion* by H. Byron Earhart and *Chinese Religion* by Laurence Thompson, both in this Dickenson series include materials on the popular Buddhism of Japan and China.

2. See bibliography, p. 232, for reference to Spiro's work.

Chapter 9

1. For additional information on Buddhism in China, see Laurence G. Thompson, *Chinese Religion: An Introduction* (Second Edition), especially chapters 6-8, and *The Chinese Way In Religion,* Parts III, V, VI, and the Postscript, both in this same series.

2. For additional information on Japanese Buddhism, see H. Byron Earhart, *Japanese Religion: Unity and Diversity* (Second Edition), Part I, chap. 5; Part II, chaps. 9, 10; Part III, chaps. 14, 16-18; and *Religion in the Japanese Experience: Sources and Interpretations,* Parts III, VIII, IX, XIII, XV, XVI, and XVII, both in this same series.

3. See Beyer, pp. 246-257.

Chapter 10

1. Tibetan words are given first in a roughly phonetic spelling, and then in a mechanical transliteration of the Tibetan orthography, which represents the pronunciation of a thousand years ago.

2. See Beyer, pp. 174-184.

Chapter 11

1. A good list of most of them, including addresses, can be found in Charles S. Prebish's *Buddhism, A Modern Perspective* (University Park: The Pennsylvania State University Press, 1975), pp. 255-258.

Epilogue

1. Or, as the Oxford English Dictionary entry for 1614 puts it, much more in the Buddhist idiom, "Farre from the madding Worldling's hoarse discords."

Glossary of Key Sanskrit Terms

This is an interlocking glossary; all key doctrinal terms that have been left in the text in their original Sanskrit form are defined in it, often using other terms which are also explained in the glossary. If not already known, these other terms, which are italicized, must be consulted as well. Learning about another vision of life, such as that of Buddhists, requires learning some of the language in which the religious experience is conceptualized. Often our English equivalents carry connotations unwarranted for a different world view. Understanding the terms in this glossary, and how they relate to one another, can substantially aid in your understanding of the Buddhist religion and the textbook you are using. Students should try to learn or be able to recognize all these terms. Teachers can help, especially with proper pronunciation, by reading them aloud and rehearsing them with the class.

Each term is cited in Sanskrit. When the Pali form of the term is sufficiently different as to cause possible confusion, the Pali form follows in parenthesis. A term immediately following in quotation marks is the literal English meaning of the word, but not a good translation equivalent. Generally, the first word that follows is the translation equivalent chosen for this text; when such a word occurs in the text in English, it stands for the Sanskrit term with which it is here joined.

References immediately after the definition are first to this text, then to the following three works: Stephan V. Beyer, *The Buddhist Experience: Sources and Interpretations,* in this same series; Henry Clarke Warren, *Buddhism in Translations* (New York: Atheneum, 1963); Edward Conze, *Buddhist Thought in India* (Ann Arbor: The University of Michigan Press, 1967).

Abhidharma. Scholastic ordering and elaboration of the meaning of ideas, involving especially psychology-metaphysics, from the *Sūtras.* See pp. 65-66.

Abhidharma Piṭaka. Collection of seven scholastic works of the *Theravāda* school, one of the three traditional portions of the Pali Canon.

Anātman (Anattā). Devoid of self *(ātman),* a term applied to all phenomena including the sense of "I" or personhood, indicating the Buddhist view that everything is transient and insubstantial, being without underlying reality or independent, substantial, continuing substrate. As applied to personhood, the anātman doctrine states that there is no ātman in the five *skandhas.* See also *śūnyatā.* Warren ("no-ego") pp. 129-159; Conze pp. 36-39, 122-134.

Anitya (Anicca). Impermanence, flux, change; characteristic of everything that arises and continues to exist due to causes and conditions, and is thus subject to eventual disappearance. See also *anātman.* Conze, pp. 34, 134 ff.

Arhant (Arahant). "One who is deserving (of reverence and offerings), worthy"; perfected saint, a person who has attained *nirvāṇa,* destroyed the *āsravas,* achieved the goal of *bodhi,* and who will be released at death from rebirth in *saṃsāra.* This term is used by *Hīnayāna* traditions; see *bodhisattva* for a corresponding *Mahāyāna* ideal.

Āsrava (Āsava). Outflow, the destruction of which is equivalent to attaining release (arhantship), the final goal of Buddhist practice. Listed as four: the outflows of sensual desire, desire for continual physical becoming, wrong (or speculative) views, and ignorance.

Ātman (Attā). Self; substantial, independent entity existing apart from the phenomenal personhood (the *skandhas,* in the Buddhist view), giving continuity and essential identity to individual beings; against this ātman view espoused by Hinduism (in the Upaniṣads and the Bhagavad Gītā, for example), Buddhism propounded its anātman doctrine.

Avidyā (Avijjā). Ignorance, particularly of the Four Holy Truths, the root cause of *duḥkha* and the first link in the causal chain of *pratītya-samutpāda* leading to recurrent rebirth in saṃsāra; its opposite is bodhi or prajñā. See Warren, pp. 170-179.

Bhikṣu (Bhikkhu). Buddhist monk.

Bhikṣuṇī (Bhikkhunī). Buddhist nun.

Bhikṣu-saṅgha. Order of Buddhist monks; Bhikṣuṇī-saṅgha, order of Buddhist nuns.

Bodhi. "Awakening"; enlightenment, the special knowledge of a *Buddha,* the ultimate goal of Buddhist practice.

Bodhicitta. Thought or mind of (that is, intentness upon) *bodhi;* the mental attitude which the candidate "puts forth" or "arouses" when aspiring to the *bodhisattva* path. See p. 97; Beyer, pp. 101-103.

Bodhisattva. Being who is to become fully enlightened (possess *bodhi);* especially as applied to Gautama, the future *Buddha.* More generally, in Mahāyāna Buddhism the term "bodhisattva" applies to those who have experienced enlightenment (bodhi) but who have taken a special vow to continue being reborn into saṃsāra (rather than entering nirvāṇa) so as to deliver others from their suffering by aiding in their attainment of enlightenment. This contrasts with the older ideal of the arhant, who was the product of a monastic community of individuals striving primarily for their own salvation. The Mahāyāna ideal of the bodhisattva stressed the return of the enlightened being to the world, where the suffering of others demanded compassionate action on their behalf. See "The Bodhisattva Path," pp. 96-101; Beyer, pp. 38-45, 99-115, 217-225, 229-235.

Brāhmaṇa. Ritual priest of the archaic religious tradition; continued into classical times as the upper, sacerdotal class of the Hindu social system. Anglicized form: brahmin.

Buddha. "Awakened"; an enlightened one; Gautama's title after his Enlightenment visions. Beyer, pp. 1-6, 238-240.

Dharma (Dhamma). Has many meanings in Buddhist texts, the proper one being determined by context and use. Meanings occurring in this textbook are: (1) Dharma, the teaching of the *Buddha,* the Truth; or (2) the Real; (3) dharmas, the immediate constituents of all phenomena (things, mental and physical events) in the conditioned realm. Also, dharma can mean moral law, the right, duty, or religion. See "Nirvāṇa, Early Buddhist Meditation and the Dharmas," pp. 50-56; Conze, pp. 92-106, 225-232.

Dhyāna (Jhāna). Meditative trance ("trance" here is not used to designate an unconscious or dazed state, but a special meditative attainment of calm, firm mental control, and clarity, achieved through rigorous meditative training); sometimes more loosely used to mean meditation in general rather than the specific meditative trances. See p. 28 ("four stages of dhyāna"); Beyer, pp. 85-86, 107-108, 206-211 (adds further formless dhyānas); Warren pp. 109-110, 288, 291, 347-348, 374, 384-385.

Duḥkha. "Dis-ease"; usually translated as suffering or ill; the transmigratory misery which, as the first Holy Truth states, characterizes all conditioned reality; all the dis-ease humans experience because of attachment to *saṃsāra* through the five *skandhas. Duḥkha* is equivalent to saṃsāra; its opposite, sukha, true happiness, is a synonym of *nirvāṇa.* Warren ("misery") pp. 170, 204, 369, 438-440; Conze pp. 34-36.

Hīnayāna. The Small Vehicle or Course; the whole set of sects which arose between the first and fourth centuries after the death of the *Buddha.* Hīnayāna sects and monks were numerically the majority in Indian Buddhism; one of these, the *Theravāda,* survives today in Ceylon and Southeast Asia. See p. 86 with note; Conze, pp. 119-191.

Karman (Kamman). Act, action, deed performed by body, speech, or mind, which, according to the intention it embodies, will have a

set consequence (vipāka, result or phala, fruit), experienced in this or a future rebirth. See pp. 38-39; Warren, pp. 179-182, 194-202, 209-279.

Mahāyāna. The Great Vehicle or Course; the general term for the sects which arose in India after the Sthavira-Mahāsāṅghika schism of the second century following the death of the *Buddha.* Today Mahāyāna, or northern Buddhism, is associated with Tibet, Mongolia, China, Korea, Japan, and Vietnam. See pp. 86-115; Conze, pp. 195-274.

Maṇḍala. Magic or sacred circle; cosmoplan used in *Tantric* meditation and ritual. See pp. 117, 120-122.

Mantra. "Instrument of mind"; short verse or collection of syllables used to evoke (visualize, actualize) a deity, gain protection against evil or adverse forces, or as a meditative object, especially in Buddhist *Tantra.* See pp. 117-119.

Māyā. Illusion, trick, wile; a term favored by *Mahāyāna* writers to describe the apparent "reality" of *saṃsāra,* which being only relatively real, or dependent on causes and conditions, is like an illusion (not nonexistent but deceptive), a magic show, a trick, a bubble, or a mirage, since it lacks any substantial independent reality, and soon disappears. See *śūnyatā.* Beyer, pp. 215-217, Conze, pp. 220-225.

Nikāya. Collection of *Sūtras* found in the *Sūtra Piṭaka,* also called *Āgama,* text, scripture. See pp. 64, 238.

Nirvāṇa (Nibbāna). "Blowing out, quenching (as of a fire)"; the goal of Buddhism, the extinguishing of passionate attachment or desire (rāga), fearful hostility or hatred and anger (dveṣa), and confusion or delusion (moha), the primary causes of *karman* and hence bondage to *saṃsāra*. Attained when the *āsravas* are stopped, it is the unconditioned state, emancipation, or release from rebirth and *saṃsāra's* limiting conditions *(duḥkha, anitya, anātman,* recurrent death); structurally equivalent to the Hindu goal of mokṣa (release), given the hybrid designation brahmanirvāṇa, or nirvāṇa in the absolute, in the Bhagavad Gītā. See pp. 50-56; Beyer, pp. 199-206, 212-215; Warren, pp. 59, 281 ff., 331-353, 377-383, 389-391; Conze, pp. 69-79, 159-166.

Pāramitā. "Supremacy"; perfection, practice of a virtue to the point of supremacy, especially by a *bodhisattva.* See pp. 70, 98-99; Conze, pp. 211-217.

Parinirvāṇa. "Full nirvāṇa"; loosely, the complete and final release attained at the death of a *Buddha* (see pp. 60-61), or more accurately, complete release from ignorance, desire, and attachment through the five *skandhas* to material phenomena.

Prajñā (Paññā). Wisdom, insight, understanding of the true nature of conditioned reality and the Four Holy Truths, and clearing the mind of the *āsravas,* the goal of the Buddhist path. Made possible by the disciplined practice of *śīla* and *samādhi,* and leading to release from bondage to rebirth in *saṃsāra,* the final step in the three trainings leading to *nirvāṇa.* A synonym is insight (vipaśyanā). See p. 54; Beyer, pp. 197-198 and Part III; Warren, p. 330.

Prajñā-pāramitā. The perfection of *prajñā,* the *Mahāyāna* designation of the supreme degree of *prajñā,* which sees that all *dharmas* are *śūnya,* devoid of *svabhāva;* also the designation of the earliest Mahāyāna *Sūtras.*

Pratītya-samutpāda (Paṭicca-samuppāda). Dependent co-arising, also translated in other works as "conditioned co-production," "conditioned genesis," and variations on these; the specific formula analyzing the causal links (preconditions, nidāna) in the chain connecting *avidyā,* the root cause, with the consequents, birth, aging, and dying (and the whole mass of saṃsaric *duḥkha).* See also *saṃsāra.* See pp. 31-34; Beyer, pp. 194-197; Warren ("Dependent Origination") pp. 84, 165-208; Conze, pp. 156-158.

Samādhi. Concentration; the meditative state which is the goal of Buddhist meditation, characterized by "one-pointedness of thought (on the meditative object)," calm, stability, and absence of distraction or mental disturbance; the senses are controlled, mindfulness (smṛti) is attained, false notions of "I" and "mine" (associated with a notion of a substantial independent selfhood) are stopped, and *prajñā* is possible. A synonym is calm (śamatha); more loosely used, meditation in general. See pp. 52, 63; Beyer, Part II; Warren, pp. 291 ff.

Saṃsāra. "That which turns around forever," "the great run-around"; the round of existence, transmigration, the realm into which *karman*-laden beings are reborn and die recurrently; made up of six rebirth realms as illustrated in the Wheel of Life (see pp. 34-38); saṃsāra is characterized by *duḥkha, anitya, anātman* (the three marks, lakṣaṇa, of all conditioned things) and *śūnyatā;* it is often synonymous with *pratītya-samutpāda,* while its opposite is *nirvāṇa;* a term used by both Buddhists and Hindus.

Saṅgha. "Assemblage"; the Order or Community of Buddhist monks, nuns, and laity. In *Theravāda* it often refers only to the monastic order. See pp. 56-60; Beyer, pp. 65-73; Warren, pp. 392-486.

Śīla. Morality, virtue, conduct conducive to progress on the path to *nirvāṇa;* rules (especially the ten precepts, p. 74) to correct and purify a person's karmic endowment, preparatory to the double practice of *samādhi* and *prajñā.* See pp. 45, 63, 78, 89; Beyer, Part I; Warren, pp. 285-287.

Skandha (Khandha). "Heap, mass"; appropriating group or personality aggregate, a term used to indicate that all aspects of personhood which exhibit permanence or unity, either separately or as a group, giving a sense of "ego" or "self," are in reality only impermanent, causally produced aggregations or groups. The five skandhas are: (1) form (rūpa, the body or physical skandha), (2) feeling (vedanā), (3) conception (saṃjñā), (4) karmic dispositions (saṃskāras, plural), and (5) consciousness (vijñāna). The five skandhas constitute the phenomenal world-and-person; are the five basis for clinging to (appropriating) existence which results in continued rebirth; are characterized as well by *duḥkha, anitya,* and *anātman.* See pp. 43, 46, 47; Conze, pp. 107 ff.

Srotāpanna. Stream-winner, one who has entered the stream leading to *nirvāṇa,* and will not relapse; one who has been "converted" to Budhism; the lowest of the four stages or grades of saint; these four stages or paths of sanctification are, in ascending order, (1) srotāpanna,

(2) sakṛd-āgāmin, once-returner, one who will have to be reborn in this world as a human being only once more to become an arhant, (3) anāgāmin, nonreturner, one who will never have to be reborn in this world as a human being but will be spontaneously reborn in the highest heavens until attaining *nirvāṇa,* and (4) arhant, one who will never be reborn again in any rebirth realm. See pp. 44, 66, 79, 97; Warren, p. 287.

Stūpa. Memorial shrine or reliquary, especially to the deceased *Buddha.*

Sukhāvatī. "Happiness-having"; Pure Land or land of happiness of Buddha Amitābha (Amitāyus). See pp. 112-115; Beyer pp. 123-124.

Śūnya. "Swollen, hollow"; empty, devoid, that is, of any *ātman* or substantial independent underlying reality (cf. *svabhāva),* the favorite Mahāyāna explication of the older anātman doctrine; the claim is that on the surface things appear substantial, but, when seen with penetrating insight *(prajñā),* they are found to be empty inside, without independent reality or enduring substantiality.

Śūnyatā. Emptiness (see *śūnya);* characteristic of all *dharmas.* See pp. 89-92; Conze, pp. 59-61, 242-249.

Śūnyavāda. The teaching that all *dharmas* are *śūnya.*

Śūnyavādin. "Empty-ist," follower of the Śūnyavāda.

Sūtra (Sutta). A Buddhist text, especially the dialogs or discourses (in Pali) of the *Buddha,* collected in the *Sūtra Piṭaka,* the Basket of Discourses, and the principal texts of the early *Mahāyāna* (in Sanskrit), also attributed to the *Buddha.* See pp. 64, 86-87, 238.

Svabhāva. Own-being (as opposed to a state of being dependent on causes and conditions); the notion held by some Indian thinkers (Svabhāvavādins, followers of the svabhāva theory as opposed to the Śūnyavādins) and perceived through ordinary common sense that things somehow have independent, continuing, substantial reality, that is, svabhāva; countered by the Buddhist assertion that everything arises in dependence on causes and conditions, and therefore has no independent, or substantial, unchanging existence or reality. See pp. 89-91; Conze, pp. 220-225.

Tantra. Ritual manual, for which the school of Buddhist Tantra is named. See pp. 116-123; Beyer, pp. 124-161, 258-261.

Tathāgata. "He who has come or gone thus (that is, on the path of all the *Buddhas),*" or "He who has reached what is really so, the True"; the term used by the Buddha to speak of himself after Enlightenment. See p. 42.

Theravāda (Pali for Sthaviravāda). The teaching of the Elders; originally an early sect which became established in Ceylon, at the Great Monastery of Anurādhapura, about 240 B.C. Today the term is used to designate the older, more conservative school of southern or Pali Buddhism found in Ceylon, Burma, Thailand, Laos, and Cambodia. Contrasts with *Mahāyāna.* See p. 68.

Theravādin. One who holds to the teaching of the Elders.

Tṛṣṇā (Taṇhā). "Thirst"; desire, craving, the cause of *duḥkha;* includes desire for sensual pleasure, for continued becoming, and for no becoming. To gain *nirvāṇa,* tṛṣṇā must be eliminated since it binds a person to its objects, thus causing continued rebirth in *saṃsāra.*

Vinaya. Monastic discipline and the collection of texts, originally included in the Pali Canon, containing rules for monastic discipline; more generally, the rules of Buddhist morality and canon law. See pp. 64-65, 70-77; Beyer, pp. 69-73.

Yogācāra. The "yoga practice (that is, the following of the yoga or discipline of the *Bodhisattva*'s path)" school of Buddhism which thought nothing exists outside the mind (hence: "Mind-Only School"). See pp. 92-95. Yogācārin, follower of the Yogācāra School.

Yogin. Practitioner of yoga and meditative self-discipline.

Selected Readings

This book is a short introduction to the Buddhist religion. Because of its brevity, many important subjects have received only passing reference. Even major doctrines have been but briefly explained; it is hoped that many students will want to read more. The Glossary already includes some references to further readings. In addition, throughout the text, foreign terms not covered in the Glossary have been set in parentheses to facilitate reference to other works where more information may be found. For those desiring a deeper knowledge, the following bibliographies select materials that substantially add to the picture of Buddhism presented here. Note: Books listed with a French title require a reading knowledge of French since English translations are lacking.

GENERAL SOURCES

Since this book was closely tied by its authors to textual sources, students can easily supplement it by reading selected Buddhist texts, using it as a guide to understanding. Stephan V. Beyer's companion volume to this book, *The Buddhist Experience: Sources and Interpretations,* in this same Dickenson series, is the best single source of such texts. Already, throughout this book references have been made to Beyer's collection. He includes texts translated from all major Buddhist canonical languages. Carefully organized and clearly introduced, they make up an invaluable companion to this introduction to the Buddhist religion.

A second source for a student who wants to learn more is *Buddhism: A Modern Perspective,* edited by Charles S. Prebish (University Park and London: The Pennsylvania State University Press, 1975, both paperback and hardcover henceforth referred to as Prebish, Buddhism). This book, written by former students of Richard Robinson, has summaries of almost all major topics in Buddhist history and thought. Included is an extensive glossary with many proper names, titles of texts, and brief historical sketches, as well as a long bibliography. This is a fine one-book guide to more advanced studies of Buddhism. In it a student can immediately find more information on almost all the subjects introduced in this textbook, so it is the reference to turn to first.

The following works, almost all available in paperback editions, should provide beginning students with sufficient materials to supplement what has been presented in this book.

Bapat, P. V., ed., *2500 Years of Buddhism.* New Delhi: Government of India, Publications Division, 1956. Issued to commemorate the 2500th anniversary of the Buddha's Parinirvāṇa, this book is a good source of information on the whole of Buddhism.

Basham, A. L., *The Wonder That Was India* (hereafter referred to as *Wonder).* New York: Grove Press, 1959. A survey of the culture of the Indian subcontinent before the coming of the Muslims; a many-splendored classic. Contains much historical information on the background and context of Buddhism in India, comparisons with Hinduism, and material on Buddhism itself. Includes examples of art and literature.

Coomaraswamy, Ananda K., *Buddha and the Gospel of Buddhism.* New York: Harper Torchbooks, 1964. Though written many decades ago, this reissue is an excellent survey of Indian Buddhism, including many subjects omitted by others; thoughtful, engaging presentation, beautifully illustrated. A book about Buddhism, with heart.

Conze, Edward, *Buddhism: Its Essence and Development*. New York: Harper Torch-books, 1965. Succinct introduction to major Buddhist ideas written by a world-famous Buddhist scholar obviously committed to the Buddhist vision; mixes insight with controversy.

——, *Buddhist Meditation*. New York: Harper Torchbooks, 1969. A useful introduction to Buddhist meditation through texts.

——. *Buddhist Texts through the Ages* (hereafter referred to as *Texts*). New York: Harper Torchbooks, 1964. Collection of texts including translation of Pali excerpts by I. B. Horner, of Mahāyāna texts by Edward Conze, of Buddhist Tantra by David Snellgrove, and of Chinese and Japanese Tantra by Arthur Waley. Excellent translations, but somewhat difficult to use due to lack of continuity and introductory materials.

——, *Buddhist Thought in India*. Ann Arbor: The University of Michigan Press, 1967. The best survey of Indian Buddhist thought, comprehensive, well-documented. A detailed, more advanced source than others; should be of interest to those who like philosophy and doctrine.

Horner, I. B., *The Living Thoughts of Gotama the Buddha*. London: Cassell, 1948. Excellent anthology from Pali sources, with a brilliant introduction by Ananda K. Coomaraswamy. Miss Horner has also written an excellent, succinct summary of Theravāda Buddhism, "Buddhism: the Theravāda," in *The Concise Encyclopedia of Living Faiths*, pp. 267-295, ed. R. C. Zaehner. New York: Hawthorn Books, Inc., 1959. In the same source, Edward Conze summarizes Mahāyāna, pp. 296-320; and Richard H. Robinson describes Buddhism in China and Japan, pp. 321-347.

Johansson, Rune E. A., *The Psychology of Nirvana*. New York: Doubleday & Company, Inc., 1970. Careful study of early Pali Buddhist thought on nirvāṇa and its attainment; systematically covers major points of doctrine, closely tied to representative Pali texts.

Morgan, Kenneth W., ed., *The Path of the Buddha*. New York: The Ronald Press, Inc., 1974. Good survey of Buddhism throughout Asia written by prominent Asian Buddhist scholars. Similar to, but less complete than P. V. Bapat, *2500 Years of Buddhism*, cited above.

Rahula, Walpola, *What the Buddha Taught*. New York: Grove Press, Inc., 1974. A very popular work, read widely both in the West and Southeast Asia.

Warder, A. K., *Indian Buddhism*. Delhi: Motilal Banarsidass, 1970. A recently published survey of Indian Buddhism.

Warren, Henry C., *Buddhism in Translations*. New York: Atheneum, 1963. Judicious, comprehensive selections from Pali texts in graceful but dated translations.

Watts, Alan, *The Way of Zen*. New York: Vintage, 1957. This is only one of Watts's many books available, not always on Buddhism, but one of the best by this late, popular writer. Some caution is required when reading Watts to distinguish what he says which derives from his own thought and what he writes that attempts more strictly to describe Buddhism itself. This latter is often very little.

OTHER SOURCES FOR THE STUDY OF THE BUDDHIST RELIGION

The books listed above are good, scholarly accounts of the Buddhist religion. But there are other ways of learning about it, too. Some different kinds of sources are listed below to help those beginning their study of the subject.

On Buddhist Art

Art has always been a major part of religious practice and a major expression of religious experience. Buddhist art is particularly rich since it is multicultural and has a tradition

Various seating postures *(āsana)* and hand gestures *(mudrā)* of Buddhist sculpture, including (a) the Buddha in full lotus seating posture, his hands in the teaching gesture ("turning the wheel of the law mudrā"); (b) the "half-lotus" leg position for seated meditation. Additional hand gestures: (c) meditation; (d) assurance against fear; (e) reasoning and explaining; (f) veneration and reverence; (g) touching the earth; (h) boon-bestowing.

which spans more than two thousand years. Buddhists have produced an enormous amount of art; the books listed below are only a sample of the kinds available.

The most complete single source on Buddhist art is P. M. Lad, *The Way of the Buddha* (New Delhi: Government of India, Publications Division, 1956?). Issued on the occasion of the 2500th anniversary of the Buddha's Parinirvāṇa, this book selects Buddhist art from all sources to describe the background of Buddhism, the Bodhisattva's life, the Buddha's message, the growth of Buddhism, the Buddhist pantheon, and the spread of Buddhism beyond India. Complete notes accompany the many illustrations. A book that duly honors not only the Buddha's parinirvāṇa, but all Buddhist artists too. Other worthwhile studies of Buddhist art are:

Buddhadasa, Bhikkhu, *Teaching Dhamma by Pictures*. Bangkok: Social Science Association Press of Thailand, 1968. This book presents a traditional Siamese Buddhist manuscript which illustrates the entire Buddhist Path and world view, with excellent commentary on its rich symbolism by the author, Ven. Buddhadasa Bhikkhu. A wonderful approach to Buddhism through its art. The drawings on pages 37, 51, and 52 were redrawn from this source.

Bussagli, Mario, *Painting of Central Asia*. Geneva: Editions d'Art Albert Skira, 1963. Magnificent Buddhist paintings from the rich finds of Central Asia.

Coomaraswamy, Ananda K., *Elements of Buddhist Iconography*. Cambridge, Mass.: Harvard University Press, 1935. An early interpretation of symbolism in Buddhist art.

——, *History of Indian and Indonesian Art*. New York: Dover Publications, 1965. Excellent survey, including Buddhist art.

Ghosh, A., ed., *Ajanta Murals*. New Delhi: Archeological Survey of India, 1967. Beautiful illustrations, sensitively interpreted.

Hisamatsu, Shin'ichi, *Zen and the Fine Arts.* Tokyo: Kodansha International, Ltd., 1971. Large selection of Zen-related arts.

Mitra, Debala, *Buddhist Monuments.* Calcutta: Sahitya Samsad, 1971. Excellent description of sacred Buddhist sites in India.

Rawson, Philip, *The Art of Southeast Asia.* New York: Frederick A. Praeger, 1967.

Saunders, E. Dale, *Mudrā, a Study of Symbolic Gestures in Japanese Buddhist Sculpture.* New York: Bollingen Foundation, 1960.

Singh, Madanjeet, *Himalayan Art.* New York: The Macmillan Company, 1971.

The interested student should also consult works on the arts of each Buddhist country. This short bibliography only begins to list sources for the study of the Buddhist religion through its artistic heritage.

Different Genres of Buddhist Literature

Apart from the rich, strictly textual Buddhist tradition, Buddhism may also be studied through other types of literature composed by Buddhists. From Beyer's selection of passages in *The Buddhist Experience,* a student can gain some idea of the great diversity of literary genres Buddhists have used. Discussed below are a few samples of works in which a person may find the Buddhist religion expressed in a literary mode.

There are not (yet) many traditional Buddhist autobiographies. One extended authobiographical account of at least part of a Buddhist's life was written in the seventeenth century by Japan's most famous *haiku* poet, Matsuo Bashō (Banana Tree). A lay Buddhist who practiced Zen meditation, at the relatively late and frail age of forty Bashō became a wanderer, going against all personal inclinations to settle down in his older years. He left five sketches of his resulting travels, which filled the remaining ten years of his life. They are a magnificent literary self-portrait of a Buddhist, as great as the one left by Henry David Thoreau in *Walden.* Bashō made his wanderings to see faraway parts of Japan into an extended journey of (Buddhist) self-discovery, much as Thoreau did, though ostensibly he only described his stay at Walden Pond. Bashō's sketches are translated by Nobuyuki Yuasa in *Bashō: The Narrow Road to the Deep North and Other Travel Sketches* (Baltimore: Penguin Books, 1966). Hidden below the surface of his compressed writing are some of the best glimpses into a Buddhist's experience of the Path ever recorded.

Another Japanese Buddhist poet (1763-1827) also left a lyric diary; it, too, has been translated by Yuasa: Issa's *The Year of My Life* (Berkeley: University of California Press, 1960).

One can learn also from the biographies of famous Buddhists. Two remarkable works have come to us from the biographies of eminent Tibetans: Herbert V. Guenther, (trans.), *The Life and Teaching of Nāropa* (London: Oxford University Press, 1963) and W. Y. Evans-Wentz, *Tibet's Great Yogī Milarepa* (London: Oxford University Press, 1969).

There have been many Buddhist poets. Han Shan's poems have captured the reality of the experience of Buddhist transformation. The poems, as arranged by his translator, Burton Watson, in *Cold Mountain, 100 poems by the T'ang [Chinese] Poet Han-shan,* (New York: Columbia University Press, 1970), describe his transformation from a carefree youth and subsequent life as a family man through difficult, bitter years which led eventually to the "Cold Mountain"—both a place where he took refuge and his own state of mind. Like Bashō, Han Shan never became a monk but remained a lay Ch'an Buddhist. His poems similarly go to the heart of the search for nirvāṇa.

Another Chinese Buddhist poet, one who deserves to be read more by Westerners, is Li Ho: J. D. Frodsham, translator, *The Poems of Li Ho* (791-817). (Oxford: Clarendon Press, 1970).

Shih-te, Han Shan's companion, in a moment of realization has a Buddha-smile for the broken banana leaf, symbol of the frailty of human life which, like the banana, has no sub-stantiality. (From a Chinese ink painting scroll by Yin-t'o-lo, Yüan dynasty.)

The "most popular book in the history of the Far East" describes *Monkey*, the sixteenth-century Chinese folk novel by Wu Ch'eng-en (New York: Grove Press, Inc., 1958). *Monkey* is the best of popular Chinese Buddhist literature, a work of consummate fantasy that should make it more popular than it is in this Hobbit world. Supposedly the account of Hsüan-tsang's journey to India to fetch Buddhist scriptures for the Chinese emperor, the novel tells of a fabulous stone monkey who, in typical Indian fashion, (the book uses a Sino-Buddhist world view) pursued and gained power *(siddhi)* from a venerable patriarch. Running amok on a spree through Heaven, he made too many powerful enemies and was only released from imprisonment in a mountain when he was forced by the goddess of compassion, Kuan-yin, to accompany the priest Tripitaka (Hsüan-tsang) to India, thus putting his formidable power to practical purpose. The "real" story of Hsüan-tsang is equally fascinating, and is told by Arthur Waley in *The Real Tripitaka* (New York: Macmillan, 1952). It is well worth reading as the semilegendary history of a famous Asian Buddhist's life.

Modern Buddhists have written novels, too. One, by Michio Takeyama, *The Harp of Burma* (Rutland: Charles Tuttle, 1968), describes in poignant terms a Japanese soldier who becomes a Burmese monk rather than return to Japan at the end of World War II. It was also made into a fine Japanese film, "The Burmese Harp." Both call forth deep feelings.

Essays written by a contemporary North American poet, Gary Snyder, a Buddhist, can be found in his collection *Earth House Hold, Technical Notes and Queries To Fellow Dharma Revolutionaries* (New York: New Directions, 1969). In one he describes his own experience of a *sesshin* (period of intense meditation) in a Japanese Zen temple. Another he calls "Buddhism and the Coming Revolution." This same poet's Pulitzer Prize-winning *Turtle Island* (New York: New Directions, 1974) contains "Buddhist" poems, including one that begins, "The Dharma is like an Avocado!"

Popular Books on Buddhism

A bibliography for student readers of a textbook such as this should comment somewhere on the mass of popular books on Buddhism that are available in libraries and book stores. Best be advised to use some caution in reading these, since their factual reliability often leaves much to desire. Some are outright forgeries—at least that is the opinion of scholars who claim, for instance, that T. Lobsang Rampa's series of books beginning with *The Third Eye* was written by a Londoner who never grew up in Tibet as his writings claim. (He naturally countered that his body had been inhabited, with his permission, by a transmigrating Tibetan whose experience in that remote land his writings describe.)

On the other hand, many popular books on Buddhism are worth reading. No one can be exclusively "right about Buddhism" since there must be as many ways of being "right about it" as there are adequate interpretations or real-life experiences of it.

Adventurers have left us exciting records of their experiences in Buddhist countries. An example is Heinrich Harrer's *Seven Years in Tibet* (New York: Dutton, 1954). He escaped from an Allied prison camp in India where he was interned at the outbreak of the Second World War. Rather than staying in India, he made his way to Tibet and personally witnessed that closed society until the close of the war, eventually reaching fabled Lhasa itself. Fosco Maraini wrote *Secret Tibet,* (London: Hutchinson, 1952; New York: Grove Press, 1960), an exciting, perceptive book on his experiences in Buddhist monasteries. Lama Anagarika Govinda, a European convert to Buddhism who lives in Asia, recounted his wanderings in Tibet in *Way of the White Clouds* (Berkeley: Shambhala, 1971). Another European Buddhist, John Blofeld, described his travels through China and Thailand and his conversion to Buddhism before the Second World War in *The Wheel of Life, The Autobiography of a Western Buddhist* (Berkeley: Shambhala, 1972). Traveling scholars have also written accounts of their journeys, such as David Snellgrove's *Buddhist Himālaya: Travels and Studies in Quest of the Origins and Nature of Tibetan Religion,* (Oxford: Bruno Cassirer, 1957); similarly, Marco Pallis wrote *Peaks and Lamas* (London: Woburn Press, 1957), describing his travels in Buddhist areas of India, Sikkim, and Ladak in the 1930s. A new group of travellers, those who journey to Asia (particularly to Japanese Zen Buddhist temples) to meditate, have produced a considerable number of books on their experiences, accounts which are often found in bookstores today.

Many authors have written on Buddhism, from adventurers to churchmen-turned-lecturers (like Alan Watts). The discerning reader should examine each book and read it for what it is, relying on scholars for the most accurate knowledge. Such authoritative sources follow in the detailed bibliographies below.

Selected Sources for Material in Specific Chapters

The following is a selected bibliography on the main topics presented in this book, following its outline. This is not an exhaustive listing of sources. More extensive bibliography on specific subjects can be found in Prebish, *Buddhism* and in other books in this same Dickenson series, *The Religious Life of Man*.

Part I: THE BUDDHISM OF SOUTH ASIA

Chapter 1. Antecedents of Buddhism

Backgrounds: Indus Valley and Indo-Aryan
Basham, *Wonder*, pp. 10-43, 232-241.

The Immediate Context of the Birth of Buddhism
The Upaniṣads:
Basham,, *Wonder*, pp. 247-256.
Keith, Arthur Berriedale, *The Religion and Philosophy of the Vedas and Upanishads*. Cambridge, Mass.: Harvard University Press, 1925. Authoritative; difficult for beginners.
The Ascetic Movement:
Basham, A. L., *History and Doctrines of the Ājīvikas*. London: Luzac & Company Ltd., 1951. Excellent, detailed survey of the Buddha's competitors.
——, *Wonder*, pp. 243-247, 287-297.
Davids, C. A. F. Rhys, "Asceticism (Buddhist)," in Hastings' *Encyclopaedia of Religion and Ethics (ERE)*, vol. 2, pp. 69b-71b.
Eliade, Mircea, *Yoga: Immortality and Freedom*. Princeton: Princeton University Press, 1970. Asceticism, pp. 101-111 and *passim*.
Jacobi, Hermann, "Jainism," in *ERE*, vol. 7, pp. 465a-474a.
Jayatilleke, K. N., *Early Buddhist Theory of Knowledge*. London: Allen & Unwin, 1963. A masterpiece. Sometimes hard reading, always rewarding. Excellent survey of ascetic movement thought, pp. 69-168.

Chapter 2. Gautama's Enlightenment

Gautama the Buddha: Birth to Enlightenment
Conze, Edward, *Buddhist Scriptures*. Baltimore: Penguin, 1959. Gives a condensed translation of Aśvaghoṣa's *Buddhacarita (Acts of the Buddha)*, pp. 34-66.
Cowell, E. B., trans. "The Buddha-Carita of Aśvaghoṣa" in *Buddhist Mahāyāna Texts*. Delhi: Motilal Banarsidass, 1965 (Reprint of vol. 49 of *Sacred Books of the East*).
Foucher, A., *The Life of the Buddha*. Middletown, Conn.: Wesleyan University Press, 1963. A poor English translation of *La Vie du Bouddha*. Paris: Payot, 1949. The

author, a great historian of Buddhist art, expresses many questionable opinions on doctrine and religion.

Johnston, E. H., *The Buddhacarita, or Acts of the Buddha*. Part II, Translation. Calcutta: Baptist Mission Press, 1936. Chapters 1-14, in scholarly and readable translation, the best (reprinted, New Delhi: Oriental Books Reprint Corporation, 1972). The rest of the text is translated by Johnston in *Acta Orientalia*, vol. 15, (1937).

Ñāṇamoli, Bhikkhu, *The Life of the Buddha*. Kandy: Buddhist Publication Society, 1972. Life and teachings of the Buddha selected from Pali sources.

Nārada, Thera, *The Buddha and His Teachings*. Colombo, Ceylon: Vajirārāma, 1964. Good translations of basic Pali texts, with authoritative commentary by a Theravāda scholar-monk. On the Buddha's life, see pp. 1-64, 318-331.

Thomas, E. J., *The Life of the Buddha as Legend and History*. London: Routledge & Kegan Paul, 1927. Readable, scholarly, standard.

Warren, *Buddhism in Translations*, pp. 38-83, 331-349.

The Twelve Preconditions of Dependent Co-arising
Jayatilleke, *Theory of Knowledge*, pp. 445-457. Sets Keith straight.

Keith, Arthur Berriedale, *Buddhist Philosophy in India and Ceylon*. 1st ed., 1923. Reprint, Banaras, Chowkhamba, 1963. Masterly but quirky. Causation, pp. 96-114.

Nārada, *Teachings*, pp. 418-431.

Thomas, E. J., *The History of Buddhist Thought*. London: Routledge & Kegan Paul, 1933. Very good as an account of early Buddhist thought according to the Pali Canon. On dependent co-arising, see pp. 58-70.

The Wheel of Life and the Hierarchy of Beings
Nārada, *Teachings*, pp. 432-452.

Renou, Louis et Jean Filliozat, *L'Inde Classique*. Tome I (Nos. 1-1357). Paris: Payot, 1947. Tome II (Nos. 1358-2494). Paris: Imprimeris Nationale, 1953. The standard topical encyclopedia of Indology. Tome II, pp. 315-608, presents everything the fledgling scholar should learn about Buddhism, and much that is new to veterans. On pantheon, see Nos. 1029, 1077-9, 1086-7, 2266-72.

Waddell, L. A., "The Buddhist Pictorial Wheel of Life", *Journal of the Asiatic Society of Bengal*, vol. 61 (1893), pp. 133-155. Describes in detail the Tibetan Wheel of Life.

Warren, *Buddhism in Translations*, pp. 289-291, 308-330.

Chapter 3. The Buddha as Teacher

Commentary on the First Sermon
Dutt, Nalinaksha, *Aspects of Mahāyāna Buddhism and Its Relations to Hīnayāna*. London: Luzac, 1930. A great book. Doctrine of *nirvāṇa*, pp. 129-202.

Jayatilleke, *Theory of Knowledge*, pp. 382-401. On faith.

Nārada, *Teachings*, pp. 74-102.

Poussin, Louis de La Vallée, *Nirvāṇa*. Paris, 1925. His mature view, well developed.

———— , *The Way to Nirvāṇa*. Cambridge, 1917. Popular lectures by one of the greatest modern Buddhologists.

Robinson, Richard H., "The Classical Indian Axiomatic," in *Philosophy East and West*, vol. 17 (1967), pp. 139-154. On being, non-being, and the Middle Way.

Stcherbatsky, Theodore, *The Conception of Buddhist Nirvāṇa*. Leningrad: Office of the Academy of Sciences of the U.S.S.R., 1927. An attack on La Vallée Poussin by another great master.

Warren, *Buddhism in Translations*, pp. 380-391, 117-128.

Welbon, Guy Richard, *The Buddhist Nirvāṇa and Its Western Interpreters*. Chicago: University of Chicago Press, 1968. A readable and discerning history of the West's intellectual encounter with Buddhism as instanced in the problem of *nirvāṇa*.

Nirvāṇa, Early Buddhist Meditation and the Dharmas (On nirvāṇa, see references for "Commentary on the First Sermon," above)

On Early Buddhist Meditation:

Ñāṇamoli, Thera, (trans.) *The Path of Purification* (Buddhaghosa's *Visuddhimagga*). Colombo: R. Semage, 1956.

Nyanaponika, Thera, *The Heart of Buddhist Meditation*. New York: Samuel Weiser, 1973. Deals with Satipatthana (Mindfulness) meditation.

Swearer, Donald K., *Secrets of the Lotus*. New York: Macmillan, 1971.

Vajirañāṇa Mahāthera, *Buddhist Meditation in Theory and Practice*. Colombo: Gunasena & Co., 1962.

On Buddhist Abhidharma (see also below, "Early Schisms and Sects"):

Guenther, Herbert V., *Philosophy and Psychology in the Abhidharma*. Berkeley: Shambhala, 1974.

Ñāṇatiloka, Mahāthera, *Guide through the Abhidhammapiṭaka*. Colomgo: Bauddha Sāhitya Sabhā, 1957.

Nyanaponika, Thera, *Abhidhamma Studies*. Kandy: Buddhist Publication Society, 1965.

Rhys Davids, Mrs. C.A.F., *The Birth of Indian Psychology And Its Development in Buddhism*. London: Luzae & Co., 1936.

Founding the Saṅgha

Nārada, *Teachings*, pp. 103-225.

Thomas, *Life*, pp. 89-142.

The Parinirvāṇa

Nārada, *Teachings*, pp. 233-269.

Thomas, *Life*, pp. 143-164.

Warren, *Buddhism in Translations*, pp. 95-110.

Chapter 4. Development of Indian Buddhism

Formation of the Canon

Conze, Edward, *Thirty Years of Buddhist Studies*. Oxford: Cassirer, 1967. A collection of articles. The first, "Recent Progress in Buddhist Studies," first published in 1959-60, summarizes the state of scholarship on the Buddhist scriptures.

Inde Classique, Nos. 1940-2169. The best scholarly précis on Buddhist literature.

Law, Bimala Churn, *A History of Pāli Literature*. (2 Vols.) London: Kegan Paul, Trench, Trubner & Co., 1933.

Macdonell, A. A., "Literature (Buddhist)," *ERE*, vol. 8, pp. 85*a*-89*b*.

Nārada, *Teachings*, pp. 270-278.

Thomas, *Thought*, pp. 261-287. A survey of the Pali Canon and other Buddhist scriptures.

Winternitz, Moriz, *A History of Indian Literature*. Calcutta: University of Calcutta, 1933. vol. 2, pp. 1-21, 34-165.

Early Schisms and Sects

Aung, Shwe Zan, trans., and C.A.F. Rhys Davids, ed., *Compendium of Philosophy*. London: Luzac, 1910 and 1956. Translation of the *Abhidhammattha-saṅgaha,* a medieval Theravāda textbook on Abhidhamma. Excellent introduction and notes.

Bareau, André, *Les Sectes Bouddhiques du Petit Véhicule*. Saigon: École Française d'Extrême-Orient, 1955. A definitive scholarly work.

Conze, Edward, *Buddhist Thought in India*. Ann Arbor: The University of Michigan Press, 1967. Hīnayāna sects, pp. 119-191.

Funahashi, Issai, *et al.*, "Abhidharmakośa-śāstra," in *Encyclopaedia of Buddhism* (*EB*), vol. 1, pp. 58*a*-63*a*.

Karunaratne, W.S., H.G.A. van Zeyst, and Kōgen Mizuno, "Abhidhamma," fascicule 1, pp. 37*b*-49*a*, in *EB*, ed. G.P. Malalasekera, published by the Government of Ceylon. Fascicule 1 appeared in 1961. Subsequent fascicules (parts) come out from time to time. This encyclopedia is an outstanding piece of Asian international cooperation. The best articles in it are really excellent.

Kao Kuan-ju, "Abhidharma-mahāvibhāṣā," *EB*, vol. 1, pp. 64*b*-80*a*.

Mizuno, Kōgen, "Abhidharma Literature," *EB*, vol. 1, pp. 64*b*-80*a*.

Poussin, Louis de La Vallée, *L'Abhidharmakośa de Vasubandhu*. Paris: Geuthner, 1923-1931. Annotated translation of the crowning masterpiece of the Abhidharma movement.

Stcherbatsky, Theodore, *The Central Conception of Buddhism and the Meaning of the Word "Dharma"*. London: Royal Asiatic Society, 1923. Reprint by Susil Gupta, Calcutta, 1956. A brief interpretive exposition of the *Abhidharmakośa's* doctrine.

Religious Life in the Early Centuries

Anesaki, M., "Ethics and Morality (Buddhist)," *ERE*, vol. 5, pp. 477*b*-455*b*.

Auboyer, Jeannine, *Daily Life in Ancient India* (from approximately 200 B.C. to 700 A.D.). New York: Macmillan, 1965. Contains information on early Indian (including Buddhist) worship and life.

Dutt, Nalinaksha, *Early Monastic Buddhsim*. Calcutta: Calcutta Oriental Book Agency, 1960.

Dutt, Sukumar, *Buddhist Monks and Monasteries of India*. London: George Allen & Unwin, 1962.

———, *Early Buddhist Monachism*. Bombay: Asia Publishing House, 1960.

Geden, A. S., "Monasticism (Buddhist)," *ERE*, vol. 8, pp. 797*a*-802*b*.

Horner, *Living Thoughts*, pp. 74-75, 88-138.

Prebish, Charles S., *Buddhist Monastic Discipline*. University Park and London: The Pennsylvania State University Press, 1975. Translates two discipline texts, with an introduction on the rise of Buddhist monasticism.

Warren, *Buddhism in Translations*, pp. 91-94, 392-421, 441-481.

Chapter 5. The Beginnings of Mahāyāna Buddhism in India

Bareau, *Les Sectes Bouddhiques*, pp. 296-305.

Conze, *Buddhist Thought in India*, pp. 195-204.

Dutt, Nalinaksha, *Aspects of Mahāyāna Buddhism*. London: Luzac and Co., 1930.

Lamotte, Étienne, "Sur la formation du Mahāyāna," *Asiatica* (*Festschrift F. Weller*). Leipzig, 1954, pp. 381-386.

The Teaching of Emptiness

Conze, Edward, *Buddhist Wisdom Books*. London: Allen & Unwin, 1958. (also New York: Harper and Row). Contains Diamond-Cutter Sūtra and Heart Sūtra; translation with commentary.

——, *Selected Sayings from the Perfection of Wisdom*. London: The Buddhist Society, 1955.

——, *Buddhist Thought in India*, pp. 238-249.

Inada, Kenneth K., *Nāgārjuna, A Translation of His Mūlamadhyamaka-kārikā with an Introductory Essay*. Tokyo: The Hokuseido Press, 1970.

Lamotte, Étienne, *L'Enseignement de Vimalakīrti* (Vimalakīrtinirdeśa). Louvain: Publications Universitaires, 1962. Excellent French translation, with copious notes and introduction, one of the most important and well-written Mahāyāna Sūtras.

Murti, T.R.V., *The Central Philosophy of Buddhism*. London: Allen & Unwin, 1955. A great book on Mādhyamika, somewhat obscured by the author's thinking in Sanskrit and writing in the vocabulary of 1910-ish British idealism.

Ramanan, K. V., *Nāgārjuna's Philosophy as Presented in Mahā-Prajñāpāramitā-Śāstra*. Tokyo, 1966.

Robinson, Richard H., *Classical Indian Philosophy*. Madison, Wis.: College Printing and Typing, 1968. Summary of Mādhyamika on pp. 71-79.

——, *Early Mādhyamika in India and China*. Madison, Wis.: University of Wisconsin Press, 1967. Read pp. 21-70.

Sprung, Mervyn, ed., *The Problem of Two Truths in Buddhism and Vedānta*. Boston: Reidel, 1973.

Streng, Frederick J., *Emptiness: A Study in Religious Meaning*. Nashville: Abingdon Press, 1967. A study of Nāgārjuna and his vision with respect to the relation between religious awareness and symbolic expression. Contains complete translations of Nāgārjuna's two chief works.

The Doctrine of Mind-Only

Chatterjee, Ashok Kumar, *The Yogācāra Idealism*. Banaras Hindu University Press, 1962. A weak book, but the only one in English.

Conze, *Buddhist Thought in India*, pp. 250-260.

Fukaura, Seibun, "Ālaya-vijñāna," *EB*, vol. 3, pp. 382b-388b.

Lamotte, Étienne, *La Somme du Grand Véhicule d' Asaṅga* (Mahāyānasaṃgraha). Tome II traduction et commentaire. Louvain, Muséon, 1938. A basic manual of Vijñānavāda.

Poussin, Louis de La Vallée, *La Siddhi de Hiuen-tsang*. Paris: Geuthner, 1928-1948. Translation of Hsüan-tsang's *Ch'eng-wei-shih-lun*, a synthesizing commentary on the *Thirty Verses* of Vasubandhu.

Rahula, Walpola, "Asaṅga," *EB* II, vol. 113b-146b.

Robinson, *Classical Indian Philosophy*, pp. 79-85.

Suzuki, D. T., trans., *The Laṅkāvatāra Sūtra*. London: Kegan Paul, 1932 and 1956.

——, *Studies in the Laṅkāvatāra Sūtra*. London: Routledge, 1930. A fine treatment of the Sūtra's version of Yogācāra.

Chapter 6. Soteriology and Pantheon of the Mahāyāna

The Bodhisattva Path

Dayal, Har, *The Bodhisattva Doctrine in Budhist Sanskrit Literature*. London: Kegan

Paul, 1932. Reprint: Delhi: Motilal Banarsidass, 1975.

Guenther, Herbert V., trans., *The Jewel Ornament of Liberation*, by Sgam-po-pa. London: Rider, 1959. An excellent Tibetan manual of the Bodhisattva Course. Hard to read because the translator uses nonstandard equivalents for technical terms.

The Celestial Bodhisattvas
Inde Classique Nos. 2336-39.

Lamotte, Étienne, *Histoire du Bouddhisme Indien.* Louvain: Publications Universitaires, 1958. Great scholar, great book. Maitreya, pp. 775-788.

———, "Mañjuśrī," *T'oung Pao,* vol. 48 (1960), pp. 1-96.

Warren, *Buddhism in Translation,* pp. 480-486.

The Celestial Buddhas
"Akṣobhya," *EB*, vol. 3, pp. 363-368*a*.

"Amita," EB, vol. 3, pp. 434*a*-463*b*.

Kern, H., trans., *The Saddharma-puṇḍarīka or the Lotus of the True Law*, in *SBE*, vol. 21. Oxford: Clarendon, 1909. An obsolete masterpiece.

Müller, F. Max, trans. (1) *The Larger Sukhāvatī-vyūha,* in *Sacred Books of the East,* vol. 49, pp. 1-72, (2) *The Smaller Sukhāvatī-vyūha,* in *SBE,* vol. 49, pp. 89-103.

The Shinshu Seiten ("The Holy Scripture of Shinshu"), compiled and published by the Honpa Hongwanji Mission of Hawaii, Honolulu, 1955. The three chief Pure Land Sūtras translated from the standard Chinese versions, plus other texts from Chinese and Japanese.

Takakusu, J., trans., *The Amitāyur-dhyāna-sūtra*, in *SBE,* vol. 49, pp. 161-201.

Chapter 7. Buddhist Tantra

Bharati, Agehananda, *The Tantric Tradition.* New York: Doubleday & Company, 1970. Treats both Buddhist and Hindu Tantra.

Dasgupta, Shashibhusan, *An Introduction to Tantric Buddhism.* Berkeley: Shambhala, 1974.

———, *Obscure Religious Cults.* Calcutta: Firma K. L. Mukhopadhyay, 1962.

Guenther, Herbert V., *The Life and Teaching of Nāropa.* New York: Oxford University Press, 1971. Study of a great Tantric adept.

———, *The Royal Song of Saraha.* Berkeley: Shambhala, 1973.

Lessing, Ferdinand, and Wayman, Alex, trans., *Fundamentals of the Buddhist Tantras*, by Mkhas-grub-rje. The Hague: Mouton, 1968. Useful translation of a schoolman's marginalia on Tsongkhapa's Tantric writings.

Snellgrove, David L., *The Hevajra Tantra.* Part I, Introduction and Translation. London: Oxford University Press, 1959. The only complete Tantra available in English. Readable and well-informed introduction.

Tucci, Guiseppe, *The Theory and Practice of the Maṇḍala.* New York: Samuel Weiser, 1973.

———, *Tibetan Painted Scrolls.* Rome: Libraria dello Stato, 1949. vol. 1: "The Religious Ideas: Vajrayāna."

Hinduism and Buddhism
Coomaraswamy, Ananda K., *Hinduism and Buddhism.* New York: Philosophical Library, n.d.

Upadhyaya, K. N., *Early Buddhism and the Bhagavadgita.* Delhi: Motilal Banarsidass, 1971.

Part II: THE DEVELOPMENT OF BUDDHISM OUTSIDE INDIA

General Works

Conze, Edward, *A Short History of Buddhism*. Bombay: Chetana, 1960. A fine synoptic history of Buddhism in India and its spread throughout Asia.

Zürcher, Erik, *Buddhism, Its Origin and Spread in Words, Maps, and Pictures*. Leiden: E. J. Brill, 1959, New York: St. Martin's Press, 1962. Very useful for tracing the spread of Buddhism from its beginnings in India throughout its spread to the rest of Asia.

Chapter 8. The Buddhism of Southeast Asia

Bunnag, Jane, *Buddhist Monk, Buddhist Layman*. London: Cambridge University Press, 1973.

Byles, Marie M., *Journey into Burmese Silence*. London: Allen & Unwin, 1962 A plucky Australian lady in Burmese meditation centers. Informative about Burma and its religion, as well as about what happens when one meditates.

Cabaton, Antoine, "Cambodia," *ERE*, vol. 3, pp. 155*a*-167*a*. An overall picture of Cambodian religious life.

Coedès, George, *The Indianized States of Southeast Asia*. Honolulu: East-West Center Press, 1968.

———, *The Making of Southeast Asia*. Berkeley: University of California Press, 1966.

Damais, Louis-Charles, "Le Bouddhisme en Indonésie," in *Présence du Bouddhisme*, pp. 813-824. Saigon: France-Asia, 1959.

Evers, Hans-Dieter, *Monks, Priests And Peasants: A Study of Buddhism and Social Structure in Central Ceylon*. Leiden: E. J. Brill, 1972.

Gombrich, Richard F., *Precept and Practice: Traditional Buddhism in the Rural Highlands of Ceylon*. London: Oxford University Press, 1971.

King, Winston L., *A Thousand Lives Away: Buddhism in Contemporary Burma*. Cambridge: Harvard University Press, 1964. A perceptive outsider assesses the state of Theravāda thought and values in contemporary Burma.

Lester, Robert C., *Theravada Buddhism in Southeast Asia*. Ann Arbor: University of Michigan Press, 1973.

Ludowyk, E. F. C., *The Footprint of the Buddha*. London: George Allen & Unwin, 1958. Description of the monuments of "old Ceylon."

Rāhula, Walpola, *The Heritage of the Bhikkhu*. New York: Grove Press, 1974. Description of the monk's life in Ceylon with illustrations.

———, *History of Buddhism in Ceylon*. Colombo: Gunasena, 1956. History and culture in the classical period, well-described by a scholarly bhikṣu.

Spiro, Melford E., *Buddhism and Society*. New York: Harper and Row, 1970. Excellent survey of Buddhism in Burmese society.

———, *Burmese Supernaturalism*. Englewood Cliffs: Prentice-Hall, 1967. An anthropologist looks at the total religious system of the Burmese. See especially "Supernaturalism and Buddhism," pp. 246-280. Good, up-to-date bibliography.

Tambiah, S. J., *Buddhism and the Spirit Cults in Northeast Thailand*. Cambridge: University Press, 1970.

Wells, Kenneth E., *Thai Buddhism, Its Rites and Activities*. Bangkok: Christian Bookstore, 1960. A straight description of ceremonies, liturgies, and festivals.

Yoe, Shway (pseudonym of James George Scott), *The Burman, His Life and Notions*. London: Macmillan, 1896. Now in paperback. A sympathetic and informative classic.

On Southeast Asian Buddhism, see also the separate bibliographies in Prebish, *Buddhism: A Modern Perspective*.

Chapter 9. The Buddhism of East Asia

General Reading on Chinese Buddhism

Ch'en, Kenneth, *Buddhism in China, A Historical Survey*. Princeton: The Princeton University Press, 1964. Has at least something on everything. Excellent on historical facts, weak on doctrine and interpretation; extensive bibliography.

———, *The Chinese Transformation of Buddhism*. Princeton: The Princeton University Press, 1973.

de Bary, Wm. Theodore, ed., *Sources of Chinese Tradition*. New York: Columbia University Press, 1960. Pages 306-408 contain Chinese Buddhist texts, well-chosen and well-translated by Leon Hurvitz.

Robinson, Richard H., *Chinese Buddhist Verse* (hereafter referred to as *Verse*). London: John Murray, 1955. Didactic and liturgical hymns from the Chinese Canon.

Takakusu, Junjiro, *The Essentials of Buddhist Philosophy*. (3rd ed.) Honolulu: Office Appliance Co., 1956. Data-rich but opaque textbook material on the Sino-Japanese sects.

Thompson, Laurence G., *Chinese Religion: An Introduction*, Religious Life of Man Series, Encino, Calif.: Dickenson Publishing Co., 1969. Places Buddhism within the total panorama of Chinese religiosity.

Waley, Arthur, "Texts from China and Japan," in Conze, *Buddhist Texts*, pp. 269-306. Choice morsels that Waley happened to like.

Wright, Arthur F., *Buddhism in Chinese History*. Stanford University Press, 1959. Readable, strong on history, weak on doctrine. See review by Richard H. Robinson, *Journal of the American Oriental Society*, vol. 79 (1959), pp. 311-318.

First to Sixth Centuries

Robinson, *Early Mādhyamika*. Concerns the years around 400 A.D., the Buddho-Taoists, and the first serious Chinese attempt to master an Indian treatise system.

Zürcher, Erik, *The Buddhist Conquest of China*. Leiden: Brill, 1959. Social and doctrinal history till 400 A.D. A great book, perspicacious on all facets of the subject.

T'ien-t'ai

de Bary, *Chinese Tradition*, pp. 349-368.

Hurvitz, Leon, *Chih-i* (538-597): *An Introduction to the Life and Ideas of a Chinese Buddhist Monk*. Mélanges Chinois et Bouddhiques, XII, Bruges (Belgique), 1963. The only good book in English on T'ien-t'ai.

Takakusu, *Essentials*, pp. 126-141.

San-lun

de Bary, *Chinese Tradition*, pp. 333-343.

Takakusu, *Essentials*, pp. 96-107.

Fa-hsiang

de Bary, *Chinese Tradition*, pp. 343-349.

Takakusu, *Amitāyur-dhyāna-sūtra*, pp. 80-95.

Waley, Arthur, *The Real Tripitaka*. London: Allen & Unwin, 1952. Scholarly popular book on Hsüan-tsang.

Hua-yen

Chang, Garma Chen-chi, *The Buddhist Teaching of Totality: The Philosophy of Hwa-yen Buddhism*. University Park: The Pennsylvania State University Press, 1971. The only book in English on the thought of the *Hua-yen* (Kegon) school.

Kao Kuan-ju, "Avatamsaka Sūtra," *EBII*, vol. 3, pp. 435a-446a.

Suzuki, D. T., *Essays in Zen Buddhism*, Third Series. London: Rider, 1953. Zen and the Gaṇḍavyūha, 21-214.

Takakusu, *Essentials,* pp. 108-125.

Pure Land

de Bary, *Chinese Tradition*, pp. 374-386.

Robinson, *Verse*, pp. 41-45, 64-74. The Pure Land liturgical hymns.

Shinshu Seiten, pp. 109-157 from the masters' treatises; pp. 327-338 notes on the masters.

Ch'an-Zen

Briggs, William A., ed., *Anthology of Zen*. New York: Grove Press, Inc., 1961. A handy collection of Zen writings by contemporary Asians and Westerners. Contains translations from Japanese and other materials difficult to find elsewhere. The section on Buddhism in the West is interesting but dated.

Chang, Chung-yuan, *Original Teachings of Ch'an Buddhism*. New York: Vintage, 1971. Useful translations from the *Transmission of the Lamp*.

Chang, Garma Chen-chi, *The Practice of Zen.* New York: Harper and Row, 1959. Presents Zen from the viewpoint of a modern Chinese practitioner who has also worked with Tibetan Tantra. Contains some good practical tips on meditation, in addition to history and teachings.

Dumoulin, Heinrich, *A History of Zen Buddhism*. Boston: Beacon Press, 1969. Readable and scholarly, though the author's interpretations sometimes depend on Catholic apologetic concepts.

Johnston, William, *Silent Music—The Silence of Meditation*. New York: Harper and Row, 1974. Father Johnston has practiced Zen in Japan for over twenty years and has done much to introduce the use of some Buddhist techniques into Catholic contemplation. He is a major participant in the on-going Christian-Zen dialog.

Kapleau, Philip, *The Three Pillars of Zen*. Boston: Beacon Press, 1967. How Zen is practiced in Modern Japan. Lectures by Zen masters, interviews, letters, testimonials. Especially good for its numerous accounts of meditation experiences of both Japanese and Westerners. A lotus among the thistles of writings by Western Zen enthusiasts.

Luk, Charles, *Ch'an and Zen Teaching*. London: Rider, Series I, 1960; Series II, 1961; Series III, 1962. Sloppy translations of many important texts otherwise not accessible. See review by Richard H. Robinson, *Journal of Asian Studies*, vol. 21, no. 3 (1962), 368.

Satō, Giei, *Unsui: A Diary of Zen Monastic Life*. Honolulu: The University Press of Hawaii, 1973. Illustrates all aspects of Rinzai training in Japan, based on the artist's experiences; a humorous insider's view of Zen.

Shibayama, Zenkei, *A Flower Does Not Talk*. Rutland, Vermont: Charles E. Tuttle, 1970. Contains an interesting set of six ox-herding pictures which contrasts with the more common set of ten.

Suzuki, D. T., *Essays in Zen Buddhism*. Series 1, 2, 3. London: Rider & Co., 1949, 1953. A treasure of information and insights by the man who made *Zen* an English word.

Suzuki, Shunryū, *Zen Mind, Beginner's Mind*. New York: Walker/Weatherhill, 1970. The author's approach is that of Sōtō Zen—"just sitting" without seeking to become a Buddha. The book serves as a balance to the writings of D. T. Suzuki, who, following the Rinzai tradition, emphasized grasping *satori* (enlightenment) through intense struggle.

Thich Nhat Hanh, *Zen Keys: A Zen Monk Examines the Vietnamese Tradition*. New York: Anchor Books, 1974. Another view of Zen from the Vietnamese tradition.

Welch, Holmes, *The Practice of Chinese Buddhism*. Cambridge: Harvard University Press, 1967. Based on interviews with refugee Ch'an monks. Readable, scholarly, reliable. The best book on any regional variant of modern Buddhist monastic life.

Yampolsky, Philip, *The Platform Sutra of the Sixth Patriarch*. New York: Columbia University Press, 1967. Translation, introduction, notes. The best scholarly treatment in English of this major scripture.

Modern China

Welch, Holmes, *Buddhism under Mao*. Cambridge: Harvard University Press, 1972. Excellent information on Buddhism in China since 1949.

———, *The Buddhist Revival in China*. Cambridge: Harvard University Press, 1968. Readable and authoritative.

Japan

Anesaki, Masaharu, *Nichiren, the Buddhist Prophet*. Harvard, 1916. A fine book on a fascinating personality.

de Bary, Wm. Theodore, ed., *Sources of the Japanese Tradition*. New York: Columbia University Press, 1958. Essayettes and translations of Buddhist texts, pp. 93-110, 116-175, 190-266. Basic and excellent.

Dumoulin, *History of Zen*, pp. 137-268. The best part of the book.

Earhart, H. Byron, *Japanese Religion*. Religious Life of Man Series, Encino, Calif.: Dickenson Publishing Co., 1969. Treats Buddhism as a major strand in the overall complex of Japanese religion. The best thing to read next on Japanese Buddhism.

Eliot, Charles, *Japanese Buddhism*. London, 1935 and 1959. A great book in its day. Obsolete but not superseded.

Kitagawa, Joseph M., *Religion in Japanese History*. New York: Columbia University Press, 1966. Up-to-date, well informed and informative.

Renondeau, G., *Le Bouddhisme Japonais—Textes fondamentaux de quatre grands moines de Kamakura*. Paris: Albin Michel, 1965.

Shinshu Seiten, pp. 157-315. Writings of the Japanese Pure Land masters.

Suzuki, D. T.,*Zen and Japanese Culture*. New York: Pantheon, 1959.

Vietnam

Thich Thien-An, *Buddhism and Zen in Vietnam, in relation to the development of Buddhism in Asia*. Rutland, Vt., Tuttle, 1975. Survey of Buddhism in Vietnam. Illustrated.

On the Buddhism of East Asia, see also the bibliographies in Prebish, *Buddhism: A Modern Perspective* and the introductions by Thompson (China) and Earhart (Japan) in this same Dickenson series referenced in this bibliography on p. 000.

Chapter 10. Buddhism in the Tibetan Culture Area

Beyer, Stephan V., *The Cult of Tārā*. Berkeley: University of California Press, 1973. The first treatment of Tibetan Tantric ritual-meditations as they are actually practiced. The author based his account on field work among Tibetan refugees in India. An excellent work.

———, *Tibetan Mystic Song* (Lyricord Disc LLST 7290) and *Songs of Gods and Demons: Ritual and Theatrical Music of Tibet* (Lyricord Disc LLST 7291). Recorded in Tibetan communities in India, these long-playing discs present some lesser-known Tibetan music from the traditions of mystic song and the Tibetan opera and epic. Each record has complete translations of texts, as well as photographs and commentary.

Blofeld, John, *The Tantric Mysticism of Tibet*. New York: Dutton, 1970.

Demiéville, Paul, *Le Concile de Lhasa*. Paris: Impr. Nationale de France, 1952. Describes the debate held in Lhasa between representatives of Indian Mahāyāna and Chinese Ch'an. The Indian party won, and from that time Tibet turned to India for spiritual culture.

Evans-Wentz, W. Y., *The Tibetan Book of the Dead*. Oxford University Press, 3d ed., 1960.

———, *Tibetan Yoga and Secret Doctrines*. Oxford University Press, 2d ed., 1960.

———, *Tibet's Great Yogi Milarepa*. Oxford University Press, 2d ed., 1951. Evans-Wentz is a Theosophist who worked with a bilingual Tibetan to produce translations that are readable, and notes that are often inane.

Guenther, Herbert V., *Tibetan Buddhism without Mystification*. Leiden: Brill, 1966. Translation of four eighteenth-century Gelukpa tracts, with introduction and notes.

Hoffmann, Helmut, *The Religions of Tibet*. London: Allen & Unwin, 1961. A standard work. Weak on doctrine.

Sierksma, Fokke, *Tibet's Terrifying Deities*. The Hague: Mouton, 1966. An interpretation of aspects of Tibetan art and culture perhaps too Freudian.

Snellgrove, David and Hugh Richardson, *A Cultural History of Tibet*. New York: Praeger, 1968. Readable and authoritative. Gives a prominent place to religion. Good bibliography and maps.

Chapter 11. Buddhism Comes West

Ellwood, Robert S., Jr., *The Eagle and the Rising Sun: Americans and the New Religions of Japan*. Philadelphia: Westminister Press, 1975. Excellent account of five new Japanese sects in the United States.

———, *Religious and Spiritual Groups in Modern America*. Englewood Cliffs, N.J.: Prentice-Hall, 1973.

Humphreys, Christmas. *Sixty Years of Buddhism in England* (1907-1967). London: The Buddhist Society, 1968.

Hunter, Louise, *Buddhism in Hawaii, Its Impact on a Yankee Community*. Honolulu: University of Hawaii Press, 1971.

Needleman, Jacob. *The New Religions*. New York: Pocket Books, 1970.

Riepe, Dale, *The Philosophy of India and Its Impact on American Thought*. Springfield, Ill.: Charles C. Thomas, 1970.

West, Martin L., *Early Greek Philosophy and the Orient*. Oxford: Clarendon Press, 1971.

An Overview of
the Buddhist Scriptures

A. The Pali Canon: The *Tipiṭaka* ("Three Baskets")
  See Thomas, *Thought*, pp. 265-276, and *Inde Classique* No. 1947-1979.
  I *Vinaya-piṭaka* ("Basket of Discipline")
  1. *Sutta-vibhaṅga* ("Division of Rules")—the rules of the Pātimokkha code
     with explanations and commentary.
     (a) *Makāvibhaṅga* ("Great Division")—the 227 rules for monks.
     (b) *Bhikkhunī-vibhaṅga* ("Division Concerning Nuns")
  2. *Khandaka* ("Sections")
     (a) *Mahāvagga* ("Great Group")—rules for ordination, Observance Day,
         rainy-season retreat, clothing, food, medicine, and procedures of the
         Saṅgha.
     (b) *Cullavagga* ("Small Group")—judicial rules, miscellaneous rules, ordi-
         nation and instruction of nuns, history of the First and Second Councils.
  3. *Parivāra* ("The Accessory")—summaries and classifications of the rules.
     This is a late supplement.
  II *Sutta-piṭaka,* ("Basket of Discourses")
  1. *Dīgha-nikāya* ("Collection of Long Discourses")—34 suttas.
  2. *Majjhima-nikāya* ("Collection of Medium Discourses")—152 suttas.
  3. *Saṃyutta-nikāya* ("Collection of Connected Discourses")—56 groups of
     suttas.
  4. *Aṅguttara-nikāya* ("Collection of Item-more Discourses")—over 2300 suttas.
  5. *Khuddaka-nikāya* ("Collection of Little Texts")
     (a) *Khuddaka-pāṭha* ("Little Readings")—a breviary.
     (b) *Dhammapada* ("Verses on Dharma")—423 verses in 26 chapters.
     (c) *Udāna* ("Utterances")—80 exalted pronouncements of the Buddha,
         with circumstantial tales.
     (d) *Itivuttaka* ("Thus-saids")—112 short suttas.
     (e) *Sutta-nipāta* ("Collection of Suttas")—short suttas, mostly in verse
         of high poetic quality.
     (f) *Vimāna-vatthu* ("Tales of Heavenly Mansions")—gods tell the deeds
         that earned them celestial rebirths.
     (g) *Peta-vatthu* (Tales of Ghosts")—how various persons attained that
         unfortunate rebirth.
     (h) *Thera-gāthā* ("Verses of the Elders")—stanzas attributed to 264 male
         personal disciples of the Buddha.
     (i) *Therī-gāthā* ("Verses of the Eldresses")—stanzas attributed to about
         100 female personal disciples of the Buddha.
     (j) *Jātaka* ("Lives")—tales ostensibly reporting the former lives of
         Śākyamuni. The verses in each tale are supposed to have been uttered

by the Buddha, and so are considered canonical; but the 547 tales themselves are extracanonical.

(k) *Niddesa* ("Exposition")—verbal notes to part of the Sutta-nipāta. The Niddesa is second or third century A.D.

(l) *Paṭisambhidā-magga* ("The Way of Analysis")—Abhidharma-style treatment of some doctrinal topics.

(m) *Apadāna* ("Stories")—lives and former lives of the saints.

(n) *Buddhavaṃsa* ("Lineage of the Buddhas")—lives of 24 previous Buddhas, of Śākyamuni, and of Maitreya, presented as being told by Śākyamuni.

(o) *Cariyā-piṭaka* ("Basket on Conduct")—verse retellings of Jātakas illustrating the Bodhisattva's practice of the perfections.

III *Abhidhamma-piṭaka* ("Basket of Scholasticism")

1. *Dhamma-saṅgani* ("Enumeration of Dharmas")
2. *Vibhaṅga* ("Divisions")—more on sets of dharmas.
3. *Dhātu-kathā* ("Discussion of Elements")
4. *Puggala-paññatti* ("Designation of Persons")—classifies people according to their spiritual traits and stages.
5. *Kathā-vatthu* ("Subjects of Discussion")—arguments about theses in dispute among the Hīnayāna schools.
6. *Yamaka* ("The Pairs")—arranged in pairs of questions, deals with the basic sets of categories.
7. *Paṭṭhāna* ("Activations")—24 kinds of causal relation.

B. The Chinese Canon: The *Ta-ts'ang-ching* ("Great Scripture-Store")

See Ch'en, *Buddhism in China,* pp. 365-378, and *Inde Classique,* No. 2107-2162. The first printed edition was produced in Szechuan, in 972-983 A.D. It consisted of 1,076 texts in 480 cases. The standard modern edition is the *Taishō Shinshū Daizōkyō* (Ta-ts'ang-ching newly edited in the Taishō reign-period). It was published in Tokyo, 1924-1929, and consists of 55 Western-style volumes containing 2184 texts. A supplement consists of 45 volumes. The following analysis is of the Taishō edition.

I *Āgama* Section, vol. 1-2, 151 texts. Contains the Long, Medium, Mixed (= Connected) and Item-more Āgamas (i.e., Nikāyas), plus some individual texts corresponding to parts of the Pali Khuddaka.

II Story Section, vol. 3-4, 68 texts. *Jātakas,* lives of various Buddhas, fables, and parables.

III *Prajñā-pāramitā* Section, vol. 5-8, 42 texts.

IV *Saddharma-puṇḍarīka* Section, vol. 9, 16 texts. Three complete versions of the Lotus Sūtra, plus some doctrinally cognate Sūtras.

V *Avataṃsaka* Section, vol. 9-10, 31 texts.

VI *Ratnakūṭa* Section, vol. 11-12, 64 texts. A set of 49 Mahāyāna Sūtras, some in more than one translation.

VII *Mahāparinirvāṇa* Section, vol. 12, 23 texts. The Mahāyāna version of Śākyamuni's last days and words.

VIII Great Assembly Section, vol. 13, 28 texts. A collection beginning with the Great Assembly Sūtra, which is itself a suite of Mahāyāna Sūtras.

IX   Sūtra-collection Section, vol. 14-17, 423 texts. A miscellany of Sūtras, mostly Mahāyāna.

X   Tantra Section, vol. 18-21, 572 texts. Vajrayāṇa Sūtras, Tantras, ritual manuals, and spells.

XI   Vinaya Section, vol. 22-24, 86 texts. Vinayas of the Mahīśāsakas, Mahāsāṅghikas, Dharmaguptakas, Sarvāstivādins, and Mūla-sarvāstivādins. Also some texts on the Bodhisattva discipline.

XII   Commentaries on Sūtras, vol. 24-26, 31 texts—on Āgamas and on Mahāyāna Sūtras, by Indian authors.

XIII   Abhidharma Section, vol. 26-29, 28 texts. Scholastic treatises of the Sarvāstivādins, Dharmaguptakas, and Sautrāntikas.

XIV   Mādhyamika Section, vol. 30, 15 texts.

XV   Yogācāra Section, vol. 30-31, 49 texts.

XVI   Collection of Treatises, vol. 32, 65 texts. Works on logic, anthologies from the Sūtras, and sundry treatises.

XVII   Commentaries on the Sūtras, vol. 33-39, by Chinese authors.

XVIII   Commentaries on the Vinaya, vol. 40, by Chinese authors.

XIX   Commentaries on the Śāstras, vol. 40-44, by Chinese authors.

XX   Chinese Sectarian Writings, vol. 44-48.

XXI   History and Biography, vol. 49-52, 95 texts.

XXII   Encyclopedias and Dictionaries, vol. 53-54, 16 texts.

XXIII   Non-Buddhist Doctrines, vol. 54, 8 texts. Sāṃkhya, Vaiśeṣika, Manichean, and Nestorian Christian writings.

XXIV   Catalogs, vol. 55, 40 texts. Successive catalogs of the Canon beginning with that of Seng-yu published in 515 A.D.

C. The Tibetan Canon

    See *Inde Classique,* Nos. 2033-2044, and Kenneth Ch'en, "The Tibetan Tripiṭaka," *Harvard Journal of Asian Studies* 9 (1945-47), pp. 53-62.

  I *Bka'-'gyur (Kanjur)* ("Translation of Buddha-word") The number of volumes and order of sections differ slightly from edition to edition. The following is according to the Snar-thang (Narthang) version.

    1. *Vinaya,* 13 vols.

    2. *Prajñā-pāramitā,* 21 vols.

    3. *Avataṃsaka,* 6 vols.

    4. *Ratnakūṭa,* 6 vols. A set of 49 Mahāyāna Sūtras.

    5. *Sūtra,* 30 vol., 270 texts, three-quarters Mahāyāna Sūtras and one-quarter Hīnayāna ones.

    6. *Tantra,* 22 vol., over 300 texts.

  II *Bstan-'gyur (Tenjur)* ("Translation of Teachings"). In the Peking edition, this consists of 224 volumes and 3626 texts, divided into:

    1. *Stotras* (hymns of praise), 1 vol., 64 texts.

    2. *Commentaries on Tantras,* 86 vols., 3055 texts.

    3. *Commentaries on Sūtras,* 137 vols., 567 texts.

      (a) *Prajñā-pāramitā* commentaries, 16 vols.

      (b) *Mādhyamika* treatises, 17 vols.

      (c) *Yogācāra* treatises, 29 vols.

(d) *Abhidharma,* 8 vols.
(e) Miscellaneous, 4 vols.
(f) *Vinaya* Commentaries, 16 vols.
(g) Tales and dramas, 4 vols.
(h) Technical treatises: logic (21 vols.), grammar (1 vol.), lexicography and poetics (1 vol.), medicine (5 vols.), chemistry and sundry (1 vol.), supplement (old and recent translations, indices; 14 vols.).

Index